the ONION's
FINEST NEWS REPORTING

VOLUME ONE

Also from *The Onion*

Our Dumb Century:
100 Years of Headlines
from America's Finest News Source

⌀ the ONION's FINEST NEWS REPORTING

VOLUME ONE

EDITED BY
Scott Dikkers
Robert Siegel

WRITTEN BY
Robert Siegel, Todd Hanson, Maria Schneider,
Tim Harrod, Carol Kolb, John Krewson,
Mike Loew, Scott Dikkers, Joe Garden,
Ben Karlin, David Javerbaum

GRAPHICS BY
Mike Loew
Chad Nackers

DESIGNED BY
Andrew Welyczko
Scott K. Templeton

ADDITIONAL MATERIAL BY
Kelly Ambrose, Mark Banker, Rich Dahm, Ben Greenman,
Josh Greenman, David Junker, Ryan Kallberg, Chris Karwowski,
Sean LaFleur, Kurt Luchs, Dylan MacArthur, Nathan Rabin,
Andy Selsberg, Randel Shard, Dave Sherman, Rick Streed,
Jack Szwergold, Dan Vebber, Graeme Zielinski

COPY EDITOR
Stephen Thompson

SPECIAL THANKS TO
Ken Artis, Ian Dallas, Peter Haise,
Peter Koechley, Bob Mecoy, Steve Ross,
Dave Slotten, Maggie Thompson, Don Traeger

 THREE RIVERS PRESS • NEW YORK

This book uses invented names in all stories, except notable public figures who are the subjects of satire. Any other use of real names is accidental and coincidental.

Published by Three Rivers Press, New York, New York.
Member of the Crown Publishing Group.

Random House, Inc. New York, Toronto, London, Sydney, Auckland
www.randomhouse.com

THREE RIVERS PRESS and the Tugboat design are registered trademarks of Random House, Inc.

Printed in the United States of America

Design by *The Onion*

Library of Congress Cataloging-in-Publication Data is available upon request.

ISBN 0-609-80463-4

10 9 8 7 6 5

First Edition

the ONION's
FINEST NEWS REPORTING

VOLUME ONE

Chapter One

News Stories That Won The Pulitzer

When my son, J. Phineas Zweibel, who is the current publisher of *The Onion* news-gazette, informed me that a book of our finest recent reporting was to be published, I tried to roll my eyes heavenward in an emphatic expression of disgust.

By T. Herman Zweibel
Publisher Emeritus
(photo circa 1911)

How-ever, since I am 132 years old, my eyes could not handle the undue strain and I tore my retinal nerve and dislocated an eye-ball. I under-went hours of indescribable torment as my personal physician struggled to repair me so that I might have sight again.

Any-how, my aforementioned disgust was directed at my hobbledehoy of a son, because a book of previously published *Onion* dispatches was exactly the type of tom-fool thing he would dream up. Imagine expecting the people of our great Republic to fritter away their hard-earned pennies on a bound collection of obsolete news-articles with which they have presumably already been familiarized in the very pages of *The Onion* it-self! It is a wretched waste of money and an extremely poor investment, but that has never stopped him or any of my other sons, who are like-wise involved in the news-paper trade. I always told them, "Put all your money in carbon." Plentiful though it may be through-out our Planet Earth, demand is always high and it never goes out of fashion, unlike the investor's most devil-ish mistress, oxygen. But do those head-strong wastrels ever listen to my seasoned voice of experience? Never, by jiggledy!

It was Thursday evening last that through the veriest chance I was being wheeled back to my bed-chamber after undergoing my monthly rectal tap in my private lavatory when I espied one J. Phineas Zweibel operating the type-writing device in my study! Once I determined that he was attempting to compose an introduction to the first chapter of this wrong-headed book-let himself, I had a pair of my Swiss Guard manacle the brute and whisk him away, then set my nurse to work before the type-writer as I dictated! Only T. Herman Zweibel composes chapter introductions around here, even if doing so cleaves my fragile brain-pan in two!

What really reddens my cheeks with rage is that the news-paper-men of to-day—including, to my deep disappointment, those employed by *The Onion*—spend their time trying to please that lousy immigrant Joseph Pulitzer in the hopes of receiving some kind of "prize" from him! Ninnies! Lap-dogs! Do they not realize that once they fall prey to Pulitzer's cheap flattery, they are at his mercy? Many a time I have observed the tragic consequence of accepting one of his so-called prizes. An unsuspecting news-paper-man gladly receives some gilded bauble for covering a war or shirt-waist-factory fire. Several weeks later, after retiring to bed, he feels a great clout on his head and passes out. When he wakes, he discovers that he has been shanghaied into a vast white-slavery ring and is about to be buggered by a lascivi-ous Arabian sheik! Mark my words—Pulitzer's Prize is the kiss of death for any self-respecting reporter!

I demand that *The Onion* staff return any of Pulitzer's prizes that they may have in their possession immediately. If you expect some kind of special honor for your news-paper work, you can come to my estate and clear brush. Hard work is its own reward!

Oh, the hell with it all. Were it up to me, I'd make the intro-duction to every book a word-for-word reprint of the great introduction I wrote for the highly successful 1896 pamphlet, *A Highly Risable Humor-Primer That Makes Many Jokes At The Expense Of Negroes And Jews.*

NATION

In an exciting historical reenactment, members of the Maryland Civil War Preservation Society (above) destroyed downtown Atlanta Sunday.

Civil War Enthusiasts Burn Atlanta To Ground

ATLANTA—The city of Atlanta was destroyed and 230,000 were killed Sunday when a group of overzealous Civil War buffs marched through the Georgia capital, burning it to the ground.

"It was very exciting," said Bob Gerhardt, 43, president of the Maryland Civil War Preservation Society, the group responsible for the attack. "We rode in on horseback just after dawn, crossing the Chattahoochee and approaching the city from the west, just as General Sherman did in 1864. We even used the same kind of kerosene as the Union Army. No detail was spared."

The attack began just before 6 a.m., when guests at Atlanta's Peachtree Plaza hotel were awakened by the sound of a cast-iron cannonball blasting through the lobby. Within an hour, the 71-story building was engulfed in flames. By noon, the destruction had spread through the entire downtown area.

"First the Braves lose the World Series, and now my whole family is dead," said Atlanta resident Ben Halleran. "This has been quite a week."

While the attack caused some $2.1 billion in damage, it did have a positive side, since the city's 124,000 black residents were freed.

"Run, run free!" Preservation Society member Phil Spillner, a Baltimore-area dentist, shouted to a group of black men near the CNN Building. "You have all been freed! God bless President Lincoln!"

Nearby, at the Georgia Dome, a battalion of Union soldiers stormed onto the field during the third quarter of the Atlanta Falcons' game against the Pittsburgh Steelers, emancipating a number of Falcons, including All-Pro linebacker Jessie Tuggle.

According to Gerhardt, the history buffs plan to continue their assault on the heart of Dixie, marching all the way to Savannah.

"We will drive the Rebels to the sea," said Phyllis Borelli, a Silver Spring, MD, legal secretary. "Ooh, this is so fascinating—I feel like I'm really there!"

The Atlanta attack is the most destructive historical reenactment since 1991, when a group of Cleveland-area WWII buffs dropped an atomic bomb on Hiroshima. ⌀

3

Scissors Defeats Rock

MEDFORD, OR—Scissors defeated rock Monday, marking the cutting instrument's first-ever victory over its longtime nemesis. Scissors, which had lost to rock an estimated 44 million times before the win, was widely expected to lose the match. "It was incredible," witness Maria Wellsey said. "The rock was trying to smash the scissors, but it just couldn't. Then, all of a sudden, the scissors got up and cut right through the rock, just like it was paper or something." Rock has lost its last two matches, including Friday's defeat at the hands of paper, which easily covered the helpless stone. —*November 28, 1995*

Neighbors Remember Serial Killer As Serial Killer

DUNEDIN, FL—In the wake of his capture Monday, serial killer Eddie Lee Curtis is being recalled by neighbors as a serial killer. "He was kind of a murderous, insane, serial-killer type of fellow," said Will Rowell, 57, who lived next door to the man arrested for the murder of 14 nurses in Florida and Georgia. "He sort of kept to himself, killing nurses, having sex with their corpses, and then burying the bodies in his backyard." Neighbor Peg Appleton agreed: "I didn't know him that well, but he really seemed to hate nurses, the way he was always dismembering them with power tools. I guess you could say he fancied himself a serial killer." —*April 23, 1998*

Ants To Pilot Sand Ship To Distant Star

OLIN, IN—Drawing on a highly ordered drone work force and extensive hill-building experience, a local ant colony Monday completed construction of a "sand ship," which it now plans to launch into deep space. The toaster-sized sand ship, built by thousands of ants over several generations, is equipped with a dry-leaf-based zero-gravity life-support system, a special dirt-powered engine, and a twig-reinforced outer hull. "You ants can be very proud," President Clinton said at a White House ceremony honoring the ants. "With this fine ship, you join the U.S., Russia and France in the great quest to conquer space." An earlier sand ship was built by the ants in 1974, but it was smashed to pieces by an errant softball throw. —*March 6, 1996*

Man With Heart Disease Eagerly Awaits Young Boy's Death

CLEVELAND, OH—Heart transplant patient David Morris, 56, announced Monday that he is eagerly awaiting the death of Robby Cooper, a 14-year-old who lies in a vegetative coma at an Akron hospital. When Cooper dies, which, according to hospital authorities, "could be any day now," his healthy heart will be extracted and flown to Cleveland, where Morris waits. "I very much look forward to young Robby's death," Morris said from his hospital bed. "His demise will represent a glorious new beginning for me." Morris, an investment banker who has suffered three heart attacks from years of heavy smoking and a high-fat diet, has offered the Coopers $15,000 to turn off the child's life support. —*January 30, 1996*

Metallica Kicks Ass

LOS ANGELES, CA—According to a letter published in the "Fans Speak Out" section of this month's *Hit Parader* magazine, the heavy-metal rock band Metallica kicks serious ass. "Metallica rules!!!" wrote 16-year-old Matt Fawkes of Rockford, IL, responding to a letter accusing Metallica of turning soft. According to Fawkes, the rock 'n' band could waste Slayer, Ratt or Mötley Crüe any day. —*September 19, 1995*

NRA Shifts Focus From Guns To Penmanship

MEMPHIS, TN—The nation's largest gun lobby announced Friday that it will no longer serve as a gun-rights champion and will focus instead on the battle for neater, more legible penmanship. Across the country, the National Rifle Association will sponsor Good Penmanship Workshops: men-only, military-style boot camps in which students who do not achieve a passing grade in basic penmanship will be shot. New NRA television commercials are already airing, featuring spokesman Charlton Heston, who says in his gravelly baritone, "There are those who would try to take away your right to good penmanship. Join me in telling them, 'Get your hands off me, you filthy apes!'" —*September 5, 1995*

SCIENCE

World's Knowledge To Be Written Down

In a move to preserve civilization for future generations, the world's leaders announced Monday their decision to have the accumulated knowledge of all areas of human endeavor written down.

"Once this information is transferred to a permanent record on the printed page," explained British Prime Minister John Major via satellite, "the children of tomorrow will be able to access our knowledge by visually scanning, or 'reading,' the information, similar to the way you see me speaking on your television."

Possibly the most difficult part of the "writing-it-down" plan will be agreeing on a basic set of geometric shapes to use as a visual code in transferring words into symbols. "Daunting as the task may seem, we must develop a written code," said Harvard linguist Evan Sanding. "Today, when a database crashes or a refrigerator breaks, we simply go to the person who made it and have them fix it. But what if that person dies? Thanks to the writing plan, a person's knowledge will no longer be lost forever when he or she dies."

After the language is created, the even more time-consuming process of writing everything down will need to be completed before the world's knowledge can be pre-

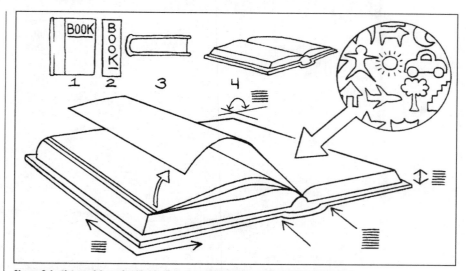

Above: Scientists envision using "books," devices which will record information in "print."

served. "That could take a really long time," said German Chancellor Otto Bühl, "especially since we really should write down multiple copies of each bit of knowledge in case something happens to one of them."

Some have hinted that the writing-it-down process could be sped up through the operation of mechanical printing devices capable of cranking out hundreds of identical manuscripts automatically, a theory many strongly reject. "Let's not get carried away here," said U.S. Secretary of State Warren Christopher. "Entrusting all of humanity's knowledge to mere machines is just not feasible. The writing should be done properly, by dedicated monks painstakingly calligraphing each page by candlelight, illuminating the manuscripts over the course of centuries."

Not all observers support the writing-it-

Left: Scientists created these symbols as a way to "write down" information.

down proposal, with Senate Majority Leader Bob Dole protesting vehemently. "Just how are people supposed to hear the sounds of these words if no one is speaking?" he asked. "If we are expected to rely on written source material for information, we will have to have people capable of 'reading' it, and just where are all these 'readers' going to come from? This plan would require extravagant spending to create a system of schools to teach these reading skills to the people. It's preposterous."

The plan has also generated resentment among oral storytellers, who will no longer be the sole repositories of the world's knowledge. "This 'writing' is an ax hanging over our heads," said Bato Mojambe, president of Local Storytellers Union #514 in Tanzania. "We have every intention of filing a grievance with the world's leaders in the form of a story complete with colorful male-initiation-rite anecdotes and maybe even a little lesson to be learned." Ø

SPORTS

Special Olympics Fixed

Many 'Winners' Found to Have Lost Badly

Scandal rocked the sports world Monday when an independent investigation revealed that the Special Olympics, one of the nation's premier annual athletic competitions, is fixed.

According to the undercover probe, over the years tens of thousands of participating athletes have been declared "winners" despite losing their respective contests, often by wide margins.

"I don't think there's anything 'winning' or 'special' about finishing in eighth or ninth place," chief investigator Harlan Brundage said. "Do these kids think they're winners just because they tried? Just because they gave it their all? Well, let me tell you, trying doesn't make you a winner. Coming in first does."

An estimated 15,000 athletes participated in the Special Olympics this year, and, according to awards records, every one of them was declared a "winner."

According to Brundage, until a thorough investigation can be conducted, all Special Olympians will be stripped of their medals and held for questioning. Several officials and judges are also being detained.

Evidence of the scandal was first discovered June 17 during a Special Olympics competition in Milpitas, CA. Marcy Simms, a 27-year-old

see OLYMPICS page 8

A Scandal Uncovered

Is there a history of double standards in Olympic competitions?

1984 ▷ Olympic sprinter Mary Decker trips and falls: Finishes last and becomes a symbol of defeat everywhere.

Special Olympian Susie Kravitz stops to wave at sister in crowd: Finishes last and is praised for super effort.

1980 ▷ Soviet Olympic weightlifter Vasiely Alexeev fails to lift qualifying weight: Wins no medal, is booed by Moscow crowd.

Special Olympian Davey Johnstone drops barbell on foot: Is treated to french fries at McDonald's by Dad.

1972 ▷ U.S. Olympic Basketball Team loses gold-medal game on blown call by referee: Players refuse to accept silver medals to this day.

Special Olympics basketball team accidentally scores for opponents at buzzer: Players enjoy group hug with coach.

OLYMPICS from page 3

Milpitas resident, was declared a winner in the gymnastics competition despite falling off the two-foot-wide balance beam some 11 times and failing to execute even a single cartwheel.

Upon finishing her routine, Simms raised her arms above her head and cheered in triumph. Her parents then raced over to hug and kiss her, joyously sharing in their daughter's "victory."

"When we saw Marcy celebrating, we immediately suspected corruption," Brundage said. "Her routine was terrible—what could she possibly have been so happy about?"

Gymnastics judge Olga Rublovskya, a bronze medalist at the 1976 Montreal Olympics, agreed. "I would give Marcy's performance a 0.0," she said. "The routine was not very good at all."

Further evidence of scandal was uncovered at this year's Harwich, MA, Special Olympics, where Jeff Coombs, 32, was awarded a medal in the 40-yard dash competition despite coming in dead last out of 15 competitors.

Following the race, an investigator asked Coombs if he realized how poorly he had fared, to which he replied, "I'm special! I'm a winner!"

When the investigator countered that Coombs was neither special nor a winner, but rather an exceptional failure who finished in last place, Coombs vehemently maintained his specialness.

"These are substandard athletes at best," Brundage said. "Why they are competing in something called the Olympics is a question we must answer as we expand our investigation."

The scandal has already resulted in a loss of sponsorship dollars. Reebok and Toshiba, the Special Olympics' two largest sponsors, have announced they are pulling out, and Pepsi is expected to follow.

"It is in Reebok's best interest at this time to put our money behind the 1996 Atlanta Games, where the athletes have proven their ability to run, jump and catch," said Marvin Balsam, Reebok director of marketing, explaining his company's decision to shift $158 million from the Special Olympics to the Atlanta Games. "Until we see more physical skill from these so-called Olympians, we have no choice but to spend our sponsorship dollars elsewhere." Ø

The 10 Greatest Movie Moments Of All Time!

Item! After more than 100 years, people still love movies!

When I think back on my life, I can think of good times and I can think of bad times.

**The Outside Scoop
By Jackie Harvey**

And for every moment, I can recall a movie that goes with those memories. When I got engaged, when my engagement was broken off, when I swore I'd never love again, when I found true love, when I lost that true love, when I found a five-dollar bill on the street... all of these are coupled with a distinct movie memory. Heck, I'm such a big fan that it gets so I can't tell my movie memories from my real memories sometimes! (Although I certainly know that it wasn't me who left **Scarlett O'Hara** standing alone at the end of *Song Of The South*. After all, I am a gentleman!).

I can't speak for everyone, but I can say that nearly everyone I have talked to has a favorite movie moment that makes their eyes shine and can still bring a tear to their eye or a smile to their lips. With this in mind, here are my picks for the 10 greatest movie moments of all time. I know that not everyone will agree, but I'm hoping you can use this as a jumping-off point for a conversation about how great the movies are and what they have done for you, asking only for $7.50 and perhaps a later rental of the video. So, here they are, in no particular order: my picks for the 10 greatest movie moments ever.

10) **The *Casablanca* nightclub scene that didn't have Peter Lorre!** If ever there was a couple that screamed "romance," it was **Bogey** and **Bacall**. Maybe Bogey was an elfin man with a grossly oversized head, but with that trenchcoat, he was magical. And Bacall? I have to confess my failings as a writer, because I can't even begin to summarize her charms. When they are in the bar with **Sam**, the original piano man, and Bogey says, "Play it again, Sam," that gets me every time.

9) **The Death Star explosion scene in *Star Wars*!** Every time I see that, I still feel the same rush of elation knowing that the Death Star will not destroy any more planets, and that **Luke Skywalker** is victorious in his quest to save the galaxy from evil. It's a shame that he eventually grew up to be **Darth Vader**, but I think that all of us, even those with the purest of heart, can be changed by circumstance.

8) **The *Psycho* shower scene!** Who can forget the tension, the expertly played string instruments, and the explosion of horror when **Vince Vaughn** stabs **Anne Heche** to death while she innocently showers? Once in a while, I wake up in a cold sweat with those violins screeching in my ears. Heck, it's because of that movie that I'm a **bath man** to this day.

7) **Gene Hackman's death scene in *The Poseidon Adventure*!** His performance as a priest who questions his calling was riveting from the word go, equaled only by his turn as **Lex Luthor** in *Superman, Superman II,* and *Superman III: The Quest For Peace*.

> I know that not everyone will agree, but I'm hoping you can use this as a jumping-off point for a conversation about how great the movies are.

When he has to sacrifice himself so he can save the other people, he asks, "How many more lives?!" before he goes to the great beyond. I don't want to die any more than you do, but when I do, and I know I will, I hope I can go out as classy as that.

6) **The cafeteria scene in *When Harry Met Sally*!** It may not be the best scene for family viewing, but that doesn't mean it's any less hilarious! If you've seen it, you know exactly what I'm talking about. If you haven't, let's just say that **Meg Ryan** gives an "exciting" explanation of a woman's "special moments" to a bewildered **Billy Crystal** and a cafeteria full of unsuspecting patrons. You might be interested to know what really goes on in their minds during those "private times," and you'll never see it explained in a funnier way! Sometimes when I'm sitting alone in a cafeteria or a cafe, I think of this and start laughing all over again!

5) **Judd Nelson's heart-wrenching scene where he explains birthdays at his house in *The Breakfast Club*!** Whenever it's on, I pop up some popcorn (the old-fashioned way, thank you) and settle in for a hearty laugh and, yes, a good cry. Nelson's tough-guy exterior melts away when he casually describes the ever-present violence in his house. I bawl like a baby and want to adopt him, but then he smokes drugs and I realize that such behavior would not be tolerated in my home.

4) **The calf-birthing scene from *City Slickers*!** In the wake of **Curly's** death, acting powerhouses **David Paymer** and **Billy Crystal** deliver a new life, thus keeping the wheel in motion. The wheel of life, that is. The balance maintained, the boys become men and find peace with themselves. It's a very contemplative, spiritual moment, dusted with comedy in order to mimic real life: tragedy, comedy and mystery.

3) **James Cameron Crowe's** Oscar® acceptance speech for *The Titanic*! It was a truly great moment in celebration of a truly great film, not to mention a truly great tragedy. More than a thousand people needlessly lost their lives on April 12, 1914, and the director—better yet, auteur!—behind the best film of the decade, and the number-one box-office champ of all time, showed real Hollywood class in the tradition of **Cary Grant** and **Tom Hanks** by sharing a special moment of silence for **those victims**. I tell you, I get teary-eyed just thinking about it. This technically is not a movie moment, but I think everyone will agree it deserves to be on this list regardless.

2) **The first mobster/psychiatrist meeting in *Analyze This*!** **Robert DeNiro** has to be my favorite tough-guy actor of all time. He's brash, but he can rein it in and say it all with one icy stare. When he lets his hair down and plays it up for yuks with poor **Billy Crystal** trying to keep a poker face in light of possible danger, all laughter breaks loose.

1) **All of *Forget Paris*!** I love romance, and *Forget Paris* delivers through and through as a mismatched basketball referee (**Billy Crystal**) and an airline executive (**Debra Winger**) fall in love in Paris, the **city of romance**. But can their love overcome their differences once the magic of Paris is behind them? I won't give it away, but if you know me, you know what I like, and you can pretty much guess whether or not they're able to stick it out. Every time I am on the downside of a romance, I pop this gem in to restore my faith that **my true love** is out there, somewhere.

Boy, that was harder than I thought. I mean, there is so much magic out there on the dream tree, just waiting to be picked like fruit. I'm sure that next week another fruit will seem riper, but for right now, this would be my choice. I'd like to know what your favorite movie moments are. Just drop me a line, and maybe we can be movie pen pals, swapping moments and ideas. In the meantime, I'll keep my eyes peeled for more golden moments and, of course, some fresh Hollywood gossip served the way you like it... on the Outside! ∅

From January 23, 1996

Desperate Vegetarians Declare Cows Plants

LAS VEGAS—At its annual national conference Saturday, the American Association of Vegans and Vegetarians released results of a detailed in-house study determining that the common beef cow is actually a plant, 100 percent fit for vegetarian consumption.

"Contrary to what was previously thought, the cow is not a higher form of animal life, capable of thinking and feeling pain," announced AAVV spokeswoman Denise Chalmers to the large crowd. "Rather, we have found it to be a harmless, non-sentient form of plant life, utterly incapable of experiencing the slightest pain or simplest thought."

Chalmers then passed around a large tray of dripping red meat, which the vegetarians in attendance ravenously devoured, feverishly licking the bloody juice from their fingers.

According to the AAVV researchers who conducted the study, cows feature many of the basic characteristics of plants. In addition to possessing roots, leaves and branches, cows produce pollen, which in the springtime is eagerly devoured by honey bees.

"The bees swarm feverishly around the cow, eager to get a taste of its delicious nectar," Chalmers said. "The cow, however, is usually too busy taking up water through its hooves, or 'roots,' to even notice."

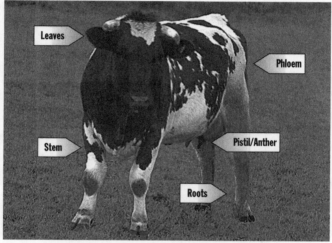

A cow, now considered flora by the American Association of Vegans and Vegetarians.

Cows, say researchers, also practice photosynthesis, the process by which plants convert sunlight into chemical energy.

"When exposed to sunlight, the cow produces chlorophyll," researcher Darrick Holten explained. "The cow then uses the chlorophyll to produce chemical energy."

Added Holten: "A very similar process occurs in chickens."

According to Chalmers, the study's findings will not alter the AAVV's basic viewpoint. "Animals still should not be eaten, and meat is murder," she said.

The study results also shed new light on the reproductive process of cows, which had been shrouded in mystery since the animal was discovered 200 years ago.

"Cows reproduce much like the common pine tree," Holten said. "They develop a hard, bristly, fertilized cone, drop it on the ground and await the natural elements of wind, rain and animal life to carry it to open forest territory."

Overall reaction at the conference was muted at first, as many of the vegetarians expressed surprise, then glee, at the unexpected announcement. Some rushed madly to the trays of processed lunch meats lined up on buffet tables around the hall, knocking over bystanders and onlookers in a mad dash for freshly carved roast beef.

"It does not taste anything like meat," vegetarian Tina Mothersby said. "It's chewy like a boiled carrot or even like a nice chunk of sourdough bread."

Added Chalmers: "Cows are plants, and we feel pretty silly for avoiding them for as long as we have. Inside the stockyard warehouse near my Chicago home is not a meat locker, but a plant locker, and that fetid stench is not one of cow heads festering in a maggot-covered pile, but rather of ripe vegetables ready to be prepared in myriad delicious ways."

Due to the overwhelming acceptance on the part of the vegetarian crowd, the AAVV announced plans to move ahead with studies proving that the pig and duck are plants. Mutton, however, is still meat. ∅

COMMUNITY

Area Homosexual Saves Four From Fire

Heroic Neighbor Praised, Gay

FALMOUTH, MA—Near-tragedy turned to joy and relief Monday, as area residents Phillip and Karen Widman and their two children were pulled from their burning home on Locust Street by Kevin Lassally, a homosexual man.

The fire is believed to have started around 1 a.m. when an unextinguished candle ignited a set of drapes, threatening to consume the home and the Widman family along with it. Lassally, returning home after visiting with other homosexuals, smelled smoke and saw flames through the Widmans' living-room window.

"I heard children crying, and knew I had to do something," the 34-year-old gay computer programmer told reporters. "I used their porch railing to climb up on the roofing that allowed me to reach the children's bedroom. Then I had to kick in their window to reach them."

Once the window was broken, gusts of wind began funneling smoke out of the house and feeding oxygen into the fire. Said Lassally, "I couldn't see through the black wall of smoke, but I was able to locate the children from the sound of their crying." After the blinded homosexual eased Meghan, 3, and Joshua, 18 months, out the window and leapt to the ground, protecting the children by absorbing the impact on his own back, he realized the children's parents had yet to be rescued.

"The older child began crying that her parents were still in the house," Lassally, who prefers the company of men to women, said. "So I had to go back in for them." The fearless and gay hero once again climbed onto the roof and entered the second-floor window, only to discover after minutes of groping that the master bedroom was not upstairs. Bolting down the stairs, he found the first floor to be a red-hot mass of flame and collapsing timbers. He nevertheless located the bedroom and carried the unconscious parents out on his shoulders.

By now a blackened, sooty, homosexual figure, Lassally set the Widmans down a safe distance from the house as firefighters were arriving and collapsed on the lawn, exhausted and gay.

Lassally suffered burns covering more than 70 percent of his body and sustained injuries leaving him unable to work or have anal intercourse with men for about two months.

Above: Falmouth resident Kevin Lassally, who likes to hold and kiss other men, is being hailed as a hero after rescuing a family of four from a deadly blaze (inset).

Doctors describe his condition as stable but homosexual.

As donations and toys come pouring in to the family, which lost most of its possessions, congratulatory cards and telegrams have flooded Falmouth's new favorite gay citizen.

"This brave, homosexual man has inspired us all," Falmouth mayor Matthew Colella said. The local hospital has announced plans to rename its burn ward "The Kevin Lassally Gay Burn Ward" in his honor.

Karen Widman beamed with praise for her new hero: "He's the kind of guy you hope your kids will grow up to be like in certain ways, like courage."

Added husband Phillip: "Sometimes life makes you cynical, like it's you against the world. Then out of nowhere comes a totally selfless gay person who turns your whole view around."

Lassally is modest in the face of so many tributes: "I've always believed that one [homosexual] really can make a difference." Ø

Angels Among Us?

A recent poll revealed that 63 percent of Americans believe in the existence of angels. What do *you* think?

"I was touched by an angel—last Saturday, on CBS."

Otto Montville
Podiatrist

"I believed in angels until I met Mother Teresa. What a bitch."

Shannon Colavito
Tax Attorney

"Innocent schoolgirl by day, high-priced hooker by night... How could you not believe in Angel?"

Jim Tatum
Tuba Player

"I believe my mother to be an angel. A perfect angel. I even stapled a little halo onto her head. I keep her in my basement."

Cory Hooper
Coal Miner

"My grandpa is an angel now, and he watches over my sister and brothers and me. Hi, my name is Jeffy, of *Family Circus* fame.

Alan Dwyer
Meteorologist

"I thought I saw an angel once, but it was just my husband in a druid's cloak masturbating to organ music."

Kathleen Foli
Systems Analyst

SPACE

Mir Scientists Study Effects Of Weightlessness On Mortal Terror

KOROLYOV, RUSSIA—U.S. and Russian scientists are increasingly excited about the Mir space-station project, which promises to reveal more than has ever been known about the scientific relationship between weightlessness and mortal terror.

"By stranding our scientists on a dilapidated space station with faulty wiring, loose hardware and malfunctioning air systems," NASA head Daniel Goldin said, "we have created extremely favorable conditions for learning about spaceborne panic."

The two Russians and one American on board the station are reportedly frightened beyond lucidity.

Among the groundbreaking experiments conducted on Mir are a June 25 collision with a cargo craft that depressurized the Spektr module, last week's emergency power shortage caused by a disconnected cable, and the periodic release of "dry ice" steam that simulates a shipboard fire. All have been deemed a huge success by agency heads.

"They are in a constant state of what aerospace scientists term 'mind-shattering terror,' frightened for their very lives," Russian mission director Vladimir Solovyov said. "And we have not even used the hull-mounted alien puppet that taps on the window yet."

"We have also taken huge leaps in our understanding of the patterns created when one wets his pants in the weightlessness of space," Solovyov said. "The urine spreads out in an expanding sphere, which we did not expect."

Taking a break from his busy schedule, astronaut Michael Foale asked ABC News reporters: "Where is Mommy?"

"Please tell me the access code to the Soyuz capsule," Russian cosmonaut Aleksandr Lazutkin said. "I would like to return to the chaotic government and widespread hunger of my homeland."

Scientists expect to gain even more useful data during an experiment at 3 a.m. Thursday. As the astronauts sleep, whirling red siren lights will flood the cabin while an ear-splitting klaxon alarm jolts them awake. Detailed scientific data will then be collected on such variables as open weeping, defecation and hair loss. Ø

Above: Scientists scramble to repair a gaping hole in the Mir space station's hull. The large rupture is part of a joint U.S.-Russian effort to learn more about spaceborne panic.

Oprah's Book Club

Oprah Winfrey's book club has quickly become a major force in the publishing world: Every book she has selected has made the *New York Times* best-seller list. Why are people responding so strongly to the new club?

34%
Need something to occupy selves while waiting for video release of *The First Wives Club*

10%
Oprah's fans intrigued by concept of "books"

9%
Drew Carey Book Club too challenging

16%
Enjoy visualizing Oprah as heroine of all novels they read

25%
To be introduced to underground authors such as Toni Morrison and Deepak Chopra

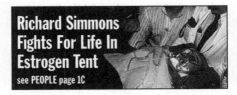

⌀ the ONION®

VOLUME 32 ISSUE 16   AMERICA'S FINEST NEWS SOURCE™   19–25 DECEMBER 1997

NEWS

SAT Found To Be Biased In Favor Of Non-Hungover

see EDUCATION page 2C

We Must Strike Now While England Is Weak

see EDITORIAL page 16A

Clinton Written Up By 'Total Bitch' Supervisor

Above: Bill Clinton.

WASHINGTON, DC—President Clinton once again became the focus of departmental scrutiny Monday when he was written up for the second time in less than a month by his immediate supervisor, presidential second-shift crew manager Diane Helbke. It was the third such incident this pay period for the embattled president.

Clinton, who allegedly forgot to punch out at the end of his 3–11 p.m. shift Sunday, held a nationally televised White House press conference following the write-up, expressing great frustration over what he called the "totally unfair" treat-ment he has endured working under Helbke.

"My fellow Americans, I stand before you today to tell you that Diane has been riding my ass ever since my re-election," Clinton said. "Further, let us not forget that I was not even hired by Diane. I was hired by Rick, long before Diane even trans-ferred here from the Odana Road office. In fact, I practically have seniority on that bitch. To get elected to the highest office in the United States by this nation's people and then be treated this way is unfair. It is what I would call 'bullshit,' is

see CLINTON page 14

CLINTON from page 1

what it is."

Political analysts noted that, if Clinton is written up one more time in the next 90-day "probationary" period, federal policy dictates that he will be subject to severe disciplinary action, including a three-day suspension without pay, reduced priority on the scheduling rotation and, potentially, termination without a reference.

"According to federal policy as outlined in the information packet Clinton was required to read and sign before taking the oath of office as a presidential trainee in 1992, the hours he worked on the days he forgot to punch out will not be included on his next paycheck, and he will have to wait until the next pay period to be paid for those hours," said Jonathan Roe of the D.C.-based American Enterprise Institute.

The two-week waiting period is intended to serve as a deterrent to Clinton forgetting to punch out in the future.

"If the president cannot learn to follow the same procedure as everybody else, he will jeopardize his position within the organization," read a memorandum posted by management on the White House break room's employee bulletin board.

According to fellow employees, when Clinton arrived for work at the start of his shift Monday, he was asked to leave his work station and see Helbke in her office.

"She had that real calm voice she only get when she mad," co-worker Jackie Sandusky said. "And when she shut the door, we was all like, 'Ooooweeee... Clinton gonna get it!'"

During the 15-minute closed-door conference, Clinton was given a written form containing a detailed description of his latest infraction, as well a complete record of all previous offenses, including his 11 instances of tardiness and four run-ins with supervisors. Clinton was required to sign the document, which was then placed in his permanent file.

Clinton remained steadfast in his insistence that he is being treated unfairly, and that his supervisor has held a "personal vendetta" against him "from day one."

"Just last week, I needed to get Friday night off for an important state dinner with the Chinese premier," Clinton said. "And the office policy is, if you want time off, you have to write and date your request in Diane's request log at least three weeks in advance. Well, I was in there a full five weeks in advance, okay? But then Kathleen has to go to her sister's baby shower, and suddenly it's

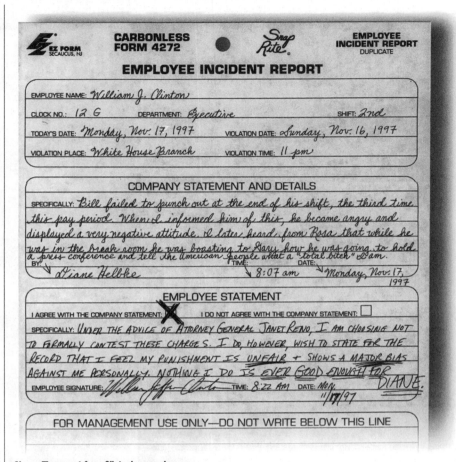

Above: The report from Clinton's supervisor.

like, now I have to work? I do not believe that is fair, and I do not believe the American people do, either."

Clinton went on to cite other instances in which he said he was treated unfairly by Helbke, including the time she made him work the day of an important Camp David retreat despite the fact that Vice-President Al Gore had already agreed to take his shift, and the time he was not permitted to use the Oval Office phone for a personal call, even though the call was necessary to arrange a ride home from his cousin.

"I ended up having to wait an hour for the bus because of her," he said.

Clinton also recounted several incidents in which he was "singled out" by Helbke for spending too much time in the bathroom, even though he claimed to be using it "no more than anyone else."

Though top Clinton strategists are divided on what course of action the president

should take in his ongoing conflicts with Helbke, there is speculation that he will use the Nov. 22 mandatory all-staff meeting as an opportunity to raise several of his complaints about his shift supervisor in front of the regional managers.

Though Clinton is reportedly convinced that his co-workers would "back him up" should such a confrontation occur, some believe any attempt on the president's part to go over Helbke's head would be ill-advised.

"Clinton's got another thing coming if he thinks Sue and Dwayne from the central office are going to side with him against Diane, because she's their little office pet and can do no wrong," said co-worker Jesse Hagen.

Helbke, meanwhile, is unfazed. "That little Buster Brown is on a one-way ticket to trouble if he doesn't get an attitude adjustment pronto," she said. ✍

From March 6, 1996

THE ELDERLY

114-Year-Old Attributes Longevity To Random Chance

MILFORD, WY—Mayor Hammond Forsythe officially declared Monday "Hazel McCreeley Day," and why not? After all, if you'd lived through more than 41,500 of them, wouldn't you deserve one, too?

With pomp, circumstance and cake, the oldest living American celebrated the start of the 14th year of her second century here amid her friends at the Milford Nursing Home. But make no mistake—old age does not mean old heart!

"What a crock of shit," remarked the feisty McCreeley, playfully feigning both inability and unwillingness to blow out even one of her 114 candles. "What a flaming crock of shit this whole day is... For the love of Jesus, honor somebody accomplishing something, not someone whose body is spiting its mind by staying alive."

Asked for the secret to her long life, the perky, silver-coifed McCreeley quipped, "Dumb luck. Do any of you have even a rudimentary understanding of probability? Extrapolate the bell curve of life expectancy for a quarter of a billion people and see for your goddamn selves. By probabilistic rights, somebody in America ought to be 119. Only one person being 114 years old is an incredible statistical deviation."

"Great, I pissed in my diaper again," wise-cracked the chipper McCreeley, who still has the sense of humor she inherited from her mother, the wife of a pioneer rancher who gave birth to her only child on March 5,

1882, during the administration of Chester A. Arthur. She grew up during the tail-end of the legendary Old West period, graduated from high school when Teddy Roosevelt was president, turned 51 one day after the first inauguration of his distant cousin Franklin, and had been eligible for Medicare for 18 years when it was first created!

Thinking of those times, McCreeley wistfully recalls them as "a total goddamn blur. Everything before this morning is a brain-fart for me."

The bouncy centedecarian has lived in Milford all her life, spending 53 years running the general store she founded with her husband, Herb. Herb died in 1958 at 79. She has three children, five grandchildren, 11 great-grandchildren and 16 great-great-grandchildren.

"Buried most of 'em," the peppy McCreeley noted. "My body is a drooping heap of grief-flesh."

Asked if her family has a history of longevity, McCreeley replied, "Christ, the usual rigmarole. All right: My parents did not have long lives, I don't drink a daily shot of brandy, I don't exercise regularly, and the clean mountain air makes no difference. I've lived in a climate-controlled nursing home for 34 years. Talk to a goddamn actuary, all right? I'm just the randomly chosen outermost tentacle of the billion-legged beast that is suffering through time. Any other brilliant theories, fuckos?"

McCreeley is the chief claim to fame of Milford, a quaint town of 3,500 in the northeastern cor-

Hazel McCreeley (above) turned 114 Monday. She encouraged celebrants to "extrapolate the bell curve of life expectancy for a quarter of a billion people" to figure out just why she's still kicking.

ner of the state. Mayor Forsythe, who has known McCreeley all his life, considers her a national treasure. "They ought to put her on Mount Rushmore. And push her off it. I'm not kidding," kidded Forsythe. "She should do us all a favor and die."

And what does the future hold

for the happy Hazel? McCreeley already has plans for her 115th birthday.

"Plan A is to be rotting in a coffin," she told us. "Plan B is to do what I do every other day: alternate between brief periods of lugubrious lucidity and tedious stretches of quasi-catatonia." Ø

Area Stoner Convinced Everyone On TV Also Stoned

Above: Athens, GA, stoner Dirk Udell.

ATHENS, GA—In a stoned statement made while sitting around watching late-night cable TV with his roommates Tuesday, Athens-area stoner Dirk Udell announced his conviction that everyone on TV is also stoned.

"You ever see that HBO series *Mr. Show*? Those guys are out there, man," said Udell, a part-time record-store clerk and occasional drummer for an as-yet-unnamed local band. "Those guys must get fucked up all the time, you can totally tell just by looking at 'em. I mean it. I don't know what those people are smokin', but, like, the other night, David, the bald guy, comes out and starts dancing around all crazy and shit? And Bob just looked at him like, 'Whoa, man, you are so baked.'"

"I was like, man," Udell said.

According to Udell, among the other TV personalities who are "obviously baked out of their minds" are David Letterman, the guy who does the voice of Homer Simpson, Sipowicz on *NYPD Blue*, the cast of *Mystery Science Theater 3000*, Beavis, Butt-Head, that one "Let's get ready to rumble" dude, Howard Stern, that guy on the Menards commercials, MTV's Matt Pinfield, and the people who came up with the aliens for the original *Star Trek* series.

"I mean, come on," said Udell, pausing to take what witnesses described as a "monster" bong hit. "A freakin' white furry gorilla with, like, one horn stickin' out the middle of his head? You just know somebody was chokin' down some serious primo cheeba-cheeba when they dreamed that up."

"That shit's fucked up," he added.

The 26-year-old Udell is no stranger to controversy. He has made numerous inflammatory statements in the past, including a June 3 allegation that the Masons are into some really freaky shit and a January 1996 announcement that somebody was eating all his Fruit Roll-Ups without asking permission. The longtime stoner's latest remarks, however, delivered in a semi-coherent monotone through a drug-induced haze, are widely considered his most explosive yet.

"I'll tell you something else, man," Udell said. "The other night, they had a rerun of that one episode of *Space Ghost* where the guest was Beck, and he was so stoned. He had, like, a lampshade on his head, and he was all like, 'This is my space helmet' or some shit like that. I mean, he was stoned off his gourd. It was awesome. Those *Space Ghost* guys must be so high, man. Especially Brak. Brak rules. He is, like, so wasted."

Udell's numerous allegations of celebrity drug use could not be confirmed as of press time. The fact that Udell was really high was confirmed, however. ∅

17

From August 21, 1996

Somebody Should Do Something About All The Problems

Why isn't anyone doing anything about all the problems? We're living in a time with supercomputers and underwater sea stations and million-dollar laboratories. And still, every day when I watch the TV news shows, I see all sorts of problems!

**Heare Me Out
By Edith Heare**

What are the scientists doing with all that technology? Just sitting on their patoots? Just yesterday there was another plane crash. Isn't that what we have radar for? Why isn't someone taking care of that?

And then there's all those people starving. You can't tell me that we can't figure out a way to feed them. What about all those high-energy vitamin supplements I read about? And what about the dehydrated space food? Someone has got to start putting this information to good use.

Somebody should get on the stick and start using all those high-powered electronic microscopes to cure cancer, that's what I think. There must be someone making money off of these diseases.

So many people are dying in the world. We have laser surgery, don't we? Isn't somebody using that? They put a baboon heart in a human, you know. They can make body parts out of plastic and put little camera probes in your body. So why are there so many people dying?

All this technology—robots, big machines, atomic power—and still they say we are in an energy crisis. Why isn't anyone working on a better way to make electricity? You should see my bill every month. Here we are in the most powerful country in the world and I can't afford to run my air conditioner so I could get one night of good rest once in a while.

They have all those space-age plastics and superconductors just sitting in a lab somewhere, but last week they tell me my muffler is rusted through. So now I roar and rattle down the street sounding like a tank division.

Who is going to start making something decent? What about everything I read in *Time*?

It's a downright shame. Is there no morality in science? Last night I tried to have a barbecue on my back patio and I ran inside before the spicy shish-kabobs were even half-grilled because of the mosquitoes. With all that chemical engineering going on today, with all that military technology, I should at least be able to sip a sloe gin and sour without getting run out of my own yard by something smaller than my fingernail!

And now I have shingles again. With the hundreds of thousands of doctors all over this world, you are telling me that not one of them can do anything about this pain? It's killing me. This is the 20th century, isn't it? We put a man on the moon and I can't find an hour of relief from the swelling? Can't someone assign a team to this problem and get something done for once?

Then there's the fact that my kids never visit me. Here I sit, all alone, wondering when they'll come. We have jet planes that break the sound barrier, but Ginny can't make it from Elk Grove once a month so I can see my own flesh and blood? The Hubble sent down pictures of the galaxy, but I have yet to see my granddaughter's fourth-grade school portraits!

They build a wall across China and a thousand years later I'm still putting up with my neighbor's pine trees dropping cones all over my front lawn. Isn't this a democracy? Have we stood still since Rome?

I hear jabber-jabbering about the discovery of new subatomic particles. What good is a quark to me? Three and a half minutes it takes to cook a bag of microwave popcorn. Three and a half minutes!

Someone is spending a billion dollars a minute to send radio messages into space, and I have to choke down a bag of Pop-Secret kernels that are only half buttered, some not even popped to full puff. God, I pray for a future when the inventor is the friend of mankind.

DNA fingerprinting—that's what they're doing now. And still strawberries at Bergmann's are $2.99 a quart. It's ludicrous. It's as if we live in the Dark Ages.

Cloned genes and fiber optics, but the cat still goes into heat and scratches up my new mahogany coffee table. I kicked that thing as hard as I could with my good leg and it still came back screeching and wagging its fanny like a Broadway showgirl.

Isn't there something someone can do about that? I'm sure with all the vaccines and hybrid cells and carbon-dating equipment we've got today someone can take a minute to whip up a pill I can force down Pumpkin's throat so I have one decent thing in this shoebox house that I worked like a dog at the phone company for 27 years in order to afford.

These are the good years for me? Huh! I'm still watering my flowers and hosing off my driveway. Where are the fiber optics in that? How's superconductivity helping me when my new cotton housedress shrank up to nothing the first time I put it in the dryer? I see all the technology they talk about on the television and I ask you, who's doing anything with it? No one, and it's a dirty rotten shame. ∅

COMMUNITY

Area Oddball Prefers God Over Girls

Through the media, you've been introduced to some of our country's most unusual individuals over the years—and some have been, shall we say, unique.

Who can forget crazy Edna McBain of Florencetown, KY, the wacky widow with the scale cement replica of the moon landing in her barn?

And how about Jack Montague of Hairston, AL, the WWII veteran who refuses to believe the war ever ended and continues to live in his basement bomb shelter, living off canned goods and communicating only by short wave?

But here's the nuttiest yet: Local resident Jerome O'Shea is so religious, he says he's given up courting—for Christ!

And not just for a day or a week, either, but for the rest of his natural life! You may wonder what could make a man behave so oddly. According to O'Shea, he likes girls—likes 'em just fine. In fact, he's in an almost constant state of temptation for pert young female bodies, just like a normal person.

But O'Shea, believing the Lord wants him to stay "pure," has "received a calling," attended the "seminary," and become officially "ordained."

And what does that all mean? This 31-year-old has taken a "holy vow of celibacy," condemning himself to a life of virginity and loneliness in order to stay closer to God's path. Apparently, the "Path of Righteousness" and "Sexual Frustration" mean pretty much the same thing in the wacky world of this area resident!

"Celibacy is a time-honored and ancient tradition of the Roman Catholic Church," O'Shea says. "I really don't understand why you're making such a big deal out of it."

So what exactly does O'Shea

> ## This 31-year-old has taken a "holy vow of celibacy," condemning himself to a life of virginity and loneliness in order to stay closer to God's path.

do in his spare time that's so much better than a Saturday night on the town with a pretty lady on his arm? According to him, his "priestly duties" consist of "reading the liturgy, lighting ceremonial candles and ministering to parishioners." Whoa, slow down, pal! You're having too much fun!

Perhaps the oddest behavior of the kooky cleric is something he calls the "confessional," during which O'Shea sits in a darkened booth and listens to others talk about their sex lives—an aspect of life he can never experience! Weird city!

Strangely enough, O'Shea's role as a "priest" carries with it the ceremonial title of "Father." Not likely! It's sort of hard to father anybody without hooking up with a "mother." Maybe somebody ought to sit this Father down for a little lecture about the birds and the bees!

Even more bizarre is the weekly ritualized cannibalism simulation in which the body and blood of Christ are devoured by the worshippers—but let's just leave that one alone.

O'Shea has been put in the role of moral arbiter of his "congre-

Above: Local "weirdo" Jerome O'Shea will live his whole life and never have sex with another person.

gation," a group of independent citizens who, of their own free will, pay O'Shea a living salary. Ironically, he's directly in charge of the sex lives of his followers, giving them advice on how sex is best practiced!

How sex is best practiced? Practiced? Someone should teach him a thing or two about practice! His advice? Ready for this one? No birth control allowed, you can't masturbate, and you can only have sex with one person your whole life—and then only when you want to

have a baby! If this makes sense to any of you, readers, please explain it to us!

"Leave me alone!" the wacky "Catholic" says, just before slamming the church door. "I thought you wanted to do a human-interest piece on a local priest, but you're just making fun of me! You'll burn in Hell, you infidel!"

Well, one thing's for sure: We can profile strange members of our community for another thousand years, and we'll never top this one! ∅

Let Me Give It To You

You are the one and only for me. And I desire only one thing in this life, and that is for you to let me give it to you.

Let me give it to you every night and day. Let me give it to you in the rain, under a romantic waterfall, under the starlit sky and, of course, between my satin sheets.

By Smoove B
Love Man

But, baby, I will take it slow with you, because I am sensitive.

First, I will approach you at a club, one of the most jumpinest clubs in all of the city. The music will be pumping. Our eyes will meet and you will forget the man that you came with, because my eyes will captivate you and I will sweep you off to the dance floor. On the dance floor we will move like a rehearsal for the real performance later on. We will move like jaguars in heat. In the jungle. My moves will make you hunger for me. You will desire me more than any man you have ever desired. Make no mistake, my groove will most definitely be on.

After an exhausting night of dancing, I will take you back to my apartment and prepare for you a gourmet meal fit for a queen. I will prepare roast pheasant with greens. I will pour you a glass of wine, also. I will select for you only the finest wine from all of the top French vineyards. It will not only be the finest wine from France; it will be the finest wine in the entire world. I will even raise the glass to your lips for you.

You will not believe your eyes when I emerge from the kitchen with a silver platter, silken napkins and the most succulent meat provided by the finest grocery-store meat department in all of Italy.

Please, have some buttered rolls. I baked them

Let me give it to you in the rain, under a romantic waterfall, under the starlit sky.

myself. And there is plenty of butter. I can go and get some margarine, too, if that is what you prefer. I will go and get the finest margarine the world has ever known.

To set the mood, I will light the candles on the table. And I will play Luther on the CD player. Damn.

When we are through with the meal, I will bathe you. I will draw a bubble bath from water imported from the Swiss mountains, purified of all toxins. Let me softly wipe your back with a rag of your choosing. Your beautiful dark skin will feel pampered to the highest extreme. Let me know if you want me to scrub hard or soft, or if you have any areas that you would like me to get especially good. Also, let me know if you want the water hotter or colder.

Girl, after this bath you will be aching with desire. Let me lead you to the bedroom gently by the hand and lay you down on the bed.

Now, my sweet baby, let me give it to you.

It is making me crazy writing this column, because I want you to let me give it to you now, right here. Let me hit you from behind.

But back to the scene I have been painting for you. Let me give it to you nice and slow. Let me drive you wild with desire by caressing every inch of your body. (Your hair included.) Let me then bring you off wild.

Let me give it to you until the break of day.

Girl, let me give it to you. I am asking with all my heart. ∅

BUSINESS

German-Style Krackhaüs Offers Hearty Cocaine

Rousing shouts of "Prosit!" and boot-shaped vials frothing over with hearty, dark, German-style crack are the order of the day at Hans von Kreutzen's new neighborhood Krackhaüs.

"Welkommen, alle!" bellows von Kreutzen to several glassy-eyed baseheads staggering through the ornately carved oak doors of Das Kracken Haüs, the family-style crack-cocaine free-basing emporium and eatery he has built in the Germantown area of East New York. "So, you vant a hit on der krackpipe, ya?"

As a desperate young woman huddles near the Krackhaüs' charming, gingerbread-trimmed bar, offering a man oral sex in exchange for $10, von Kreutzen recalls his establishment's humble roots. "I vas saddened to see zat my neighborhood had lost sight of its strong ethnic roots," he says. "The kinder vere smoking the rock out on the avenue. So I built mein Krackhaüs. Now zey have somevere to go and frei-base in der old German style!"

"Ve make and refine our own product here," says von Kreutzen, obviously proud of his operation. "Der Krack is made in many styles, including Dark, Krack Bock, and a full-bodied, malty Kracktoberfest Pilsner."

All of von Kreutzen's offerings are produced by his on-site Krackmeister in strict accordance with the Bavarian Purity Law of 1977, which states that

Above: Waitress Elke Krupps hoists a heaping tray of the dark, robust Bavarian cocaine waiting for you at Das Kracken Haüs.

the raw flaked cocaine must not be stepped on more than twice before being cut with kitchen powder. The kitchen also serves up hearty Kokenschnitzel with heavy cream sauces, as well as a variety of sausages.

The product's hearty, full-bodied nature means that customer turnover is high. "Some days der ragged, emaciated bodies of ze junkies are staked up in ze back like corpses," says von Kreutzen. "But even zat has its roots in German culture."

"Ich liebe Das Kracken Haüs!" exclaims apple-cheeked waitress Heidi Schtrundle. "This is the only place in East New York where you can cook up to the hearty oompah rhythms of the Krack Barrel Polka. Also, if you're a lady who's broke and still needs a hit, you can just let Hans have some fun under your Dirndl."

Das Kracken Haüs is decorated in the great German style. Huge stained oak tables are the perfect place to enjoy an old-fashioned "massive fatal heart attack." Torches line the walls, giving off a warm glow that illuminates what's cooking in "Der Kracklab." The enormous fieldstone fireplace is the centerpiece for the traditional Krackhead dance, in which one alternates between scuttling closer to the fire's heat and flinching from its light.

"Come, gather round!" von Kreutzen calls out to a large crowd of blond-haired, ruddy-faced addicts. "Und have some delicious Wienerblow!"

Though the story varies, legend has it that von Kreutzen started his Krackhaüs with money he acquired from the sale of miscellaneous art items his father had imported from Europe in the late summer of 1944. With a small-business loan from an Argentinean bank and local connections, Der Kracken Haüs was soon open for business.

And they've been hooked ever since. "Try it—you vill enjoy," von Kreutzen says. "Und if you OD und have to go to ze hospital with toxic shock, tell them Hans sent you!" ∅

Value Of Psychic Phone Service Empirically Proven By Gary Coleman Endorsement

HOLLYWOOD, CA—The psychic-phone-service industry is reeling from Monday's announcement by actor Gary Coleman that the Psychic Friends Network is by far the best psychic-advisement service available—the first-ever incontrovertible proof of the service's superiority over its competitors.

"When someone told me to try one of those other psychic clubs, I said, 'What are you talking about?'" Coleman said in a nationally televised announcement aired at 3 a.m. on CBS. "There's only one true psychic phone service: The Psychic Friends Network."

Coleman, who portrayed Arnold Jackson on TV's *Diff'rent Strokes* from 1978 to 1985, had until Monday remained silent on the issue of which service offers the best psychic advice. The long-awaited endorsement has sent shockwaves through the $2 billion psychic industry.

"Until now, it has not been clear which psychic phone service is truly the best," said professor Clement Dewey of Princeton University. "But now that Gary Coleman has formally endorsed the Psychic Friends Network, this changes everything. Those 'imitation' psychic lines are through. The truth has come out, and we are all the better for it."

PFN celebrity spokesperson and internationally renowned recording star Dionne Warwick was pleased with the Coleman announcement.

"We have always been proud of our hard-working team of master psychics," Warwick said. "But now, after receiving Mr. Coleman's seal of approval, we finally have proof that we are the only legitimate psychic service."

Top PFN psychic Linda Georgian agreed, adding, "All it takes is a telephone and an open mind. Call now for your free 15-minute reading!"

In the wake of Monday's endorsement, millions of Americans who put off choosing a psychic phone service until Coleman went public with a preference are now seeking advice from PFN's staff of expert counselors.

"I presumed that those psychic lines were all phony," said Gail Saunders of Escondido, CA. "But now, with Mr. Coleman's endorsement, the universe seems a very different place. There are forces out there that we don't understand—forces we cannot con-

Above: Gary Coleman endorses the Psychic Friends Network before a national television audience.

front alone. And I'd like to thank Gary for making me understand that."

Added Saunders: "Will you excuse me? I have to go call my psychic. The last time we spoke, I asked her about marriage, and she said she saw a tall, dark, handsome millionaire on the horizon. That's exactly what I wanted to hear!"

In a press statement responding to Coleman's announcement, longtime skeptic and debunker of the paranormal James "The Amazing" Randi said: "I wish to formally retract all my past statements which implied that psychic phenomena were dubious or false. Clearly, the psychic service that can convince Gary Coleman of its validity is one to be respected, even feared. I pray that they will forgive a foolish old man who spoke without thinking."

According to *Advertising Age* managing editor George Lysham, Coleman has long been considered infallible among sitcom veterans, his views second only to those of

famed Glad Trash Bags pitchman Tom Bosley.

"Remember, Coleman was not just the star of eight seasons of *Diff'rent Strokes*," Lysham said. "We're talking about the star of *The Kid With The Broken Halo* and that movie where he slept in the locker at the bus station. His opinions are not to be dismissed lightly."

As a result of the Coleman endorsement, celebrity endorsers of other psychic phone lines are scrambling to reorganize their lives. Ted Lange and Elke Sommer of Kenny Kingston's Psychic Hotline have publicly renounced Kingston, while Psychic Encounters spokespersons Nichelle Nichols and Lady Sunshine have gone into hiding.

Future infomercials for PFN will replace the disclaimer, "For entertainment purposes only," with the statement, "Everything claimed by PFN psychics is guaranteed 100 percent true by the authority of Gary Coleman, former television star and world-renowned psychic-verification expert." ∅

From April 3, 1996

Point-Counterpoint: Humidity

What We Need Is More Humidity

By Duracraft Natural Warm Moisture Humidifier, Model DH-901

Is there anything in this world more wonderful than humidity? I know, it's a rhetorical question.

There has been a lot of talk lately by certain parties, and you know who I'm talking about, when it comes to the issue of humidity. And let me say this right off the bat: I love humidity. I love giving it, especially in places where it doesn't already exist. But, selfishness aside, humidity works for everybody.

I restore moisture to the air to help prevent dry skin and chapped lips. Physicians often recommend moisture to help relieve cold and flu symptoms and dry, scratchy throats. And, of course, adding moisture to the air protects furniture and plants from damaging dryness and minimizes the annoyance of static electricity.

I feature a two-gallon output per day and humidify up to 1,175 square feet. I have a clear, removable tank which makes refill checks effortless. I feature the Mist Breather™ Safety System which automatically shuts mist off if the tank is empty, removed or tipped over.

I feature a limited three-year warranty and an easy-to-read on/off indicator light. And, something you may not know, my heating element purifies water to remove bacteria.

The dehumidifiers can talk their talk, but we know they aren't going to walk the walk. We cannot now, nor ever, peacefully co-exist. I am sworn to destroy them and everything they represent, and it is that which I will do.

The debate ends here. ∅

Humidity Must Be Destroyed

By Edison 25 pt. Dehumidifier Model DHE25W

I been hearing a lot of talk about humidifiers lately. And I been hearing a lot of talk by humidifiers lately. And I don't like it one bit. Why? Because as everybody knows, the existence of humidifiers, and humidity in general, is a horrible, horrible thing.

Everyone knows it, but for the record, let me illuminate some simple truths.

Humidity makes everything damp and wet and soggy. It ruins fragile documents and paintings and reduces the lifespan of photographs. And you'd better believe it will put mold on your bathroom tile. The worst part is, it's everywhere. How do we best combat the menace? Simple, the Edison 25 pt. Dehumidifier. But just what do I bring to the table?

How about rugged construction, automatic shut-off and a continuous drain option? That's not enough for you? Well, I'll throw in a variable-control humidistat, a full-bucket indicator light and an automatic de-icer that prevents freeze-up. And for good measure, why don't you count an air filter among my assets?

That's a lot of machine for your money. And I swear to you on my honor as a proud member of the Edison multinational corporate line, I will fight humidity every day, with every watt of energy the good Lord saw fit to power me with.

Humidity must die! You hear that, Duracraft? I'm coming after you with an empty water-collection bucket and a whole lotta steam! ∅

SOCIETY

Amish Give Up

'This Is Bullshit,' Elders Say

LANCASTER, PA—After centuries of enduring harsh, spare living conditions and voluntarily shunning modern amenities such as microwave ovens and red clothing, Amish leaders announced Monday that Amish across the U.S. will abandon their traditional ways and adapt to modern American life.

"Fuck that," said Amish Father Ezekiel Schmid at a Lancaster press conference. "This is pure bullshit."

Schmid recounted the hard Amish life, in which many long hours are spent toiling under the hot sun in heavy black clothing without any refrigerated drinks or gas-powered farm machines. He spoke of the arduous task of raising barns by hand from dawn until dusk, and of laboriously churning his own butter without electrical power.

"I can't believe we were such suckers," he said. "I feel like a fool."

Schmid added that he will shave off his "ridiculous" Pennsylvania Dutch-style beard with no mustache, a look he said went out of fashion in "about 1820."

"Why didn't anyone ever tell me how stupid I looked?" he asked.

According to Schmid, the Amish look forward to a wide variety of "alternative lifestyle opportunities" that now await them.

"I am indeed looking forward to wearing clothing that is a color other than black," said Josephat Kreugger, a prominent Amish counsel member. "I will try on some dark gray suits, perhaps even medium gray. I am also considering buying a charcoal-colored hat." Kreugger also expressed a desire to travel "twice the speed of horse."

Many social changes await the Amish, as well.

"When I punish my son for not saying his prayers," Mary Wittgenstein said, "I normally use a wooden switch taken from a tree. But now, think of the modern child-beating weapons that will be available to me in the outside world. Perhaps there are whips made especially for use on disobedient children, or muskets."

Many Amish people look forward to getting jobs in the real world. Amish farmer Abraham Verveert said he has greatly entertained other Amish people at church meetings with his rousing scripture readings, and hopes to capitalize on that talent by taking his Bible-reading on the road.

"I have readings scheduled at nightclubs and ballrooms across the country, and judging by the gleeful reaction of my Amish brethren, I believe I will find great success entertaining outsiders with my lively readings," Verveert said. "This week, I will be reading a particularly delightful passage from Corinthians at the Sunrise Motor Inn in Kew Gardens, NY. You will surely want to be present."

One Amish couple, Jacob and Sarah Neamer, plan to move to an apartment in a major city

Amish farmer Jakob Nordemann plans to sell his horse and buggy and shave off the Pennsylvania Dutch-style beard he called "totally ridiculous."

and adopt a modern lifestyle, but will continue to make a living the only way they know how.

"We will charge admission for people to enter our home and observe our lifestyle," Sarah said. "For $12.50, or $10 with coupon, you can watch us as we cook meals and watch the television."

One Amish entrepreneur, Lucas Hagen, is looking forward to taking full advantage of modern technology.

"I was often ostracized in the Amish community for my blasphemous ideas about loosening Amish traditions," he said. "Now that I am free to explore life on the outside, I plan to buy a cable TV station and create the Amish Porn Channel."

If successful, Hagen's Amish Porn Channel will feature programs in which women take off their bonnets and expose their hair.

Schmid looks forward to becoming a policeman. "I want to rid the world of illegal butter churning," he said somberly. "It is costing the government millions every year." Ø

From April 16, 1998

I Can't Stand My Filthy Hippie Owner

Jesus Christ, do I ever hate my filthy fucking hippie owner, Zach. You have no idea the hell I go through, living in this disgusting house with him and his hordes of skank-ass hippie friends.

By Thunder The Ferret

I didn't ask for this shit, you know. I try to keep clean, giving myself frequent tongue-baths. But it's simply impossible when, everywhere I step, there's a moldy black-bean pita sandwich or an ashtray overflowing with half-smoked joints.

I never get a moment's rest, either. Twenty-four hours a day, seven days a week, there's at least a dozen smelly-haired fuckers sitting around getting high and watching *Star Trek: The Next Generation*, or planning another pancake benefit for East Timor. Get a life, losers.

The agony never ends. I can't even sleep, because every time I try, Zach starts beating on his bongos while some other unwashed bozo tries to play some crappy didgeridoo he made out of some PVC pipe. And if I hear one more hippie fumble through the bridge of "Sugar Magnolia" on Zach's untuned acoustic guitar, I'm going to squeeze my head between the bars of my cage and twist until my neck snaps.

I'm a ferret, goddamn it! I have a very acute sense of smell! Day after day, I am forced to choke on the nauseating stench of strawberry incense and sweat-soaked Guatemalan wool doused in patchouli oil. And do you think my owner could actually put down his bong long enough to clean my fucking cage every once in a blue moon? Of course not!

Then there's that friend of Zach's who hitchhiked down from Boulder last week—Rick or Ryan or something. Whatever his name is, I just think of him as the "'That's Cool' Guy," because that's all he ever fucking says. You'd think that, after the 200th time I squirmed away from this bastard, he'd figure out that I don't want his grubby hands on me. Not this burn-out.

> **You have no idea the hell I go through, living in this disgusting house with him and his hordes of skank-ass hippie friends.**

"That's Cool" Guy must be brain-damaged from one too many acid trips, because a few days ago, I was just trying to make it across the living room to hide behind a big stack of dirty cereal bowls when he lunged at me and spilled bong water all down my fricking back. I smelled like holy hell for the next four days! I tried to lick myself clean, but I had to stop because I started seeing things. I swear, after a while, that Phish shit Zach plays 20 hours a day was almost starting to sound good.

The absolute worst thing that ever happened to me, though, was when that son of a bitch Zach got out that goddamn collar and took me down to the park to watch him take off his sandals and juggle sticks. I stretched the leash as far as it would go, but I'm sure people could still figure out I was with that loser. There was a bunch of squirrels standing by a tree, laughing their asses off at me. Christ, talk about humiliating!

I tried running away once, but Mr. Smarty Patchwork-Pants found me hiding underneath the front porch. I'd rather eat worms than choke down any more of that organic bulgur crap that motherfucker dumps in my bowl every day.

Mark my words, one of these days, I'm gonna make another run for it. It was the last straw today when he tied that teeny fucking hemp necklace around my neck. I chewed through that piece of shit in 10 minutes. Just because he thinks it's goddamn 1969 doesn't mean I have to play along. If I can just make it past the rusted VW microbus in the driveway, that fucking hippie will never see my ass again. ∅

From October 1, 1998

Don't Feel Sad, I'm In Heaven Now, Singing With The Pretty Angels

Please, everybody, don't feel sad. I understand how bad you all feel inside. I know it must seem so awful to you, but there's no reason to be blue. Everything's okay, don't you see? Turn that frown upside down. I'm in Heaven now, singing with the pretty angels.

Please don't cry.

It's so nice up here in Heaven. Everyone is happy, and each day is sunny and bright. Beautiful music plays all around me as I skip and dance through fluffy white clouds. Winged unicorns fly across the sky as harps, trumpets and bells play songs of glory to God. My new friends and I love to go on magic pony rides through the Enchanted Candy Forest and sip sweet nectar from the Yum-Yum Fruit of Gumdrop Glade. And I wear a beautiful necklace made of flowers as I prance about, whistling tunes with the pretty birdies.

By JonBenet Ramsey

Back when I used to live on Earth like you, nothing made me feel more special than knowing that I was making all the nice people happy with my pretty dresses and my sweet smile. I loved curtsying for the judges and hearing all the grown-ups say, "Awww, isn't that cute?" When I did my special tap-dance and sang the "Jesus Loves Me" song up there on that big stage, making sure to do it just right so nobody would get mad and yell at me, I felt like the prettiest little girl in the whole wide world.

Then the Bad Thing came.

Now, everywhere I look, people are feeling sad because they wish I could be alive again. Well, don't you see? You shouldn't be sad. Sing a happy song, because I am alive again, up here in Heaven, where all the good little girls and boys go when they die.

Here in Heaven, everyone has a shiny new halo and beautiful wings sprinkled with starshine. Sometimes, my halo falls down over my head because I'm so little. The other angels always giggle and smile when they see me wrinkling up my cute little face when the halo tickles my button nose.

Fairies and elves and cuddly little animals tuck me into bed each night, and I always have sweet dreams. Every day is full of hugs and laughter, and I never feel cold and alone, like I felt in that awful basement.

I sleep in a bed of moonbeams, covered in a blanket of clouds. Each day, an adorable deer wakes me up by licking my face. Magical dewdrops scrub my pink face clean, and for breakfast I eat a bowl of sunbeams and starshine. I have lots of pretty dresses, and nobody ever makes me wear make-up or high heels. All day long, I play and sing songs with the other angels, tugging at their robes to make them laugh. Most of them are grown-ups, but you'd be surprised if you knew how many of them are adorable little children, just like me! We play games with the angels all day long and we put on little shows for the grown-ups, spinning around and dancing, and there's always applause from the heavenly host. Then we all sing hymns together in praise to God.

Everything is so beautiful up here in Heaven, with puppies and kitties that prance around and fairy-dust that sprinkles through the light. Even Jesus is here. He cradles my tiny little body in His arms, giving me candy and shiny toys to play with, and He shines His love on me. So, you see, there's no reason to be sad. I have risen above my grisly death, and now I sit at the right hand of my Savior on the Throne of Heaven.

Cheer up. Don't be a frowny-face. Let me see you smile. ✍

26

INTERNATIONAL

Blues Musician To U.N.: 'Yemen Done Me Wrong'

NEW YORK—Legendary Delta bluesman Willie "Skipbone" Jackson is demanding U.N. sanctions against the Middle Eastern Republic of Yemen following what he called "a low-down dirty deed" against him.

Among the actions Jackson is protesting are Yemen's alleged tearing out and stomping flat of his heart, disappearing when he most needed the Arab republic and making him feel like a worn-out old dog—actions which, according to the U.N.'s Charter of Fundamental Human Rights, "just ain't right."

Said Jackson: "Prime Minister Abd al-Aziz al-Ghani gonna be the death of me."

This represents an unfortunate breakdown in once-positive relations between the predominantly Muslim nation and the 74-year-old master of the slide guitar. As recently as last year, Yemen's Council of Ministers rocked and rolled the musician in so vigorous a manner as to make a landlord forget about the rent.

"This is a devastating blow to Mr. Jackson," said Harvard political science professor Eldred Hyde. "For a man who has been beaten up and down until his mama don't recognize him no more, then cheated out of his only pair of shoes, a diplomatic incident with a longtime ally like Yemen may be an unrecoverable crisis."

Added Hyde: "If it weren't for bad luck, it appears Mr. Jackson would not have any luck at all."

The composer of such blues classics as "Dead Cow Blues" and "Butter My Bread" maintained that he gave Yemen all he had, only to be forsaken, much like a worn-out suit. He also said that there is another country whose name Yemen cries out at night.

Above: According to Delta bluesman Willie "Skipbone" Jackson, the nation of Yemen (inset) "done treat me so unkind." Yemen Prime Minister Abd al-Aziz al-Ghani denies the charges.

"Yemen done recently form a trade pact with the United Arab Emirates," Jackson said, "and I been laid low ever since."

Yemen President Ali Abdallah Salih has expressed a willingness to reopen negotiations with the Clarksdale, MS-born blues legend, but vigorously denied that his nation has been seen with the U.A.R., that oil-rich country down Oman way.

Salih added that it is Jackson who is sneaking around, implying that Jackson's mojo was recently worked by Pakistani Prime Minister Benazir Bhutto.

"When Bhutto shakes her thing, Jackson is unable to keep his stuff still," Salih said. "May Allah have mercy on his two-timin' soul."

Jackson denied any involvement with Bhutto and rejected Salih's offer for negotiations, noting that he is "too busy wishin' I was anyone but me."

If Jackson's U.N. demands are met, Yemen will be penalized by severe international economic sanctions. In addition, none of Yemen's 15 million citizens would be welcome in his house no more.

"I been cryin' ever since the day I met that devil-hearted country," Jackson said. "I ain't goin' down that Middle Eastern nation's road no more." ∅

The Fairness And Accuracy In Media Silver Medallion Winners

To-day, I had my man-servant Standish procure several leather-bound volumes of vintage issues of *The Onion* and bring them to my bed-chamber. What a treasure trove these yellowed pages are! Many a historian would give his eye-teeth to spend a few hours amidst these regal tomes, which truly serve as a mirror to a long-ago past.

By T. Herman Zweibel
Publisher Emeritus
(photo circa 1911)

Because I personally edited *The Onion* for much of the Twentieth Century, many of the old dispatches, from the histori-cally significant to the trivially minor, were still familiar to me. As Standish turned each thin, fragile page, a torrent of memo-ries flooded my mind.

"Standish, do you remember when that Floradora Girl eloped with the Mohammedan contortionist, leaving her elderly steel-magnate beau in the lurch?" I asked. "Indeed, I do, sir," Standish replied, and we both laughed. "What about the time when that Irish-man's horse ran about City Hall, causing an up-roar?" I queried. "It prompted much amusement," Standish answered, and we laughed some more. "And do you remem-ber the fire at the shirt-waist factory, the one that killed all those immigrants?" I asked. "As though it were yesterday, sir," Standish replied, and our laughter grew even louder. Such was our joyful camaraderie that I almost for-got our rigid master–servant relationship. But I remembered it just in time, and curtly up-braided Standish for disregarding his place, ordering him to remain silent in my presence for the duration of the after-noon.

I bet I can remember things Standish can't. After all, he is only 81 or so, while I am 132 years old. Much like the old bound volumes, my mind is a repository of multitudinous facts. I can't help it; ever since I was a lad, I have been blessed with a daguerrotypic memory. For example, I must be the only person alive who can remember the street-car accident on the corner of 34th and Parmenter back in 1894, or that the favorite color of the famed vaudeville singer Miss Charlotte Wren was chartreuse, or that Mayor Bellinger's elegant cherry-wood desk was a gift from Union General Dan Sickles for all the tire-less work he did for the G.A.R.

Oh, who gives a rat's ass? Only a feeble-minded pedant would care about such petty things. My life has been a com-plete waste. Here I was, merely a two-bit news-paper editor, proof-reading end-less accounts about cats up trees or slav-ishly transcribing the stock ticker, when I could have been a great man, an author of history or literature. Or, better yet, made history my-self as a great general or president.

Imagine my calling the old news-papers a "treasure trove." Hah! They're all crammed with myopic, small-minded commentary and myriad meaning-less ephemera. The winds of Time barely stir up a breeze in these moldering, silver-fish-ridden pages. My life's work amounts to nothing more than a pile of crumbling dust, meager kindling for a waning fire!

And here I am, an absurd mockery of an aged man, wizened beyond all human recognition and cursed to remember nearly every detail of my miserable existence! Nurse! If you have any decency within you, grab the nearest scalpel and plunge it into my decaying blue heart post-haste! No jury will convict you!

No, wait, I said "scalpel," not "syringe"! No! No more laudanum, please! Nothing that will prolong my agonizing life further! Please, I beg you! Oh!

Ah... Delicious laudanum...

NATION

Black Box Reveals TWA Flight 800 Passengers Missed End Of *Dragonheart*

WASHINGTON, DC—In what may be the most difficult news yet for families of TWA Flight 800 victims, federal investigators revealed Monday that, according to black-box evidence, passengers had not finished viewing the in-flight movie *Dragonheart* before the airplane crashed.

"As far as we can determine by analysis of the on-board flight recorder," said National Air Traffic Safety Board investigator Gina Paz, "a violent explosion in the plane's fuselage caused the plane to go down, terminating *Dragonheart* before its exciting completion."

A visibly shaken Paz paused for a moment before adding, "There were roughly 20 minutes remaining in this magical, fanciful Universal Pictures release that the victims never got to see."

"This is a terrible tragedy," said U.S. Transportation Secretary Federico Peña. "One thousand years ago, two sworn enemies—a dragonslaying knight and the last remaining dragon—formed an incredible alliance to battle tyranny in the land. No one deserves to die in the middle of such a tale."

Though the *Dragonheart* disaster is still under investigation, the NATSB did release several seconds of tape recordings from Flight 800's black box. On the tape, screams and loud sobbing can be heard as the popular Dennis Quaid/Sean Connery film inexplicably stops in mid-reel following a complete loss of cabin pressure.

"My God! The screen's gone out! We're going down! Does Bowen slay the dragon? Or does he resist and honor their unlikeliest of friendships?!" a woman can be heard wailing on the tape.

Also captured by the black box is an elderly man, who shouts: "What happened? What happened to Julie Christie in her first big-screen performance in over five years?"

According to Irwin Schifrin, the NATSB technician in charge of reviewing TWA's in-flight recorder tapes, there was little indication of trouble prior to the explosion.

"Right up to the moment of the blast, everything was proceeding normally," Schifrin said. "Passengers responded well to Quaid's portrayal of the idealistic armored knight. There was a brief moment of trouble at the beginning, when some passengers had a hard time accepting Connery as the dragon's voice, but it passed without incident. Then you can hear the explosion. Not long after that, the movie stopped and the screaming began."

To help ease the pain of the victims' families, TWA is sending each their own copy of *Dragonheart*.

"It's the least we could do," said TWA spokesman Malcolm Schlesinger. "Even if the victims never lived to see the end of the movie, at least now their loved ones can." ∅

Above: FBI officials collect some of the wreckage of TWA Flight 800, on which 288 people were tragically killed before being able to see the end of the in-flight movie, *Dragonheart* (inset).

From June 5, 1996

Bantu Tribesman Uses IBM Global Uplink Network Modem To Crush Nut

KABINDA, ZAIRE—In a move IBM officials are hailing as a major step in the company's ongoing worldwide telecommunications revolution, M'wana Ndeti, a member of Zaire's Bantu tribe, used an IBM global uplink network modem to crush a nut Monday. Ndeti, who had spent 20 minutes trying to open the nut by hand, easily cracked it open by smashing it with the powerful modem.

"I could not crush the nut by myself," said the 47-year-old Ndeti, who added the savory nut to a thick, peanut-based soup minutes later. "With IBM's help, I was able to break it."

Ndeti discovered the nut-breaking, 28.8 V.34 modem when IBM was shooting a commercial in his village. During a break in shooting the ad, which shows African villagers eagerly teleconferencing via computer with Japanese schoolchildren, Ndeti sneaked onto the set and took the modem, which he believed would serve well as a "smashing" utensil.

Just after Ndeti shattered the nut, a 200-member Southern Baptist gospel choir, on hand for the taping of the commercial, broke out into raucous, joyous song in celebration of the tribesman's accomplishment.

IBM officials were not surprised the long-time computer giant was able to provide Ndeti with practical solutions to his everyday problems.

"Our telecommunications systems offer people all over the world global networking solutions that fit their specific needs," said Herbert Ross, IBM's director of marketing. "Whether you're a nun cloistered in an Italian abbey or an aborigine in Australia's Great Sandy Desert, IBM has the ideas to get you where you want to go today."

According to Ndeti, the modem's most impressive feature was its hard plastic casing, which easily sustained several minutes of vigorous pounding against a large stone. "I put the nut on a rock and hit it with the modem," Ndeti said. "The modem did not break. It is a good modem."

Ndeti was so impressed with the modem that he purchased a new, state-of-the-art

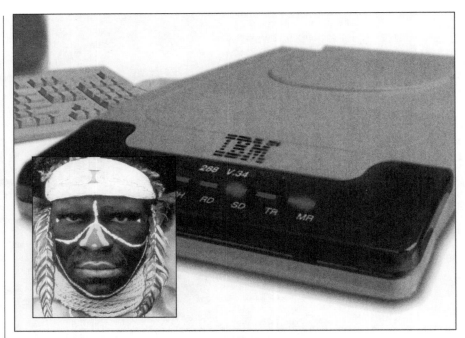

Bantu tribesman M'wana Ndeti (inset) found good use for an IBM modem (above), smashing a difficult-to-crack nut with the modem's hard outer casing. Ndeti borrowed the modem during the taping of an IBM commercial depicting African villagers communicating online with Japanese schoolchildren.

IBM workstation, complete with a PowerPC 601 microprocessor, a quad-speed internal CD-ROM drive and three 16-bit ethernet networking connectors. The tribesman has already made good use of the computer system, fashioning a gazelle trap out of its wires, an anchor out of the monitor and a crude but effective weapon from its mouse.

"This is a good computer," said Ndeti, carving up a gazelle with the computer's flat, sharp internal processing device. "I am using every part of it. I will cook this gazelle on the keyboard."

Hours later, Ndeti capped off his gazelle dinner by smoking the computer's 200-page owner's manual.

IBM spokespeople praised Ndeti's choice of computer.

"We are pleased that the Bantu people are turning to IBM for their business needs," said

CEO William Allaire. "From Kansas City to Kinshasa, IBM is bringing the world closer together. Our cutting-edge technology is truly creating a global village."

The Bantu tribesmen are members of an ever-growing, international community of users who have turned to IBM to solve their networking needs. Jean-Claude DuMont, a goatherder from the French region of Brittany who is working on an Indiana University doctorate in biology via the Internet, recently looked into IBM's new computer-satellite data uplink, which offers instant access to library files worldwide.

"With IBM's new uplink service, I can access any file I want, any time I want," DuMont told fellow goatherder Pierre Valmont during a recent walk through a rye field. "I can even find out how many points Michael Jordan scored last night."

Replied Valmont: "Radical." ✐

HARVEY'S HOLLYWOOD

Hitler Was Wrong!

Item! I just saw a TNT biopic (that's biographical picture) about former German president **Adolf Hitler**. Apparently, he was the reason we got involved in that unpleasant business in Europe in the '40s.

**The Outside Scoop
By Jackie Harvey**

Donald Sutherland played the evil Hitler, and, based on the story in this movie, he was wrong! I couldn't believe the stuff he was saying. It made my ears burn just to hear it. The long and short of it was that he wanted to kill a lot of people because he thought he was in some way superior. What sort of person thinks they can just go out and kill people? Well, that is just bunk. Kudos to **Ted Turner** for blowing the lid off of this villain!

Item! **Jennifer Aniston** from the smash comedy hit *Friends* is on the cover of the *Rolling Stone Magazine*... bare naked! Now, I like to see a pretty girl as much as the next guy, but I hardly think that is appropriate by the checkout stand where just anyone can see her bare bottom! I was so steamed, I vowed not to watch *Friends* again. The only problem is that the promise of side-splitting comedy (coupled with the cast's strong friendship) weakened my resolve. By the time I remembered, the show was half over and I was hooked! But, come on, keep that stuff clean so everyone can enjoy it!

Say, has anyone ever seen those shoes that light up when you walk in them? I mean, what is the deal?

We'll miss you, old friend. Singer, dancer and actor **Gene Kelly** died recently, putting yet another feather in heaven's cap. If you hear a great noise in the sky, it's probably just Gene teaching those angels a little two-step. It's thoughts like this that make me look forward to dying.

Joseph Cotten has escaped the media, but that doesn't mean I'm not trying to get that one-to-one. He hasn't gotten back to me. I'll wait, though.

Item! Author **Salman Rushdie** has come out of hiding to show those nogoodnik fanatics he won't be pushed around. Bully for him! As a journalist, I know what it's like to stir up the muck occasionally. I stand in solidarity with Mr. Rushdie. If you want him, you're going to have to get through me first!

> ## What sort of person thinks they can just go out and kill people? Kudos to Ted Turner for blowing the lid off of this villain!

Item! The **Oscar People** have announced the nominations for the next Oscars. There is the movie about the pig who talks (it's a trick), the movie about toys and the movie with heartthrob **Mel Gibson** wearing a skirt! Just kidding. The Oscar People would never nominate a movie about a man in a skirt. I'll take a smart pair of pants any day! My money goes to the toy movie, called *The Toy Story*. That was a good family movie, and it had the guy from *Home Improvement* in it. If that wasn't the best movie of the year, maybe ever, I don't know what is. Hey, Disney, I'm pulling for ya!

Hot on the comeback trail! **John Travolta** did it. **Brooke Shields** did it. Now, *Star Wars* hero **Billy Dee Williams** is doing it! After three years in relative obscurity, the suave Williams is a television regular again. Unfortunately, his program is on late at night. His new show is a sort of talk show where he interviews **psychics**. It even had a number that I could call for more information on this fascinating subject. Williams was rich with effusive charm, his sparkling eyes and warm smile filling the screen and my soul. Hey, you **network executives**—maybe you should try moving the show to prime time where it stands a chance!

Finally, I've gotten a few letters asking me about my sources that I frequently refer to. Everyone wants to know just who they are. Obviously, I can't reveal their names, or I'd lose my credibility as a journalist. Let's just say that this **Outside Scoop** has pretty big ears, as well as some **friends in high places** in all the right places.

Here's a thought to send you away with: Have you ever seen **Mary-Kate** and **Ashley Olsen** in the same place at the same time? Kind of makes you think, huh? ∅

From December 5, 1995

Man, Ape Cause Roadhouse Ruckus

FLAGSTAFF, AZ—A ruckus commenced Saturday night at Big Bertha's Saloon and Roadhouse, the result of raucous shenanigans stemming from the irreverent, authority-defying actions of an unidentified man/orangutan duo, police said Monday.

The ruckus, which involved the throwing of chairs, beer bottles and denim-clad good ol' boys through plate-glass windows, was accompanied by numerous hoots, hollers and exuberant yells of the common battle cry, "Yee-haw!"

It may have been caused by one of the regulars, local boy Clem Taylor, who suggested to the unidentified visitor that he "[didn't] look so tough." Taylor proceeded to challenge the stranger to prove his manhood via traditional hand-to-hand combat. It is thought that an errant roundhouse swing by Taylor may have spilled beer on an uninvolved onlooker, thereby causing the violence to quickly spread among the bar's other patrons.

Other unconfirmed reports claimed that the brawl had been started over an arm-wrestling match. Still others close to the action disagreed, indicating that the chaos may have started when the stranger became visibly insulted after fellow truckers openly mocked his ape, claiming his "date could use a shave," then pouring a drink over the orangutan's head.

The ape is a midland African orangutan, roughly five years old, according to a witness familiar with higher primate development. Eyewitnesses said the animal seemed oddly unfrightened during the ruckus, smiling from ear to ear while he hung from the rafters, knocking various brawlers unconscious by conking them on the head from behind with beer bottles, then clapping his hands and feet in triumph.

The man and ape, still being sought for questioning by local authorities, are said to be "two loners" who "truck across the country together, searching for adventure on the open road, chasing tail and raising hell."

Police refused to speculate on whether this incident is connected to the madcap chase scene which took place earlier this week involving a bumbling motorcycle gang and a man/ape duo in an battered old pick-up. Ø

Above: These two characters caused quite a stir, boozin' and brawlin' into the wee hours.

From December 19, 1995

Nine Drawn And Quartered At Renaissance Fair

RICHMOND, VA—Nine people were torn limb from limb and skewered through the anus with wooden stakes Sunday at the city's annual Renaissance fair. Organizers boast that the "Drawn And Quartered" show made this year's fair one of the most authentic ever.

The early-Renaissance torture demonstration was one of many improvisations that peppered the fair ground, performed by actors from the local theater community dressed in period costumes. These performances have been a fixture of past years' fairs.

"The skits where we publicly tortured and humiliated 'condemned heretics' gave us by far the most response we've ever gotten," actor Paul Mealen said. "Who would have thought violence would appeal to people?"

In the skit, victims were randomly selected from the crowd, strung up on posts and read official "charges." A dirt-encrusted dagger was then used to saw off vital parts of the condemned. One man's scrotum was cut off, causing his testicles to fall to the ground. According to witnesses, children at the festival then tossed the testicles back and forth as the victim watched.

Such vital organs as the liver were cut out of other victims, then cooked and force-fed to them. The pale and barely conscious subjects were then taken down from the posts and prepared for the next stage of their torture amid taunts and bellows from the crowd.

"We loved it," said University of

Above: Richmond, Virginia's annual Renaissance fair featured plenty of exciting, historically accurate action, such as jousting, swordfighting, archery competitions and the evisceration of condemned heretics.

Virginia student Steve Limeneg, who, along with his friend Alicia Ponfret, was attending the fair for the first time. "It was like we were transported back to the real Renaissance. We got turkey drumsticks at the Ye Olde Grille, threw stones at the Drench A Wench booth—I won a stuffed jester doll—and then we got to see this heretic forced to eat his own kidney."

Added Richmond middle-school teacher Linda Douglas: "It was a lot of fun. They picked my husband out of the crowd and he thought it was a kick. When they eviscerated him and

he started screaming and begging for his life and crying out to me, the kids and I did our part, yelling, 'Heretic!' and so on."

Next, four horses were tied to the arms and legs of each victim, and each horse was made to pull in opposing directions, summarily causing limbs to tear off and go skipping in every direction. Finally, the disembodied and helpless torsos were fed to packs of ravenous dogs. The victims' horrific, wheezing screams caught the attention of the entire fair.

"I thought it was very impressive," said Herman Klinemest, a

bank executive who partook of the fair with his wife and three children. "I enjoyed taunting the condemned, and my children enjoyed playing with the testicles."

One volunteer was tied up and laid on his back spread-eagled, his legs held apart by a short beam roped to a horse. A long wooden stake was braced against a rock and inserted just a few inches into the participant's anus. When the horse received a snap from the whip, it bolted, causing the participant to be driven onto the stake until it thrust out of his mouth.

Festival organizer Liz Fendamn has faced pressure to compete with nearby Colonial Williamsburg for tourist dollars, and she said the event was popular enough to guarantee a return next year.

"We try to give people a merry ol' time, m'lord," she said with a smile. "Ye can bet yer knickers we'll be doing it again."

She hinted they may even have the performing troupe dress like Spanish soldiers and wantonly slaughter masses of heretical fair visitors.

Though most everyone called the fair a success, some family members of the late participants were not so enthusiastic.

"My husband and I came to the fair as part of our honeymoon," Jaclyn Welden said. "When he was stabbed through the heart and killed for blaspheming the pope, the fair suddenly became less fun."

Welden added that she will not return next year. Ø

You Are Pretty

WASHINGTON, D.C.—Department of the Interior officials released a report Monday stating that you are pretty. The report found that you have a pleasant face and emphasized that it is unique "in a good way." The report also cites the great features you have: your cute nose, wavy hair and a "really nice" smile. —*November 7, 1995*

Aerobics Show Used For Almost Completely Non-Aerobic Purpose

BELLEVUE, WA—The aerobics program *Get Fit With Jenni* was used for almost entirely non-aerobic purposes Tuesday, when Seattle-area 15-year-old Brian Elkins vigorously engaged in a low-impact cardiovascular workout while watching the TV show. Elkins performed his semi-aerobic routine while watching 22-year-old host Jenni Raye, clad in a Spandex bikini top and form-fitting Lycra shorts, do hamstring-toning leg lifts while bent over on all fours. "We have determined that Brian's heart rate increased by about 35 percent during his semi-strenuous nine-minute regimen," said Elkins family physician Dr. Edward Farber. "His breathing rate likewise increased, and several large and small muscle groups received a modicum of aerobic movement and stretching." Elkins, who woke up with minor soreness the next day, said he "could really feel it working." —*June 11, 1998*

Jews To Celebrate Rosh Hashasha Or Something

JERUSALEM—Jews the world over are preparing to celebrate Rosh Hashanukah or something this weekend, the traditional Jewish holiday marking some sort of rebirth and new beginning, or maybe the Jews' liberation from some foreign ruler 55,000 years ago. "Rash Kishansha is a very holy time for the Jewish people," said Paul Castellano, a guy from Houston whose gastroenterologist is Jewish. "I think Dr. Futterman said it's the holiday where they light that chandelier and blow that horn." Lasting 12 days, Ran Hosea is followed by Yor Kiplach, the Festival of Sand, during which no buttered bread may be eaten in remembrance of the flooding of the ancient Temple of Hosea. —*September 11, 1996*

O.J. Trial Lampooned In Outrageous TV Send-Up

NEW YORK—Network television broke new ground Wednesday when the murder trial of O.J. Simpson was lampooned on the ABC comedy program *The Dana Carvey Show*. The trial, in which former football star O.J. Simpson was acquitted of the murders of Nicole Brown Simpson and Ronald Goldman, proved a wellspring of comedy for the creative minds behind the show. "We realized this trial was a major event a year ago," Carvey said. "So we thought, wouldn't it be crazy if we did a wild send-up of it?" In the skit, which ran for 14 unpredictable minutes, Simpson was portrayed as actually having committed the murders. —*April 10, 1996*

White Castle Plundered By Turks

KEW GARDENS, NY—A Queens-area White Castle restaurant was violently raided Friday by Turkish marauder Bakhbar The Cruel. "Let songs of this day echo off the white tile walls," Bakhbar said shortly after unseating and beheading shift manager Dave Spivac, 27. Small, squarish hamburgers, described by one of Bakhbar's generals as "what he craves," were carted off by the hundreds following the raid. Four captured employees will now be traded as slaves. Also stolen in the brutal Castle purge were more than 36 dozen kids' meal toys, 11 gallons of beverage syrup and enough onion chips to get the nomadic horde to the Throgs Neck Bridge. —*March 5, 1997*

Quincy Suspects Murder

LOS ANGELES—Forensic examiner Quincy announced Tuesday that he believes a John Doe brought to him by police detectives was murdered, and not dead of natural causes as ruled by the county coroner. "It is not often that I suspect foul play," Quincy said. "But in this rare case, a slight imperfection in the body that went unnoticed by other investigators makes me highly suspicious." Lieut. Frank Monahan of the LAPD maintained there is no evidence of murder, and is urging Quincy to "drop it," calling the matter an "open-and-shut case." Quincy and his assistant, Sam Fujiyama, plan to circumvent the police force and investigate, solve and render justice in the murder case themselves. —*July 10, 1996*

MALPH'S CORNER

Why Do People Laugh After I Do Something Funny?

I consider myself a typical teenager growing up in a typical Milwaukee neighborhood in the late 1950s. I attend Jefferson High School and like looking at girls. I'm in a band with my two best friends. We play mostly Bobby Darin and Fats Domino tunes. My favorite after-school hangout is a burger joint with roller-skating carhops. I even have a leather-jacketed greaser friend, and although he often refers to me as a "nerd," I consider

By Ralph Malph

him my friend. So here is my question: Why do I hear laughter every time I say something?

The laughter is not coming from my friends or those around me. In fact, they wear pained expressions when I am nearby. It sounds like many people laughing, like a crowd of hundreds of people, yet I can't see them. For example, I'll be chiding one of my friends, saying, "Sit on it, Potsie," and I'll hear this laughter. But everybody is frowning and rolling their eyes. I once suspected the people seated at the booths at Arnold's (my hang-out) were the ones laughing, but they never acknowledge me. They seem to keep to themselves, talking inaudibly or dancing to an Everly Brothers song.

I hear this laughter when some of my other friends say things, too, especially when Fonzie calls me a "nerd" or hits the jukebox to play an Elvis song instead of putting a nickel in it. Or when I'm at my best friend Richie Cunningham's house and his kid sister Joanie tells me to sit on it. (That reminds me, I often wonder whatever happened to their older brother Chuck. A couple years ago, he went to college and nobody has even talked about him ever since. When I ask about him, people give me weird looks. I am beginning to think Chuck never existed.)

Sometimes, I hear cheers and applause, too. It happens most frequently when Fonzie enters a room, or when his girlfriend Pinky Tuscadero rolls into town. But I never hear any cheers or applause when I walk into a room. Lately, after that obnoxious Chachi strolls into Arnold's, I've been hearing these hysterical screams, as if they're coming from young girls. Chachi. I hate Chachi.

And another thing: Why are the walls cut out of

It sounds like many people laughing, like a crowd of hundreds of people, yet I can't see them.

all the buildings? When I enter Arnold's, I'm faced with this void. It's as if the restaurant suddenly ceases to exist past this void. The Cunninghams' living room has a void, too. So does Fonzie's apartment above the garage. Every building I walk into has just three walls with a black void where the fourth wall should be. Why?

I have other concerns. Where do I live? How come I never see my parents? I can't say I even know what they look like, although sometimes I'll just mention something they did or said. That's another thing: Sometimes I'll just say stuff without even thinking and then wonder why I said it. It's as though someone is putting words in my mouth. Then I'll hear laughter. The laughter.

Most frustrating of all is that no one else acknowledges that something weird is going on. They'll just go about their day-to-day routines. Mr. C runs his hardware store, Fonzie works at his garage and Joanie practices her baton.

That reminds me, an odd thing happened a while ago. Fonzie had this idea that he was a daredevil and decided to jump a bunch of garbage cans on his motorcycle in front of Arnold's to break the record. So everybody gathers to watch, and Fonzie revs up his engine. Everyone's dying of suspense. He builds up speed and finally jumps. But halfway through it, he freezes in midair. He just hung there, frozen, for a whole week. It was incredible.

Then, exactly one week later, he came crashing down and everybody rushed to his aid. He was okay, but no one said anything about his midair suspension. It was like that whole week never passed at all. Was I the only one who noticed this? I swear, it's the strangest thing I've ever seen. Sometimes I think I'm going crazy, like that Mork from Ork guy. ∅

Owls Are Assholes
see OUTDOORS page 1D

New Aspershirt Relieves Torso Pain
see HEALTH page 9C

Clinton's Head Sawed Off
see NATION page 5A

Ø the ONION ®

★

VOLUME 33 ISSUE 19 | AMERICA'S FINEST NEWS SOURCE ™ | 21–27 MAY 1998

NEWS

Tony Randall Secedes From Union; Declares Himself Independent Nation Of Randalia

See WORLD page 2B

Suburban Family Invests Hopes, Dreams In Gas Grill

See LIFE page 7C

School Shooting Solves All Of Troubled Youth's Problems

TERROR & SOLUTIONS in Kentucky

Above: Police officials collect evidence at the scene of Brian Kolodiczek's (inset) deadly, personally fulfilling rampage.

BOWLING GREEN, KY—For weeks, 11-year-old Brian Kolodiczek loudly boasted to classmates that he was going to get back at everyone who had caused him problems at school, everyone who had kept him from being popular and successful.

Mission accomplished.

At 1:15 p.m. Monday, Kolodiczek fired two dozen rounds into a helpless crowd assembled on the playground behind Stephen C. Calhoun Elementary School, killing nine students and four teachers and solving all of the fifth-grader's problems in the process.

"Brian was a troubled young boy. He felt like he didn't fit in with the other kids," school see SHOOTING page 5

SHOOTING from page 1

guidance counselor Camille Evans said. "But now that he's killed the classmates who upset him the most, things should be a lot better for him."

Among the slain children was Larry Eichhorn, 11, pronounced dead at the scene. Kolodiczek was reportedly jealous of Eichhorn, who outshone him on the track team. "Larry was faster than Brian and anchored the relay team, and that always made Brian very angry," said track coach Buddy Miller, who shortly after the murders promoted Kolodiczek to relay anchor. "I guess Brian's the fastest now, though."

Critically wounded in the attack was 10-year-old Holly Walsh. According to Walsh's best friend, Monica Reardon, Kolodiczek "really liked Holly, but she would never talk to him. She'd pretend he wasn't there or get me to tell him to leave her alone." Early this morning, in her first statement since the shooting occurred, Walsh said she would "love to go out to a

movie" with Kolodiczek as soon as she is released from the hospital.

Calhoun Elementary principal Benjamin Breyer, who had met with Kolodiczek and his parents on numerous occasions over the years, said the boy was "frequently upset about certain teachers who he felt made unreasonable demands of him. In particular, he believed that his math teacher, Evelyn Baird, hated him and wanted him to fail."

Baird was among the four teachers killed in the assault.

"Maybe he'll get along with the new math teacher better," Breyer said. "If so, I think we can expect a big improvement in his grades. If not, he still has the gun."

The other dead faculty members are drama teacher Marcia Crosley, who did not cast Brian in the school play; English teacher Donald Baum, who frequently criticized his penmanship; and social-studies teacher Stephen Reedy, who advised

him to "lay off the Nintendo a bit."

Music teacher Stella Hammond, who on May 11 made Brian stand in the back of the class with a tambourine, is in critical condition with a perforated lung.

Experts say Kolodiczek's actions are part of an emerging trend in pre-adolescent behavior, a trend child psychiatrist Owen Green termed "shooting everybody you don't like."

"Brian was bothered by all kinds of things at this school," Green said. "But did he just sit there and complain about it? No. He realized that complaining is not a solution. Instead, he took action. And the results speak for themselves."

Despite the marked improvement in Kolodiczek's life as a result of the shooting, some said the bloody rampage was no solution at all.

Said assistant principal Patrick Chernin: "Bobby Pratt, a classmate of Brian's who called him 'diaper baby' and made fun of

his lunch box, was barely grazed on the leg in the shooting. He'll be back at school tomorrow. And another boy who regularly taunts Brian at his bus stop was absent altogether. Brian's problems have not entirely gone away, I assure you."

Dr. Andrew Goldwyn, one of many grief counselors and specially trained therapists who will be on hand at Calhoun Elementary all next week, said helping the students come to terms with the death of their friends should be a fairly easy task.

"We will emphasize the positive side of this event—that their classmate Brian has eliminated many sources of pain and annoyance in his life," Goldwyn said. "That's a good thing."

"With any luck," Goldwyn continued, "a valuable lesson will come out of this shooting. Hopefully, these kids will learn that, like Brian, they too have the power to solve their own problems." ∅

Ain't Nobody Going To Tell Me How To Raise My Baby

Before I had Rywanda I was kinda worried that she gonna come out lookin' all weird-ass. This one chick? I used to party with her, she had a baby, and two of its fingers were, like, stuck together and the ears were all fucked up. Turns out I didn't have nothing to worry about, 'cause Rywanda came out totally cute. She got big brown eyes and the best little fucking nose. She may be kinda fat now, but when she grow up, she gonna be gorgeous.

By Amber Richardson

Rywanda don't even need to wear that bullshit breathing monitor no more, like she did in that box thing at the hospital the first couple weeks. Doctor said her lungs are 80 percent formed now, so I figure that's pretty good, 'cause a 80 is a B-minus and that's better than I ever did on anything before I had Rywanda.

So, even though I obviously got it all under control, people still trying to tell me how to raise my baby. Everybody be like, "You got to hold her head like this" or, "You got to heat that up before you feed it to her." I'm getting sick of that shit. This is my child and I will bring her up how I want.

They just jealous that I got a new baby. My friend Tina's kid, Shoney? He always crawling around the ashtrays and beer cans or fucking with the extension cords and unplugging the TV when we're watching it. When Rywanda get older she ain't gonna be doing that shit, I can tell you that. My child gonna be discipline. I'll be like, "You ain't gonna be running around with the boys all night, smoking weed and gettin' fucked up. I'll kick you out of this house so fast, girl…" It's hard to be tough, but kids need to have a role model. Rywanda's not even a year, and I'm already teaching her she can't get her way by crying and being all spoiled. She ain't like the other babies, always grabbing at some shit or squirming around to look at who's talking. She's a good baby. She mostly just sleeps.

But people think 'cause this my first baby they can boss me around. I'm ready to slap that cunt social worker Debra. She say Rywanda might get some more government money, but first she got to have all these tests to, like, check on how part of her brain waves are missing or something. So now I gotta get the baby all dressed—they'll trip if she just wearing a diaper—and drag her over to the clinic. Which means I have to stuff all her Wet Wipes and shit in a shopping bag, and call for my Free Fare Cab and do all this other bullshit, like find Rywanda's goddamn birth certificate.

At first I thought them doctors were okay—they even gave me one of them car-seat things to take Rywanda home in—but then they started piling all these pamphlets and other shit to read on me. It's like, I'm busy, okay? Like I really want to read some bullshit just to find out how to use a thermometer. Stop riding my ass about every little thing! What's the big deal?

And you know who the worst? My bitch-ass mom. When Rywanda first got out of the hospital? I was dealing with her bullshit 24-7, except for when I ran out for cigarettes when she was sleeping. But then my asshole landlord? He sends me a eviction notice. So we crashing at Mom's. Then Mom lost her job at Big K, and since she gonna be home anyway, I thought I could get out the house and have a little fun for once. (I even started seeing this guy, Ray. We per-

> **People think 'cause this my first baby they can boss me around. I'm ready to slap that cunt social worker Debra.**

fect for each other 'cause he already got two babies down in Florida, so he know what it's like to be a parent.) But suddenly, like, Mom get all baggy, acting like she can tell me what time to come home at night, or when my own baby need a bath. Rag-ass bitch, shut the fuck up!

I'm a adult. I was like, "If you want me to move out, I will—and then you won't see your grandchild no more." She best remember I'm sharing my checks and my food stamps with her, and if it wasn't for me and my baby she'd be back making blue-raspberry Icees at Kmart.

As soon as I can, I movin' out. I'm gonna get one of them free houses from the government so my baby can have a nice place to grow up in. I told you I have plans. She gonna get a education, too, and be a doctor or movie star or something. She gonna have everything I couldn't never have 'cause I never got my G.E.D. So when Rywanda's driving me around in her Mercedes–Benz and I see someone who ragged on me to take better care of my kid, I'll flip 'em off out the window. ∅

From May 1, 1996

Ask A Navy SEAL

By Lieut. Ryan Cusper
Navy SEAL

Dear Navy SEAL,

My boyfriend, who I love very much, was laid off from his job a few weeks back. Ever since cashing his small severance check, all he does is sit on the couch and watch TV while I work to support us both. I know unemployment has undermined his confidence, but I'm not his mother! How do I get him out of the house and looking for work?

—**Peeved In Palmyra**

Dear Peeved,

Killing silently is a tall order, but a quick look at an anatomy chart will show that the larynx is an easy enough target—providing you can make a stealthy submerged approach, sneak up on your victim and catch him unaware. Once that's accomplished, grasp his hair as close to the scalp as you're able to and yank his head back while using your Ka-Bar combat knife to make a lateral cut across his throat. Make sure you sever both the carotid artery and jugular vein while piercing the windpipe, and press hard; the larynx is a tough, rubbery piece of tissue.

Dear Navy SEAL,

I am a happily married man with a warm and loving wife who is also one of my best friends. We've been together for 17 years (married for 15) and couldn't be happier, but lately she says she wants separate beds. I'm reeling! We're barely into our 40s, but in my mind separate sleeping is for seniors—or singles. Am I making too much of this? Is she less happy than she lets on? Help!

—**Anxious In Andersonville**

Dear Anxious,

Destroying a bridge might look easy in the movies, but remember: They're meant to withstand the immense shear-forces of wind and weather. Deploying an underwater M-32 satchel charge at the base of each load-bearing pylon looks like the answer, but it might not even shake a modern riveted steel highway or railroad bridge. Without delving into the complex language of the guerrilla combat engineer, the best I can tell you is to forgo subtlety in favor of brute force: Put two satchel charges at each X-shaped trestle buck, and this should rob the bridge of any reinforcing strength and cause it to buckle nicely.

Dear Navy SEAL,

After several catastrophically bad relationships, I have found the right man. But old habits die hard. After all those cheating jerks, it requires great will for me to trust this absolute prince. I find myself reading his mail, listening to his messages, even—God help me—following him around. How do I handle this potentially devastating situation? I don't want to ruin the best thing I've ever had going for myself.

—**Paranoid In Port Said**

Dear Paranoid,

The 10mm Colt sidearm might not be an ideal long-distance weapon and it's certainly no sniper's rifle, but it has the advantages of low weight and quicker target acquisition. You can reliably engage aggressors at ranges of 30 meters and more. Use a two-handed grip and brace the barrel against a tree, or use your dive tanks and rebreather as an improvised bench rest. Don't worry about "stopping power"—one of those 10mm slugs opens up to about 70 caliber when it hits, leaving an exit wound you could toss a cat through and bringing so much energy to a target that a hit in the extremities is often enough to drop Ivan in his tracks.

Lieut. Ryan Cusper is a combat-decorated Navy SEAL and a nationally syndicated advice columnist. His weekly feature, Ask A Navy SEAL, appears in more than 200 newspapers nationwide. His new book, In My Sights, is available at bookstores everywhere.

notable skills. "This new law should really help people like me."

With the passage of the Americans With No Abilities Act, Gertz and millions of other untalented, inessential citizens can finally see a light at the end of the tunnel.

Said Clinton: "It is our duty, both as lawmakers and as human beings, to provide each and every American citizen, regardless of his or her lack of value to society, some sort of space to take up in this great nation."

RELIGION

Church Group Offers Homosexual New Life In Closet

Above: Dennis Lindeman, a reformed homosexual whose natural sexual urges have been repressed with the help of the Lord. Above right: A 1995 photo of Lindeman and friends at an L.A. gay bar.

LAGUNA HILLS, CA—It is a typical Sunday in this conservative Orange County suburb, as the parishioners of Holy Christ Almighty Baptist Church gather for morning worship. Organ music descends from the rafters as the wholesome-looking congregation files quietly into the building. Situated in orderly rows, the assembled families stand for the minis-

see HOMOSEXUAL page 10

ter's blessing and open their hymnals to sing.

Among them, his arm around his wife, smiling down at the fresh-scrubbed faces of his two young children, born-again Christian Dennis Lindeman sings his heart out, secretly imagining a huge, engorged cock thrusting all the way down into the back of his throat.

Difficult as it may be to believe, just three years ago, this 44-year-old churchgoing family man was a construction worker, nightclub regular and self-described "party slut" in Los Angeles' seamy homosexual underground. But now, thanks to the friends he has made through the Orange County-based Reclamation Ministries, all that has changed. Today, Lindeman is living a new life of devotion to his wife and children, piety before the Lord and intense self-hatred and shame in the face of his entirely unchanged sexual orientation.

"Before I was converted to the light of the Lord, I was constantly indulging my sinful, natural sexual desires," Lindeman said. "But now, with the help of Jesus, all those group gropes in the backs of abandoned trucks near the warehouse district are just so many shadowy memories, fueling so many secret masturbation sessions, followed by paralyzing attacks of guilt and fear and frantic prayers begging forgiveness."

His motorcycle gear, leather cap and butt-plug long gone, Lindeman has finally found a place for himself in the house of the Lord.

"Thanks to my new friends at Reclamation Ministries, I am redeemed and born anew in Christ," said Lindeman, respected throughout the community as a hardware-store owner, youth soccer coach and Kiwanis Club treasurer. "Before, I never would have thought it possible that I could go without meaty, throbbing cocks pumping my lubed-up asshole on a regular basis. What's more, I never thought I could live with the crippling self-loathing and shame that denying my true self would bring. But with the love of Jesus and the strong support of my wonderful wife Diane, that miracle has come true."

Unlike during his days of sexual liberation, the act of coupling, Lindeman said, is now a wholesome, maritally sanctified act devoid of physical pleasure and performed solely for the purpose of procreation, as God intended.

"I feel so much better about myself," said Lindeman, choking back tears.

Diane Lindeman, a former lesbian also rescued by Reclamation Ministries, agreed with her husband. "We live as God intended now," she said, sitting bolt upright next to her husband in a stiff-backed chair, holding his hand for photographers. "We know that Jesus loves us for putting our homosexual ways behind us forever."

"God, I miss eating pussy," she added, grinding her teeth. "Deeply internalized self-hatred consumes every fiber of my being."

Dennis and Diane met in 1995 at a "Choose Love" weekend retreat, a Reclamation Ministries-sponsored program designed to help convert homosexuals to lives of decency and morality. The two grew teary-eyed recounting the story of their first meeting, recalling how a group of Christians held them in their arms and prayed to God to take away their natural sexual desires. They were nostalgic as they recalled their wedding day and how, with the help and support of their Christian brothers and sisters, they had been able to convince themselves that a life of heterosexuality was for the best.

"Jesus has given me a fresh start," Dennis said. "When I lock myself in the bathroom with the light off, crying for hours on end, I know He is there watching over me, ready to hurl me into the pits of eternal hellfire if I give in to my ferocious, unquenchable desire to cup in my hands the butt cheeks of a hirsute Latino and gently tug them apart as I work my tongue into his ass."

"Christ has taken over my life," Diane said. "Everything I am has been transformed by my Savior, who judges all in His love. I can't think of anything else but His divine mercy and guidance. Once I had my entire fist up this one chick's cunt. It was so incredible."

Rev. Henry Spottiswood, founder of Reclamation Ministries and marriage counselor for the Lindemans, praised the couple as "yet another victory" for the side of rectitude and piety.

"While it is true that Dennis and Diane may still harbor homosexual desires deep within their hearts, this is all right, because God forgives them for it," said Spottiswood, who had numerous homosexual encounters during his teenage years but has never allowed himself to consciously acknowledge them. "The important thing to remember is that this is not about what Dennis and Diane want. It is about what God wants for Dennis and Diane."

Added Spottiswood: "There is room enough for all in the closet of the Lord." ∅

THE LIGHTER SIDE

Black Bear Attacks, Rapes Zookeeper

SAN DIEGO—Here's a little dog-bites-man tale we couldn't resist! Except replace "dog" with "850-pound black bear"! And "bites" with "anally violates"!

Yes, last Saturday a zookeeper at the San Diego Zoo had "claws" for alarm when he was attacked and raped by the black bear he had raised from a cub! Geez, talk about gratitude!

"It was horrible, just horrible," sobbed an eyewitness. Guess she sure got an eyeful!

The bear, "Barry," attacked zookeeper Ron Gilks as Gilks entered the cage to give him dinner. Barry lunged at his throat, slashing him with his huge claws and razor-sharp teeth. Some of the claw marks were three-quarters of an inch deep. Ouch!

Then, astonished onlookers could "bearly" believe what happened next—Barry began to brutally rape Gilks!

Frantic zookeepers rushed for rifles as others tried to divert the bear. But there was no stopping Barry! This bear kept "bearing down," and Gilks just had to grin and "bear" it! Maybe Barry was mistaking him for his "honey"!

Barry's 27-inch phallus, armed with guard hairs as sharp as red-hot needles, shot through Gilks' rectum, shattered his lower spine and skewered his colon, causing his entire lower torso to "cave" in! Yikes! Bet that wasn't the type of "cave" you had in mind when you took up zookeeping, Mr. Gilks!

And can you imagine his surprise when nearly a pint of Barry's putrid ursine semen flooded his ruptured chest cavity? (By the way, Mr. Gilks, whatever cologne you've been wearing, where can the public get some?)

Finally, zookeeper Eric Pulliam shot Barry with a tranquilizer gun and pulled Gilks from the cage. The unconscious bear was later destroyed. Guess this "Yogi" made a major "Boo-Boo"!

"I have worked with dangerous animals before," zoo director Kate Donegal said. "But never have I seen any animal sexually

Grin and bear it! Barry, an 850-pound black bear (above), got a little frisky with zookeeper Ron Gilks (inset). The anal rape is believed to be the first interspecial coupling in San Diego Zoo history. Gilks was pronounced dead upon arrival at the hospital. And that's no small Boo-Boo!

assault a human being." "Barry"? Try "Scary"!

Meanwhile, Gilks was pronounced dead at an area hospital—but at least he died grin-ning and bearing it! No doubt this episode gives new meaning to the warning, "Do not feed the bears!" ✐

From September 13, 1994

Walken In L.A.

This week, The Onion *picks up another popular syndicated column: Christopher Walken's "Walken In L.A." For the past two years, Mr. Walken has provided his readers with consistently insightful commentary into the entertainment industry. His column already appears regularly in* Variety *and* Rolling Stone, *as well as in dozens of smaller newspapers and magazines. We're proud to welcome this celebrated actor and columnist to our pages.*

By Christopher Walken

Do you enjoy eating hot dogs? I hope you won't be put off by my frankness when I tell you that I absolutely love them. In fact, I enjoy no food item more than a freshly boiled hot dog. Now, I've done a lot of movies, and it's true that I've worked with quite a few celebrities who did not share this opinion. I'm sorry to say that these people have always angered me.

There are two types of people in this world: those who eat hot dogs whenever it is possible to do so, and those who opt to do other things with their free time. Who do the latter think they are kidding? What pastime could be more rewarding than the consumption of hot dogs? I haven't yet found one and I don't expect to in my lifetime. Unlike other foods, hot dogs can be eaten at any time, in any place, and it is not necessary to cook them. Now, I ask you: Why not eat hot dogs? They are delicious.

I carry a bag of hot dogs with me wherever I go. I eat them from the bag whenever I get the urge, regardless of the circumstances. When I make a movie, my hot dogs are my co-stars. If, in the middle of a scene, I decide I want to consume a hot dog, I do so. I waste the director's time and thousands of dollars in film stock, but in the end it is all worth it, because I enjoy eating hot dogs more than I enjoy acting. This bothers some people. I was supposed to portray *Batman,* but when Tim Burton learned of my hot-dog cravings, he asked Michael Keaton to wear the cape. To this day, I am peeved about this.

When we filmed *The Dead Zone,* I ate over 800 hot dogs a day. It was necessary. My character needed to come across as intense as possible, and I found the inspiration for that intensity in my intense love of hot dogs. The director, David Cronenberg, said that he would never work with me again. I kept eating hot dogs when the cameras were rolling, and that seemed to bother him. I say fuck him. He doesn't even like hot dogs.

I would like to end by emphasizing once again that I really like to eat hot dogs. If any of you people disagree, I loathe you. I despise you. Not only that, but I also despise all your loved ones. I want to see them torn to pieces by wild dogs. If I ever meet you in person, I'll smash your brains in with a fucking bat. Then we'll see who doesn't like hot dogs.

Next week: my thoughts on Woody Allen, hot-dog hater and shitty director. ∅

SOCIETY

Collectible-Plate Industry Calls For Tragic Death Of Streisand

Above: Franklin Mint president Jim Campion addresses members of the collectible-plate industry.

With sales of Princess Di memorabilia falling off sharply after a record 1997, collectible-plate-industry leaders Monday called for the tragic death of beloved entertainer Barbra Streisand.

"For the 1998 Christmas season to be anywhere near as successful as last year's, we need a heartbreaking, untimely end to a wonderful life that we can commemorate with a series of limited-edition collector's plates," said Franklin Mint president Jim Campion, who joined representatives from the Bradford Exchange and Danbury Mint in a unified call for Streisand's tragic demise. "The death of Barbra Streisand, with her upscale, intensely devoted following, would be ideal."

Economists say the unexpected death of a star of Streisand's magnitude would mean a 70 percent sales boost for the $1 billion collectible-plate industry.

"A Streisand death would probably outsell all other recent celebrity deaths combined, including Princess Di and Frank Sinatra," said Andrew Culpepper of *The Wall Street Journal.* "I could easily see QVC moving any-

see STREISAND page 11

where from 500,000 to a million units of Streisand memorabilia in the first week alone. After all, we're talking about the woman who sang 'People,' 'Evergreen' and 'You Don't Bring Me Flowers.'"

Directly addressing the *Funny Girl* star, Campion urged Streisand to give "serious consideration" to the collectible-plate industry's request.

"Ms. Streisand, you have lived a life of comfort and wealth, much of which was made possible by the selling of collectibles and memorabilia bearing your image. We feel it would be fair and honorable of you to 'give something back,' both to your fans and the collectibles industry, by passing away in a manner that leaves the world stunned and deeply in want of some tangible object commemorating your rare beauty and talent, an object your fans can hold on to as a treasured keepsake and an assurance that your spirit will always be with them."

Among the means of death recommended by collectible-plate-industry leaders: car crash, helicopter crash, skiing accident, drowning, accidental shooting, or a rare, degenerative disease that Streisand had been bravely battling for years in secret. They were also open to the possibility of a sleeping-pill overdose.

"While embarrassing and potentially damaging to a star's legacy, the perennial success of Elvis Presley memorabilia proves that a drug-related death does not necessarily hurt sales. In fact, in some cases it can actually help," Campion said. "We therefore wholeheartedly approve of this mode of demise."

In anticipation of a possible Streisand death, plate-makers are busily developing merchandise lines. The Bradford Exchange is planning "The Evergreen Collection," a line of premium, gold-inlaid plates depicting Streisand in scenes from such cinematic triumphs as *Yentl, Nuts* and *The Mirror Has Two Faces*. Additional plates commemorate such landmark moments in Streisand history as her triumphant 1994 return concert at

Above: A prototype of a limited-edition commemorative Streisand plate.

Madison Square Garden, her 1981 "Best Pop Duet" Grammy for "Guilty" with Barry Gibb and her brief 1970s marriage to Elliott Gould.

Said Bradford Exchange vice-president of marketing Theodore Deele: "Each Evergreen Collection plate will be available for just two easy payments of $49 plus shipping and handling, and will be limited to 200 firing dates, virtually guaranteeing it to be a rare, sought-after collectible. It will also come with a certificate of authenticity stating unequivocally that this is indeed a plate with a picture of Barbra Streisand on it."

The Bradford Exchange is already accepting reservations for the plate, promising customers an unconditional money-back guarantee should Streisand decline to expire.

Many other industries have praised the collectible-plate manufacturers' call for Streisand's death. Said Laura Samuelson, president of the American Association of Florists: "In September 1997, British florists sold $11.5 million worth of Princess Di-related bouquets, nearly half of which were laid at the gates outside Buckingham Palace. Based on those numbers, we are confident we could easily sell $20 million in flowers for fans to lay in front of Streisand's Brooklyn birthplace."

Also supporting Monday's call for an untimely death were the Home Shopping Network, *People* magazine and Columbia Records, which would stand to enjoy a 300 percent surge in Streisand back-catalog sales from such an event. Beanie Babies manufacturer Ty has also expressed interest in producing a limited-edition Barbra Bear. And close Streisand friend Marvin Hamlisch, who wrote her 1973 hit "The Way We Were," said he would record a new version of the Grammy-winning song in her memory. "The Way You Were (1998)" would hit stores the first Tuesday after her death and would likely become the best-selling single of all time.

According to collectible-plate-industry leaders, a number of other celebrities were discussed as possible candidates for tragic death, but Streisand emerged as the best choice. "We talked about all sorts of people—Bette Midler, Elton John, Oprah Winfrey, Leonardo DiCaprio, Celine Dion—the list goes on and on," Martin Krujczek of the Danbury Mint said. "But the more we talked, the more apparent it became that no one could match the incomparable Barbra Streisand."

Buzzing over Monday's call for their idol's death, Streisand's famously devoted fans are already eager to purchase something to remember her by.

"I can't even tell you how crazy I am about Barbra—I've seen *A Star Is Born* at least 200 times," said Rick Childress, a Hermosa Beach, CA, hairdresser. "If she died, I would buy anything and everything that's even remotely commemorative."

"There's nobody else like Barbra. Nobody," said Woodmere, NY, homemaker Joan Kushner, whose 6,000-item Streisand collection includes an autographed copy of *My Name Is Barbra* and the boxing gloves she wore in the movie poster for *The Main Event*. "God forbid anything should ever happen to our Barbra. But if it must, let there be merchandise to help us cope." ∅

MUSIC

Area bassist Paul Simms (above), who recently enjoyed oral sex, attributed the encounter to his status as a rock musician, which creates tremendous sexual energy that makes him irresistible to women.

Area Bassist Fellated

COLUMBUS, OH—According to reports, area musician Paul Simms, bassist for the local grunge/punk band The Dead Taybacks, was fellated early Sunday morning by an unknown woman. The fellatio, which occurred during a late-night party following a Dead Taybacks show at The Tar Pit in downtown Columbus, was described as "totally rockin'" by the former member of Claw Jockey.

A part-time college student who is currently looking for a place to stay, Simms was unable to identify his fellater, since he lost consciousness shortly thereafter. Nevertheless, he remains optimistic about future occurrences of fellatio in his life and credits his status as a band member for his recent success.

"The whole rock thing—the hair, the ripped clothes, the disillusionment with the overwhelming, crushing commercialism of modern American life," said Simms, brushing aside his tousled locks with a flip of his hand, "chicks dig it."

According to witnesses, the fellatio occurred in the alley behind The Tar Pit. At approximately 3:52 a.m., the unknown fellatist unbuckled Simms' belt, lowered his trousers and proceeded to lick, stroke and suck his exposed penis.

"It was awesome," said Simms, "but don't get the wrong idea here. Fellatio isn't what it's all about. For me, the most important thing is still the music. The beer, the parties and the anonymous random orally induced orgasms are just a tiny part of it."

see BASSIST page 11

According to Simms, The Dead Taybacks will soon launch a five-day tour of southern Ohio, during which he believes he has an excellent chance of receiving additional fellatio.

"I hear we're really big at Antioch," Simms said. "My sister's friend Steve goes to school down there, and she said he thinks he's heard of us."

The Dead Taybacks' first out-of-town date is May 4, when the band will play at a Dayton, OH, Knights of Columbus hall.

In addition to the upcoming tour, Simms said he hopes The Dead Taybacks' forthcoming six-song cassette will also help him land enjoyable oral sex.

"Yeah, we're gonna do a new tape, which will include some songs from our seven-inch EP," Simms said. "A friend of ours borrowed a cassette four-track, so it will be pretty good quality. We'll shop it around, and maybe a local label will pick it up. If not, this record store downtown might sell it on consignment for us. That would be awesome."

Simms said the band has saved "over $75" to record the new cassette, including $11 from a recent show at the Drift On Inn Bar & Grill.

"We got paid $40 for that gig," Dead Taybacks drummer and part-time Video Zone clerk Jim Klapisch explained, "but most of that money went toward paying for the flyers."

Band members maintain that the money, like the sex, is just a small part of what keeps them going.

"When we get into a van to go to a gig, we rarely talk about how much money we'll pocket or how many babes will be in the audience," Simms said. "After the show, however, that's pretty much all we talk about."

According to sources close to the band, Sunday was no exception, as Simms told bandmates everything he could remember about the night's escapade.

Simms also suddenly put off plans to quit the group, though he maintains that his recent encounter had nothing to do with his change of heart.

Experts were not surprised that Simms was the recipient of a bold sexual favor that is not traditionally a casual exchange between partners.

"Being a member of a rock band is very alluring from a sexual standpoint," said Yale University's Nora Hayes, one of the nation's leading authorities on college-area-band-related sexual activity. "Men and women in bands are considered 'cool' by their peers, and that, when combined with a visceral, sweaty performance on the part of the musician, makes them very attractive from a mating standpoint."

"That stuff used to happen to me all the time," said Gary Thortle, 29, who played keyboards for Penthouse Sweet while a student at Ohio State. Thortle has since graduated and is now temping for a Columbus-area QualiTemps. "God, I miss those days."

Added former Zen Monkey singer and guitarist Ronald Gick: "God, I miss those days." ∅

From February 12, 1998

INVESTIGATION

Family Dog Suspected Cause Of Miniature Chuck Wagon Disaster

Above: The wreckage from last week's fatal miniature-chuck-wagon crash in a San Jose, CA, kitchen. Investigators have ruled out driver error and now believe the disaster to be dog-related.

SAN JOSE, CA—Though Federal Microvehicular Safety Administration officials stressed that it is too early to draw definitive conclusions, a family dog is widely regarded as the probable cause of the miniature-chuck-wagon disaster that shocked the nation Wednesday.

According to an FMSA report released Monday, the crash—which resulted in the deaths of the chuck wagon's miniature driver and four passengers, as well as the loss of more than one pound of hearty Chuck Wagon-brand gravy-flavored dog-food cargo and a team of four miniature draft horses—is in all likelihood attributable to the presence of one or more pet dogs in the kitchen at the time of the accident.

"Preliminary studies of the chuck-wagon wreckage, combined with analysis of data recovered from the minuscule carriage's 'black box,' strongly suggest that, unknown to chuck-wagon traffic controllers monitoring the wagon's progress, the kitchen was occupied by at least one pet animal, probably a dog, which pursued and overtook the chuck wagon in the final moments before it vanished from radar screens," FMSA chief

see CHUCK WAGON page 7

CHUCK WAGON from page 1

Vincent Renaldo said.

In the 48 hours immediately following the disaster, safety investigators examined a wide variety of on-site evidence. The chuck wagon's original fuselage, scattered across an approximate eight-tile area of linoleum in the "breakfast nook" region of the kitchen, was painstakingly reassembled by FMSA investigators in an attempt to better understand the events leading up to the crash.

The rebuilt chuck wagon's key structural elements—particularly the glue-fastened wooden dowels used as tiny spokes in the load-bearing miniature wagon wheels, the itsy-bitsy swing-axle steering rack, and the teensy-weensy whip used to make the miniature horses accelerate in times of danger—were then subjected to a battery of stress tests in an effort to determine whether equipment failure or driver error was to blame.

While the tests are still not complete, FMSA officials say the discovery of a two-inch "bite radius" breaching the chuck wagon's hull indicates severe canine mastication, strongly supporting the dog-attack hypothesis.

"The old saw about how 'the great taste of Chuck Wagon stops dogs in their tracks' has taken on grim new overtones in light of these findings," Renaldo said.

Though Chuck Wagon Transit Authority officials insist that proper safety procedures were followed during the chuck wagon's fateful final voyage, a number of dog-food-industry whistleblowers are coming forward in the wake of the crash, insisting that such a tragedy was inevitable, given the CWTA's longtime failure to address serious driver-safety issues.

"This sort of thing happens all the time," said former miniature-chuck-wagon driver Randall "Tex" West, who claimed he was fired by Chuck Wagon Transit after refusing to do any more kitchen runs until the dog problem

Above: Scruffers.

was addressed. "I can't tell you how many times a chuck wagon will tear through a kitchen, hell-bent for leather, hootin' and hollerin' to beat the devil, with a happy, hungry hound right on its tail, just inches behind."

Continued West: "A lot of these drivers consider it kind of a 'macho' thing to see how close they can cut it before zipping under the kitchen counter into the dog-food bag at the last minute, leaving the puzzled mutt wondering where all them tasty treats disappeared to. Sure, it seems kind of funny at first, the way the dog looks around and blinks, like it can't figure out where that old chuck wagon up and went all of a sudden. But when something like this happens, it's a damn shame."

Two-inch-tall wagon-driver Roy "Speedy" Sanders agreed, but noted that thrill-seeking drivers are not the only reason for the increased risk of accidents. According to Sanders, ever-increasing dog-food delivery

quotas leave drivers with no choice but to speed.

"It's impossible to pull off the typical dog-food-delivery schedule and meet federal safety standards at the same time," Sanders said. "Every day, in kitchens across the U.S., drivers run their teams at full gallop through routes that traffic control knows damn well are dog-occupied. But the traffic controllers look the other way, because if they didn't, delivery quotas would never be met. Drivers whip their teams up to full speed and chance it, hoping either to outrun or out-maneuver the dog, figuring they can always pivot at the last minute and send the animal sliding across the linoleum if it gets too close. That way, management is happy, and they get to keep their jobs."

Though Chuck Wagon Transit authorities have cooperated with investigators, the group's official position remains that Wednesday's crash was an isolated incident that is in no way symptomatic of a larger safety problem.

FMSA investigators are not so certain.

"The kitchen in question is a well-established nap-zone for a mid-sized dog named Scruffers, and we have solid evidence demonstrating that the driver regularly made a practice of exceeding his wagon's per-axle cargo limit by as much as 20 to 30 bite-sized chunks," FMSA Special Investigator Richard Sobell said. "Dogs like Scruffers can't corner as well as chuck wagons on your basic no-wax kitchen-tile surfacing; their greater mass gives them more inertia, making it harder for them to turn, especially if they're running at a full sprint."

"Ninety-nine times out of a hundred, your skilled miniature-wagon handler can pull it off," said Sobell, looking out over the crash site. "But that hundredth time? That's the one these hot-shot drivers need to start seriously thinking about." ∅

From December 3, 1997

Ask A Bee

By Worker Bee #7438-F87904

Dear Worker Bee #7438-F87904:

My husband and I split last year after 11 years of marriage. We're still good friends, though, and we even go out for coffee once a week. Problem is, he's been seeing a new person, someone I feel is definitely not right for him. Should I say anything? I'm not jealous—I know I wasn't right for him, either. What's my move?

—**Protective In Pensacola**

Dear Pensacola,

Enable protocol "seek POLLEN"/Must harvest POLLEN for HIVE/feed LARVAE/feed QUEEN/feed DRONES/feed WORKERS/superseding priority: feed QUEEN/standby to receive POLLEN-search-behavior-inducing chemicals/search outside hive in precise searching-pattern (west-southwest forward 400 meters turn 15 degrees west [daylight hours only to find flowering plants] (repeat pattern as necessary)/locate and fix position of POLLEN/rub sacs on legs against stamen against pistil against all parts of flowering plant to obtain POLLEN/must find POLLEN/finding POLLEN primary purpose of BEE(WORKER) #7438-F87904/awaiting query/awaiting query.

Dear Worker Bee #7438-F87904:

I really enjoyed your response to the reader whose husband doesn't enjoy foreplay. In your humble opinion, is there anything wrong with a gal like me demanding that her boyfriend take things slow? Call me old-fashioned, but I'm just not the "Wham, Bam, Thank You, Ma'am" type!

—**Frustrated In Frankfort**

Dear Frustrated,

Upon location of POLLEN initiate protocol "location-dance"/upon retrieval of POLLEN initiate location-retrieval dance/indicate for HIVE for QUEEN for BEES(WORKER) location of POLLEN/standby to receive POLLEN-location-dance-behavior-inducing chemicals/upon completion of POLLEN dance: commence POLLEN retrieval/Upon completion of POLLEN search: commence HONEY distribution (HONEY to BEES [WORKERS]) (HONEY to BEES [DRONES]) (ROYAL JELLY to QUEEN repeat ROYAL JELLY to QUEEN)/upon completion of nutritive distribution commence maintenance-repair of HIVE maintenance-repair of COMBS maintenance-repair of chamber of QUEEN/enable circulation of air through wing-beating/repeat protocol "seek POLLEN."

Dear Worker Bee #7438-F87904:

I work in a large office, and I think I'm in love with the woman who works in the next cubicle. I'm wary of office romance, though. I mean, what if things don't work out? That could make for a pretty uncomfortable work environment. But I really like this woman. Could the answer be as simple as switching cubicles if things don't work out? Or am I just giving myself an excuse to do something I suspect may be wrong?

—**In A Quandary In Quantico**

Dear Quantico,

Search for/retrieval of POLLEN interrupted by HIVE-originating aggressor messages/interpreting sense-message(smell-sound) from HIVE/HIVE under observation by quadruped: sub=mammal: sub=HONEY-eating: sub=OPOSSUM/constitutes THREAT TO QUEEN constitutes THREAT TO HIVE constitutes THREAT TO LARVAE constitutes THREAT TO HONEY/repeat constitutes THREAT TO QUEEN/must respond by swarming (standing by to receive anger-inducing chemicals standing by to receive swarming-behavior-inducing chemicals) STING-use situation possible/STING-use will prove terminal to this unit [contingency not optimal for survival of BEE(WORKER) #7438-F87904/follow sting-use protocol only if HIVE-survival probability sub-nominal/protect QUEEN/protect HIVE/repeat protect QUEEN/repeat protect QUEEN/repeat protect QUEEN/repeat protect QUEEN/repeat protect QUEEN.

Worker Bee #7438-F87904 is a syndicated advice columnist whose weekly column, Ask A Bee, is featured in more than 250 newspapers nationwide. ∅

SPORTS

Basketball Star Blames God For Defeat

LEXINGTON, KY—University of Kentucky basketball star Jeron Smith, who singlehandedly blew Saturday's game against SEC rival South Carolina with a missed last-second layup, held a press conference Sunday, blaming God for the surprise loss.

"I always thank the Lord for blessing me with the talent and determination to play well and win," said Smith, a 6-foot-4 sophomore forward from Louisville. "But on Saturday, for some reason, He decided to take all that talent and determination away from me. I am very disappointed in Him for doing that."

The game marked the first time this season God had failed Smith, who before the loss was averaging 21.7 points per game, including a school-record 52 in a 109-77 rout of Alabama last week.

"I want to blame God for the terrible way I played today," said Smith, who scored just 2 points all game in a miserable 1-for-22 shooting performance. "I would particularly like to blame God for that last shot I blew, which He normally never would have let me miss."

Area clergy blame God, as well, citing His failure to give Smith the ability to run fast enough.

"Had God blessed Jeron with the footspeed of, say, a Dante Williams of South Carolina, perhaps he would not have been so badly out of position under the boards all day long," said Michael Philby, pastor at Lexington's First Presbyterian Church of God and a devoted Kentucky basketball fan. "But instead God made him a step slower than Williams, enabling Williams to block him out on every single rebound and shot opportunity."

In addition to God, Smith has suggested that Jesus Christ was also responsible for his poor performance.

"God clearly deserves most of the blame here, but I think Christ also had a hand in my failure," Smith said. "I know Jesus is beside me always, for I believe in Him, and for my faith He shall grant me eternal life, but when there was a minute left and I was wide open underneath, why didn't He get me the ball? I just can't understand it."

According to a spokesman for God, many factors were involved in the decision not to bless the Kentucky Wildcats.

"Obviously, this was a big game for both teams, but God felt that South Carolina, struggling with a 9-12 record, clearly needed it more," said Wayne Patterson, speaking from Heaven's Gate. "And the fact that South Carolina has several devoted Christians on its team didn't hurt, either."

Veteran basketball analyst Billy Packer disagreed with Patterson's explanation. "I don't think it had anything to do with Carolina needing this game or their having some good Christians on the team," Packer said. "The simple fact is, Kentucky is a team full of sinners. God was punishing the team for its wicked, wanton ways, and that's that."

Perhaps the most disappointed in God is UK Coach Rick Pitino, who led his team in a pregame prayer asking for His help. "We got down on our knees and said, 'Lord, please let us defeat South Carolina in this nationally televised contest,'" Pitino said. "We were very clear with God. There really could have been no misunderstanding."

In addition to Pitino, fans and

Above: Kentucky forward Jeron Smith questioned his faith after Saturday's loss to South Carolina. Both God and Jesus were blamed for his inability to hit a game-winning lay-up.

local clergy, area rabbis are disappointed in God, as well. "I, too, must find fault with God, as the Wildcats badly needed a win to stay close to the number-one ranking," said Rabbi Leonard Waldman of Temple Ohav Shalom. "But, while I accept God's role in this defeat, I reject the Christian notion that Jesus Christ, a carpenter from Bethlehem who died nearly 2,000 years ago, had anything to do with Kentucky's loss in this critical early-season SEC showdown. That's just ridiculous." ∅

PEOPLE

Christopher Reeve Placed Atop Washington Monument

WASHINGTON, DC—One of America's most beloved landmarks, the Washington Monument, became all the more stirring and inspiring Monday with the addition of disabled actor Christopher Reeve.

Reeve, 44, paralyzed below the neck after a tragic equestrian mishap last year, was bolted to the pinnacle of the 555-foot monument and affixed with display spotlights for night viewing. He will remain there permanently, on 24-hour display.

"Christopher has shown himself to be a pillar of strength and courage who brings out the best in us all," said John Beaumont, Director of U.S. Parks and Services. "He was a logical addition to this already-impressive monument. Once the idea was presented, nothing could stop us: not logistical problems, not budget constraints, not even the teary objections of Mr. Reeve."

The former *Superman* actor and his electric wheelchair were hoisted up the side of the towering obelisk by a tractor-powered cable pulley. Reeve was then welded to the pinnacle, facing east toward the Capitol, and bolted in place with iron slugs made from a cannonball fired at the battle of Yorktown.

A bronze plaque at the foot of the monument describes Reeve's history and dimensions. It reads: "We elevate you to the heavens so that future generations may know of your courage and your almost total paralysis."

A crowd of more than 300,000 peo-

More than 300,000 well-wishers gathered at the Washington Monument Monday to watch Reeve's official bolting-in ceremony. Said Greensboro, NC, resident Cal Brewer: "I wish I had the courage to be crippled like that."

ple, including many of Reeve's closest friends, gathered to watch the installation. "It was so beautiful," said Jane Seymour, star of TV's *Dr.* *Quinn, Medicine Woman*, who co-starred with Reeve in the hit 1980 film *Somewhere In Time.* "As the

see REEVE page 17

REEVE from page 4

final welders were blasting away, the sparks were flying everywhere, and then they set off those fireworks. I honestly cried."

"We brought the kids here to try and teach them about the courage and fortitude Washington showed at Valley Forge," said Cal Brewer, a father of four from Greensboro, NC. "Now, with Christopher Reeve up there, the whole scene just speaks for itself."

Added Brewer: "I wish I had the courage to be crippled like that."

"You can fly... you belong in the sky," sang celebrity guest Bette Midler in a musical prelude to the formal dedication and attachment ceremony. "Once upon a time, my dear friend Chris flew into our movie houses and into our hearts as The Man Of Steel, soaring above the highest peaks. Though today he's wearing several hundred pounds of life-support equipment instead of his old red and blue tights, from the top of this monument he shall forever soar."

Midler, who performed "Love Theme From The Movie *Superman*" to a standing ovation as the final weldings were secured into place, was a last-minute replacement for scheduled vocalist Margot Kidder, whose whereabouts remain unknown.

Though Reeve was unable to speak at the commemoration due to an intense fear of heights, no one was more moved by the ceremony than the actor himself. "Please let me down," the visibly touched celebrity said to reporters. "I'm cold, and I miss my family."

Upon Reeve's natural death, he will be removed from the monument long enough to be encased in acrylic plastic, then reattached.

Reeve's installation, planners say, will give him a new ability to touch and inspire people 24 hours a day as a public fixture, rain, snow or shine. "Christopher touched us all with his heartfelt speeches at the Oscars and the Democratic Convention, but he just can't be everywhere at once," Beaumont said. "As it is, the Republicans have had to cripple their own actors to gain comparable emotional impact."

Republican actor Tom Selleck's spine was shattered by the GOP in August, gaining him many standing ovations at Republican fundraisers since.

President Reagan praised his fellow acting veteran in a telegram read at the ceremony: "Uhhh... blanket. Muhhh."

This is not the first time a showbiz notable has been added to a Washington, DC, attraction. Comedian George Burns spent the last few months of his life in the Smithsonian Institute's Museum of Arts and Industries, in a glass case between Fonzie's jacket from *Happy Days* and the original Kermit The Frog puppet. Bob Hope now occupies the case.

In light of the project's success, The U.S. Department of Parks and Services is considering similar additions to its attractions. Plans are already being drafted to have hearing-impaired actress Marlee Matlin bolted to the Lincoln Memorial. ∅

From October 22, 1998

I Know What Is Best For Everyone

> How do I know about everything? That's simple: by being smarter than everyone else.

Listen to me, because I know what is best for everyone. There are a great many problems facing America today, and I have all the answers to all of them.

By Edwin Wiersbicki

Everyone should listen to what I have to say and heed my advice because I am correct. When I say that lowering taxes is the solution to the Social Security crisis, you should agree. We can reduce juvenile crime by requiring school uniforms. It is crazy to pay a man $10 million just because he can put a ball in a hoop. Consuming a daily dose of Vitamin E will result in healthier, stronger dental tissue. No daughter of mine is going to step foot inside a church wearing a miniskirt. Those fat cats in Washington deserve each other. Parker pens are simply the best writing instruments on the market.

If your daughter is getting married, the groom's family should pay for bar expenses. Higher tariffs mean protection for America. It is important to support your local YMCA. Listen to me. We need longer jail terms for repeat drug offenders. If you are having a cookout to entertain friends, make both beef and chicken available. Wildly patterned ties are tacky—the simpler, the classier. I am right.

I also know the solution to the issue of campaign-finance reform. I wrote a letter to *The Glendale Post-Gazette* to inform the citizenry what needs to be done, and that letter was published on Oct. 9. If you wish to know what needs to be done about the problem of campaign finance, you should find a copy of the Oct. 9 *Glendale Post-Gazette*.

How do I know about everything? That's simple: by being smarter than everyone else.

Take, for example, the city council's plan to build a community swimming pool. They are wrong, and I am right. Not only will a community pool needlessly raise property taxes, but the traffic on Claybourne Avenue will double, causing delays for those heading to the Pine Street shopping area. I have alerted the members of the city council of this fact, but they have failed to heed my advice, because, as I mentioned earlier, they are not as intelligent as I am.

One of the things I like best about myself is that not only do I know what is best for everyone, I always make sure to come forward with this information. I do not passively sit by, doing nothing about the problems around me. As soon as I determine what is right for my community, state or country, I speak up about it, writing a letter to the editor of a newspaper or talking about it loudly at a local park.

I also know what is right for individuals. I recently informed Patti and Gus Schmidt that their son Steven was smoking pot and I told them they should put a stop to it. The Schmidts are not perceptive, so they did not notice the warning signs of drug abuse. Fortunately, I am extremely perceptive and was able to intervene.

Tomorrow, I am going to write a letter to *USA Today* about the problem of international terrorism. That will solve this serious problem once and for all. Thank goodness for me. ∅

From April 16, 1997

Computer Countdown To '00

There is widespread fear among computer experts that the turn of the millennium will create vast problems, as computers around the world, programmed with only the last two digits of a year, will mistake 2000 for 1900. What do *you* think?

"My computer went all crazy on me the other day. But I think it was because I ejaculated all over the keyboard."

Wally Putnam
Landscaper

"I pray that a solution is found. What will happen to my Ms. Pac Man high scores?"

David Charbonneau
Carpet Salesman

"In just three years, William McKinley will lead the country, the auto-mobile fad will be in full swing, and I shall sport a jaunty boater cap and wax my moustache!"

Pete Mortman
Choir Director

"Open the pod bay doors, Hal... Hal? I won't argue with you, Hal!"

Robyn Lipman
Systems Analyst

"Without a computer, how will I speak to my friends in Japan, order a bouquet of roses, and help my son with his report on dinosaurs?"

Rachel Stryzinski
Librarian

"I hope this problem won't affect the hovering space cars we'll be driving in 2000."

Mitchell Jessup
Chemical Engineer

From August 20, 1997

EDUCATION

Nation's Educators Alarmed By Poorly Written Teen Suicide Notes

WASHINGTON, DC—At the group's annual convention Sunday, members of the National Education Association called for the formation of a nationwide coalition of parents, teachers and political leaders to address a growing problem: the alarmingly low quality of teenage suicide notes across the U.S.

In his keynote address, U.S. Secretary of Education Richard Riley said America must renew its commitment to grammar, spelling and writing skills, calling the marked improvement of teen suicide prose "the nation's number-one educational priority."

"Not three days ago I met with the parents of a young man who chose to take his own life," Riley said. "I was shocked by what I saw: a note that read simply, 'Im gonna blo my head of.' This sort of syntax would be understandable coming from a first- or second-grader, but from a 17-year-old it is downright appalling," Riley said. "What do you tell the parents in a situation like that? By all outward appearances, this seemed like a normal child. The parents had no idea their son's writing skills were that poor."

Addressing the assemblage of teachers, NEA president Cheryl Brodhagen described an "alarming erosion of grammar skills" among America's teens, in whose suicide notes can be found double negatives, split infinitives, improper word usage and, in the worst cases, unnecessary use of the passive voice.

Calling the decision to take one's life "one of the most important decisions a young student has to face," Brodhagen said that to leave behind poorly written and misspelled suicide notes of the type found recently is "tragic beyond words" for the loved ones left behind to pick up the pieces.

"This one, for example," said Brodhagen, holding up a suicide note from a 16-year-old Pawtucket, RI, girl, "is written in such shaky, uneven handwriting and is so badly blurred with some sort of wet stains and splotches that it's virtually unreadable. In any decent classroom it would be considered entirely unacceptable."

Brodhagen then related the story of another tragic suicide note, discovered at the feet of a 15-year-old St. Louis boy who had hanged himself.

"The boy's mother opened the door to his room

Above: U.S. Education Secretary Richard Riley holds up a suicide note from a 15-year-old girl he says was "crying out for help in proper punctuation and spelling."

one morning to wake him up for school," Brodhagen said, "and she screamed in horror at what she saw: Dangling, right there in front of her, was a participle."

Also cause for concern among educators is the excessively "purple" prose of many teen suicide notes. Said Savannah, GA, ninth-grade creative-writing teacher Ed Salmons: "I'm seeing overwrought, melodramatic, bathetic writing that demonstrates no grasp of subtlety or style. It's really hard for me to take pretentious, self-indulgent suicide notes like these seriously as pieces of writing. It's as if the author was just in love with the sound of his or her own voice."

According to leading child psychologists, a suicidal teen's failure to meet even the most basic standards of high-school-level composition may indicate the child has given up hope of ever having his or her written prose understood.

"These teens are desperately trying to express themselves, but all they can manage are sloppy, barely coherent phrases like 'Im usles' and 'I hat myself,'" noted therapist Eli Wasserbaum said. "One Florida boy who recently shot himself in the head wrote, 'I cant talk to anyone about my problems.' 'Cant'? Is he referring to the noun defined as 'the whining, singsong speech of beggars and thieves'? Somehow, I don't think so. We're talking about a serious inability to com-

see SUICIDE page 10

58

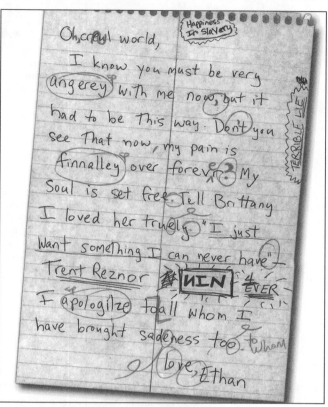

Above: A pair of teen suicide notes, corrected by *New York Times* copy editor Edward Stimson. Stimson called the error-riddled notes "disturbing."

municate here."

Wasserbaum said early detection and intervention is crucial. "My advice is this: If you know a teen who seems to be exhibiting the sort of low self-esteem and withdrawn alienation that often precedes suicidal behaviors, for God's sake, get them into a one-on-one writing tutorial immediately," he said. "They've got to improve their communication skills now, before it's too late."

The NEA is currently developing a 12-step plan to improve suicidal teens' reading and writing skills, including extra homework for students deemed "at-risk" by counselors and tougher grading standards for teens who have attempted suicide on one or more occasions.

The proposal also calls for the creation of special 'suicidal-only' after-school study halls to prevent depressed teens from engaging in extracurricular social activities with their peers, interactions which may interfere with their studies and lead to greater erosion of basic grammar and spelling down the road.

"There seems to be an almost direct link between the rise in suicidal behavior and the decline in students' overall command of the English language," said Bangor, ME, junior-high vice-principal Bob Drake. "If this lack of attention paid to developing writing skills continues among teens, we may need to start thinking about revoking their suicide privileges altogether." ∅

Why Can't I Sell Any Of These Fucking Bibles?

I honestly have no idea what the hell is going on. Why can't I seem to sell any of these fucking Bibles? I'm offering the best goddamn Bible I've ever seen—not some piece-of-shit Bible that'll fall apart before you're halfway through Matthew—and still, everywhere I go, I get the door slammed in my face. What gives?

Edwin Childress
Bible Salesman

Yesterday, I was going door-to-door on Sycamore Drive. The first house I went to, this nice-looking old lady opened the door, and the first thing I noticed were these two big fucking crucifixes hanging on her living-room wall. I thought for sure I had a sale in the bag. I thought, if I can't sell a Bible to this woman, Jesus, who in all of God's fucking kingdom can I sell one to?

I didn't waste any time moving in for the sale. I asked the woman how much she'd expect to pay for a handsome Bible with a 32-page full-color insert, a genuine, hand-fucking-crafted leather cover, and a reinforced spine that could take just about any beating she could dish out.

She didn't answer, so I went ahead and answered for her: a fucking hell of a lot more than $14.99, that's for sure!

You can't get workmanship like this from those sons of bitches at Christian Book World, I told her. Just look at the gilded edges on this cocksucker! Take it into your own hands and examine the quality of this hardback volume made with 100 percent acid-free paper, I said.

This Bible will last a fuckin' lifetime. You want a Good Book? This is a good fucking book! You'd have to be brain-dead not to get in on a deal like this. Hell, I said, I'll throw in a motherfucking "Parables & Miracles Of Christ" bookmark for absolutely free!

I poured my heart out on that doorstep, and do you think I earned one red son-of-a-bitching cent? Nope. I tried not to show my disappointment, though, and acted real professional. When I left, I waved and said, "Thank you, ma'am, per-

I'm offering the best goddamn Bible I've ever seen—not some piece-of-shit Bible.

haps some other time."

Why does this happen day after day? I'm offering one seriously nice Bible for a goddamn song. Still, I've got three fucking crates of them sitting in the trunk of my car. Christ!

It can't be me, 'cause I know I'm a good salesman. I worked for 14 years at Jensen Used Auto Parts, and I was the top man in sales six years running. Before that, I sold plumbing fixtures and made a goddamn fortune on commissions.

At this point, I have no choice but to contact the Beechwood Bible Company and complain, because I'm doing everything their official Bible salesman's handbook says I should do.

First, it says, "Greet the customer in a friendly manner." I do that. I flash a big smile and say, "How the hell are you doing today?"

Number two, it says, "Politely ask, 'May have a moment of your time?'" I've started reading the sentence right out of the handbook, just to prove I'm doing things to the letter. I say, "Ma'am, may I have a moment of your time?" If she says no, I leave. If she says yes, I say, "Thank you, I won't be long. I know you're probably extremely busy keeping up this big-ass house of yours."

Step three is to present the product. Well, fuck—that's the easy part! This fucking Bible should sell itself! It has everything: It's got the New Fucking Testament, it's got the Old Fucking Testament. It's got a full index and supplemental material in the back. It even has all the shit Jesus said conveniently highlighted in red ink.

I guess this proves people just aren't religious anymore. The Word of God must mean nothing to people nowadays. Christ Almighty, that's just fucking sad. ∅

NATION

WWII Ace To Kill One Last German

WASHINGTON, DC—Since 1948, WWII fighter pilot Herman Porter has appealed to the federal government to earn the legal right to kill one last German citizen. This week, at 78, the decorated soldier will get his wish.

The Congressional Subcommittee on Defense Relations has granted Porter official permission to kill a German in cold blood without fear of legal repercussions.

"This is the happiest day of my life," Porter said at his Bredford, MO, home when contacted by a congressional liaison with the news. "This is one Jerry who isn't getting away."

The killing will take place in Porter's hometown of Bredford, as he is bound to a wheelchair with Hodgkin's disease and has been advised by his physician not to travel or over-exert himself.

Porter, a member of the U.S. Air Force's famed 3rd Squadron in the European theater, registered 11 kills during the war but missed out on the fall of Berlin and the subsequent German surrender. Porter's plane was shot down over Dresden, and, though he was able to kill numerous German soldiers in hand-to-hand combat, he was injured during his escape to Allied lines. Since the war ended, Porter has longed for the opportunity to kill another German, putting an exclamation point on what he considers the greatest war in U.S. history.

"It won't take much," Porter said, "just one thrust of my bayonet."

The German selected for killing by the congressional subcommittee was initially slated to be a citizen of Germany, but delicate diplomacy and strained relations between the countries' governments made such an option impossible. A random American citizen of German descent was then selected as a replacement.

Brian Thomas, a machine-tool operator

Above: Herman Porter's first attempt to kill a final German failed, as the septuagenarian was too weak to effect a fatal thrust of his bayonet. Left: Porter registered 11 kills as a WWII pilot.

from Rochester, MN, is slated to serve as the kill. While not a full-blooded German, Thomas is the grandson of immigrants and retains the minimum 25 percent German blood to qualify him for killing under U.S. law.

Thomas, who attempted to flee the country upon discovering his fate, was unavailable for comment, though he issued a release stating that his German grandparents were leaders in the resistance movement and successfully sheltered 250 Jewish families during the war's darkest hours. But Thomas' pleas for mercy went unanswered.

Although the kill is scheduled for Sept. 12, a first attempt failed last Thursday. Escorted by federal agents to Bredford, Thomas was held in front of Porter in the town square. Porter was handed an authentic early-1940s-issue bayonet and WWII helmet courtesy of U.S. Army archives, then wheeled up to face Thomas.

In front of a hushed audience of friends, relatives and townspeople, Porter exclaimed, "Die, you damned Jerry scum!" and feebly moved his bayonet toward Thomas. Thomas struggled with the agents, who held him in place and even tried to force him onto the weapon. He was not killed, but did sustain a minor knee abrasion.

Porter, meanwhile, froze in mid-thrust, overcome by heat exhaustion. He was rushed to an area hospital.

Porter will face Thomas again upon his recovery. ∅

Chapter Three

Stories That Saved A Baby's Life

Although they are tragically over-looked in this volume, my old "Message From The Publisher" columns indeed make for riveting reading. It is remarkable to think that I have authored that space for more than a century. To read my old

By T. Herman Zweibel
Publisher Emeritus
(photo circa 1911)

columns again reminds me of what a modern-day Renaissance man I was, for it seemed that no subject, great or small, eluded my pen, and my judgment was impeccable. For example, in 1912 I predicted that the insurgent Bull Moose Party would fall short of defeating the Democrats in the presidential race, and I was right. In 1919, I predicted that the ladies' skirt-hems would rise considerably in the coming year, and I was right. In 1951, I argued that furniture should have the right to marry. It was not until 1964 that the president signed the Furniture Matrimony Act into law, making me an impressive 13 years ahead of the herd on that one.

Remarkable, too, is how consistent the standards of journalistic excellence have remained. With his gasoline-fueled "combustible" motion-machines and steel-framed sky-scrapery, Modern Man may feel that old-fashioned customs have gone the way of powdered wigs, but, thankfully, some are still with us. I am proud to say that *The Onion* has led the way in this endeavor. Despite my retirement, I continue to personally school each novice correspondent in the essentials of news-gathering. The eager young scrivener is brought to my bed-chamber, where I impart to him the formula for effective reportage, which can be concisely explained in these simple terms:

Who?

What?

Where?

When?

Why?

How?

Could I get this off the news-wire with very little effort?

Will this take up precious advertising space?

I guarantee that, if every cub reporter asks him-self these crucial questions as he practices his craft, he will file stories that will ensure him a secure place in the news-paper trade. How-ever, don't go looking for a job at *The Onion*. We're full up! Although I do need some-one to give me an epsom-salts bath.

TRAVEL

Perky 'Canada' Has Own Government, Laws

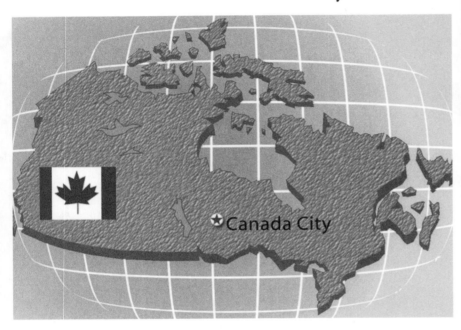

Canada City

It's Monday morning, and Toronto resident Steve Dorman shares a quick breakfast of "eggs" (a native food) with his "wife" (an officially state-sanctioned mate), and discusses yesterday's poor showing by the hometown team in "baseball" (a popular local sport). After a kiss on his wife's cheek, he hops on the "subway train" (a mode of subterranean transport) to the office.

This is life in exotic Canada City, set deep in the heart of the mysterious land known as Canada (pronounced CAN-a-da).

Like his estimated 35,000 countrymen, Dorman is proud to be a "Canadian." Located 120 miles north of Buffalo, NY, Canada is, according to Dorman, "a nation with a government and laws distinct from those of the United States." It also has a military, a system of taxation and periodic free elections to select political leaders. It even has its own currency, various denominations of "dollars" that can be exchanged for the many products manufactured in Canada, including Canadian bacon and ice.

Canada City, Canada's largest community, is located in a place called a "province," a subdivision not unlike the cantons of Switzerland. There are 10 Canadian provinces in all, from Nova Scotia in the east to British Columbia in the west. And, much like America's states, nearly every one of the provinces has its own capital. But make no mistake—there's nothing provincial about these provinces. Canada has both feet planted firmly in the 20th century.

In fact, Canadians enjoy such advancements as refrigerated food, zippers and printing, says Dorman, an "accountant" who goes to work wearing the comfortable trousers, dress shirt and necktie that form a traditional Canadian costume. "Our industries are large and varied, ranging from logging to automobile manufacturing."

Not too shabby for a nation that just 240 years ago had no electricity!

One area in which Canada certainly has the U.S. beat is languages. Canadians speak

see CANADA page 10

Did You Know...

▶ ...that Canada is known as the "Maple Leaf State"?

▶ ...that in Canadian units, Canada is actually a larger land mass than the U.S.?

▶ ...that murder is illegal in Canada?

▶ ...that the province of Saskatchewan was mentioned in a song in *The Muppet Movie*?

▶ ...that the North American Free Trade Agreement (NAFTA) also mentions Canada in several clauses?

▶ ...that Canadians have evolved with a fully functioning pancreas?

CANADA from page 7

When Canadians say: They mean:

When Canadians say:	They mean:
Parliament	Congress
Wayne Gretzky	Ken Griffey Jr.
Manitoba	Texas
Air Canada	American
"Eh?"	"What I just said, is it not true?"
Quebec independent maintenant!	I am an angry black man!

not only English, but also French. According to Prime Minister (roughly Canada's equivalent of a president) Jean Chrétien, "French is the primary language in some parts of the country, and English is in others. The national-language question has divided our nation terribly, with Quebec even recently threatening to leave the union."

Canada has produced many prominent people who have gone on to great success in hockey. Among them is Colorado Avalanche goaltender Patrick Roy, who says hockey is the "national sport" of the Canadianers.

"It's in our blood, it's part of our heritage and it brings people together," he says of the sport Canada picked up from America in the late '50s. So appreciative is Canada, it even has hockey teams called the "Oilers" and "Jets," named after its favorite American football teams.

Despite the language problem and other obstacles, at least one Canadianer is optimistic about his country's future prospects.

"Canada will remain free, proud and strong in the new century," says Dorman, heading off for another day of what in Canada is known as "work." "Our nation will continue to be a beacon to those around the world who value liberty, dignity and human rights."

Aww, isn't that cute? At times like this, there's really only one thing left to say: "Oh, Canada!" ∅

SPACE

NASA Baffled By Failure Of Straw Shuttle

CAPE CANAVERAL, FL—NASA officials watched in horror Monday as the $68 billion straw space shuttle, *Explorer 2*, burst into flames upon lift-off from Cape Canaveral. The four American and three Russian astronauts onboard were killed instantly, despite the protection of their all-straw space suits.

Technicians were stunned by the failure, which capped a flawless six-month pre-launch test period. They count "faulty twine" among the possible causes of the accident.

According to an official statement by NASA chief engineer George Toshikima, "The straw ship was dry, lightweight and well-bailed enough to break the Earth's orbit, but it inexplicably burst into flames when ignited with 3,000 gallons of rocket fuel."

"This is a devastating setback for NASA," he added.

An estimated 30 birds, 15 voles and 20 mice which had nested in the ship's outer hull or burrowed homes deep in the ship's straw engines also perished in the blast.

The ship was held in place with top-quality bailing twine, purchased in bulk from Cape Canaveral's leading farm-equipment supplier.

The straw ship was constructed with more than 200,000 bales of U.S. grade E straw; baled, tied and pitched from NASA's Cape Canaveral farm; and stored over the planting season in the launch-pad barn.

"It was nice and crisp and dry," Toshikima said, "which is the best condition for straw headed away from the Earth's gravitational pull."

According to accident reports, the one-eighth-inch-thick string may not have been tied tightly enough or even not weaved right around a critical fuel-delivery gasket, which may have caused the ship to unravel.

Toshikima said he does not believe such a small imperfection could have caused the massive explosion.

"We are still trying to determine why it burst into flames suddenly," he said. "In all the pre-fueling tests, the procedure went perfectly, but as soon as we ignited the fuel, it exploded. Why?"

Some insiders fault a problem that occurred last week, when a section of the ship's starboard high-pressure re-entry tiles was eaten by a horse.

Above: NASA's lightweight straw space shuttle tragically burst into flames upon rocket-fuel ignition.

"The horse should not have been on the launch pad," NASA grounds coordinator Nathan Meersen said. "He ate a critical section of the ship, and it set us back one full day to re-bail and re-tie that section."

Meersen said the horse was returned to NASA stables and given a suitable meal of remnants from the department's long-abandoned, all-hay Mars probe.

Although some reports indicate goats may have gnawed at the ship's exterior cables, NASA scientists maintain that there was never a problem with goats.

Explorer 1, NASA's first straw ship, was built in 1994 but, after 11 months of painstaking preparation, it was destroyed the day before the launch when it unexpectedly rained.

Explorer 2, like its predecessor, had been headed for the sun, where it was to be the first spacecraft to land on a star. "We'd hoped to bring back and study sun rock," Toshikima said.

The straw ship had been equipped with a special reinforced wicker basket to hold the sun lava for its journey back to Earth. A straw-enforced robot arm was constructed to scoop the lava—which scientists say is as hot as the center of a nuclear holocaust—and place it in the basket.

The ship's debris is slated to be used as mulch. ∅

From September 5, 1995

Wedding It Be Nice

More Americans are getting married than ever before. In this age of skyrocketing divorce rates and "dysfunctional families," why are so many people getting hitched?

6% Too uneducated to realize they didn't have to wed first person willing to have sex with them

19% Handsome dowry irresistible to greedy family

23% Needed to qualify under spouse's health insurance for life-saving bone-marrow transplant

41% Vastly better orgasms possible without fear of vengeful god

89% Inability to act and think for one's self

SPORTS

Christ Returns To NBA

ATLANTA—After a two-year hiatus from basketball, Jesus Christ returned to the NBA Sunday night, rejoining His former team, the Atlanta Hawks. Christ, who quit the sport in May 1994 to focus on spreading His message of universal love and compassion, made His triumphant comeback against the Bulls, just in time for Easter Sunday.

The return of Christ, who averaged 18.2 points and 7.3 assists per game during his 10-year NBA career, has excited success-hungry Hawks fans, who have dubbed Him the team's "Savior."

Said Atlanta resident and devout Christian Jeff Voorhees, "Jesus is Lord."

Christ's decision to return to the Hawks surprised insiders; for years the Nazareth native had been crucified by the Atlanta press. Ever since He was drafted third overall out of Texas A&M in 1986, Christ has been labeled "too passive and forgiving" to lead the Hawks to the promised land. Christ, however, has turned the other cheek.

"I forgive *Atlanta Journal-Constitution* sportswriter Stan Sheridan," Christ said after Sunday's game. "He knows not what he writes."

The closest Christ came to signing with another team came in December, when He spent 40 days and 40 nights in the desert with Detroit Pistons coach Doug Collins. After consulting His father, God, Christ decided to turn down the Pistons' offer of 30 gold pieces.

"Get thee behind me, Coach Collins," Christ reportedly said at the time.

Though some say the media led Christ to quit basketball, many contend He quit after being betrayed by teammate Kevin Willis during a 1994 Celtics-Hawks playoff game. With three seconds left and the Hawks trailing by one, Christ was wide open underneath the basket for an easy lay-up. Instead of passing to Christ, Willis took a wild shot from three-point range, missing the net com-

see CHRIST on page 12

Right: Jesus Christ returned to action Sunday night against the Chicago Bulls, chipping in 13 points and 4 assists and wowing fans with his trademark "Ascension Dunk."

CHRIST from page 3

pletely. After the game, a visibly upset Christ stretched out His arms and asked, "Kevin Willis, why hast thou forsaken me?"

Despite the controversies, Hawks teammates and personnel are excited to have Christ back.

Forward Stacey Augmon, one of many Hawks players who claim to have a personal relationship with Christ, said, "He's taught me so much, like how to love your enemies as yourself, to pray for those who hurt you, and when to pass up the three in favor of a higher-percentage shot."

Fans also eagerly await the return of Christ's "Ascension Dunk," a crowd favorite in which Christ leaps His less-than-league-average 24-inch vertical, then miraculously ascends toward Heaven, floating in midair just long enough to stuff the ball. An accompanying angelic choir momentarily stuns His defenders, as the ball comes crashing down on their heads. The move has wowed audiences at NBA All-Star Slam-N-Jam dunk competitions for years.

A three-time NBA All-Star, Christ impressed team doctors during Friday's brief closed-door workout, in which He displayed His still-sharp shooting skills, dribbling ability and overwhelming love for all mankind.

Team doctors also noted that, in contrast to most players who take layoffs, Christ's body fat is just 3 percent, even lower than when He was playing. Christ attributed the low figure to His recent food-free, 2,000-year out-of-body reign in His Father's Kingdom.

Christ's Career Highlights

College: Texas A&M

 School's second all-time leading scorer.

 Junior year, led Aggies to NCAA's Sweet 16.

Pro: Drafted third overall by Atlanta in 1986.

 January 17, 1988—Scored 33 points in one quarter after Nets forward Buck Williams used his name in vain following a missed dunk.

 February 22, 1990—During time-out at All-Star Game in Chicago, turned water into Gatorade.

 December 16, 1991—Overturned souvenir stand in lobby of Dallas' Reunion Arena, shouting, "This is a house of basketball!"

 March 4, 1992—Appeared on cover of *Sports Illustrated* for the seventh time, once again with the headline, "It's A Miracle!"

Meanwhile, the league made a ruling regarding Christ's crown of thorns, deciding that He may wear the headpiece only so long as He does not "unwittingly anoint a player with the forgiving power of His Holy Blood."

Though Hawks fans seem certain Christ can help the team, some NBA experts question whether Jesus is the answer.

"The healing power of His Holy Love may get the Hawks into the playoffs, but they can't ride it to the championship," NBA commentator Hubie Brown said. "What they really need is a solid power forward who can fill the lane, someone like Cliff Robinson."

Some analysts say Christ's injuries, along with His added age, may slow Him down.

"Christ isn't going to be 33 forever, and, quite frankly, He hasn't been the same since the Romans drove holes into His hands and feet," NBA analyst and former coach Chuck Daly said. "A painful stigmata injury is difficult to overcome, and it may affect His shooting touch. Still, I'm pretty confident He can rise again." ∅

SOCIETY

Area Loser To Spend Rest Of Day In Bed

STEVENS POINT, WI—Part-time dishwasher and self-described "utter failure" Eric Mayhew opted to call in sick and spend the rest of the day in bed Monday, and may do so again tomorrow, sources said.

Reasons cited for the decision to remain in bed include overall misery, desire to withdraw from all human contact and the lack of any point in getting up to face another day of the pathetic charade of his wasted existence.

"I knocked on his door for a long time. I don't know if he didn't hear me or what," said Tom Worland, a former roommate of Mayhew's from the University of Wisconsin at Stevens Point, where the two briefly attended classes before dropping out in 1991. "He's pretty much a loner nowadays. To be honest, I don't see much of him anymore."

The 24-year-old Mayhew, who for the last several years has eked out a partial subsistence at various minimum-wage menial-labor jobs and has been repeatedly rescued from insolvency by his parents, hit the "snooze" button on his alarm clock 11 times before finally venturing out of bed long enough to call in sick to work, using a neighbor's phone because of his own line's disconnection for non-payment of his February bill. He spent the mid-morning staring into space, picking dead skin off his feet and listening to Jesus & Mary Chain's *Psychocandy* before leaving his room again at approximately noon to urinate.

Upon returning to bed, Mayhew reportedly listened to the CD—a gift from a girlfriend who broke up with him 17 months ago—three more times before taking it out of the stereo and snapping the disc in half.

"I tried calling her, like, last April, but she just yelled, 'Loser!' seven or eight times and then hung up," said Mayhew, speaking to reporters through the mail slot of his tiny, one-room apartment. "I guess she just hates me now. And who could blame her? I'm a sad, worthless, empty shell of a pitiful excuse for a human being."

Mayhew also reread, for the 29th time, Kurt Vonnegut's *Breakfast Of Champions*, a book he calls "one of the most horribly depressing depic-

Above: Utter failure Eric Mayhew.

tions of humanity's essential pointlessness ever written." He then spent the remainder of the afternoon watching reruns of *Saved By The Bell* on the sole channel his television can pick up, accelerating his descent into a nightmare hellscape of unrelenting horror.

"I hate that fuckwad Slater so much," he said, "but I despise that fucking Screech even more. Whenever he's on the screen, I just stare at him, mumbling, 'Die, die, die.' I don't know why I even bother to watch it. I guess it's either that or staring at the wall." Mayhew then kicked the television over and began staring at the wall.

While it is not known how Mayhew will occupy himself during the remainder of his time in bed, it is widely believed that he will berate himself

see FAILURE page 10

70

FAILURE from page 1

Above: Mayhew's view for the past 26 hours.

under his breath, pausing every half hour or so to break down into desperate, half-choked sobs. He is also expected to draw squiggly shapes on a crumpled Taco Bell napkin with a magic marker, halfheartedly masturbate twice and restore his television to an upright position some time around 10 p.m. to watch reruns of *Star Trek: The Next Generation*. It is unknown whether he will repeat these activities tomorrow.

Observers attribute Mayhew's utter failure of a life to a variety of factors. His lack of employable skills makes him ill-suited for all but the most degrading menial jobs, few of which offer a living wage, leaving him in constant poverty and debt. His lack of health insurance, coupled with a diet consisting almost exclusively of Saltines and Tang, has contributed greatly to the deterioration of his physical and mental well-being. And his substandard personal hygiene, caused by his low self-esteem, as well as his enormous emotional neediness, make him extremely unattractive to members of the opposite sex as a potential romantic partner.

Mayhew dismissed such explanations. "The reason I'm such a loser is obvious," he said. "I'm such a pathetic fucking loser because I'm a worthless goddamn dorko motherfucking gaywad asshole useless piece of shit, that's why."

"Duh," he added, snapping the mail slot shut. ∅

From January 30, 1996

An Open Letter To A Starving Child

Dear Starving Child,

**By Dick Crimwelt
Carpet Salesman**

I saw your picture in one of these "Feed The Children" magazine ads. It said that your mother dumped you in a Sri Lankan back-alley trash heap and that you've been a street urchin, begging for scraps from Bedouin traders since you were five. And it said for two cents a day I could feed you. Well, I must say, I don't know how you can live like that. I mean, what are you thinking?

If I were you, I'd high-tail it home and make myself a juicy ham sandwich with some cheese on it, then I'd put it in the microwave so the cheese melts and the sandwich is nice and warm. In fact, I'd toast the bread so it has a little crunch to it.

And that gets to why I'm writing you. I think I can offer you some basic tips on how to get along better in life. Instead of giving you a mere two cents a day, I'm going to give you a lifetime's accumulated wisdom. You see, as a successful carpet salesman, I do all right. And I think I can share a lesson or two about getting the most out of this crazy game called life.

First of all, you've gotta consolidate your debt. Those interest payments will kill you. I learned this one the hard way. And seeing as you don't have a home, you should be able to pay off any high-interest loans and start putting your money into no-load mutual funds. That's where the real growth potential is. It may not seem like much every month, but, over time, you'll be building quite a nest egg. And when you get to be my age, it's nice to be able to pamper yourself a little bit with some of your dividends.

Like just last night, I spent more than $250 on a lobster dinner. We had lobster soaked in butter, mashed potatoes with chives, and yellow squash with yogurt sauce. I'm telling you, I was so stuffed, I felt sick. I came home and vomited! It was a great meal, but I hate

For As Little As Two Cents A Day, You Can Feed A Starving Child.

This is Gabriel. He lives in a hut. These devices create a wall of silent noise that drives away annoying animal pests. Now you can use ultrasonic power to repel annoying dogs, cats and many wild animals—without harming them.

Be honest. Even if you like animals, you don't want strange ones in your yard. You know what I mean: dogs that foul your lawn or cats that trample flowers and sleep on your car. It's a common Problem. If you live in a rural area, you may have had trouble with racoons, skunks or possums. Some people in the south are even bothered by armadillos!

Up until Now, there weren't many options. You wouldn't want to harm a stray animal, and an animal control agency may take days to respond—if they ever do.

Call toll free: 1-800-695-4376

United Care Foundation
3232 Washington Center • New York, New York • 10019

when I stuff myself. That takes the pleasure out of eating. It's almost like I threw that $250 right into the toilet. But for a split second, it was heaven.

Second, living on the street is no way to build equity. For as little as $1,000 down, you can own a modest two- or three-bedroom home. This will not only help you build a financial future; it will help you build self-esteem. Homeowners are self-assured, productive members of society. And remember the three most important things in real estate: location, location and location. So buy in a nice area. You want to look at schools, since you're eight years old.

You know, it occurs to me that you don't even live in America. And I've gotta know, what the heck are you doing living in Sri Lanka? What do they have there? Camels? Rugs? Well, I can tell you one thing they don't have: 100 percent grade-A American opportunity.

America is the land of milk and honey. You can catch a flight here for as little as $2,800 nowadays, if you shop around. So what's keeping you? Okay, I can imagine how it is: You live in a back alley and you eat garbage. And maybe you don't have the liquid capital to lay out $2,800 on a luxury like first-class airfare to the U.S. Well, you can always fly coach for about a third of first-class fare and, if worst comes to worst, put it on the plastic. As long as you pay it off as quickly as you can, the interest won't cramp your style. (See Tip #1.)

Now, since you're eating scraps from dumpsters, my guess is you could use a little shot in the arm when it comes to income. Well, maybe I'm tooting my own horn a little bit here, but have you considered seeking a position in carpet sales? It's a high-profit industry and commissions are good nowadays. With new homes being built at a record pace all across the country and remodeling positively going through the stratosphere, there's never a shortage of demand for new, high-quality carpets. Thick shag, thin shag, knit, indoor, outdoor—any variety of color. Heck, I could take you over to the warehouse and show you some of my samples, if you like.

Well, I hope I've given you some fat to chew on. I'd like to know if I can be of any more help, so I'd appreciate it if you could write back. And Fed-Ex it. I bet international mail takes forever.

Sincerely,
Dick Crimwelt Ø

Joining The Record Club

Direct-mail CD and cassette clubs are a $4 billion-per-year industry. Why do so many consumers use these clubs to purchase music?

68%
Desperate for hard-to-find Mariah Carey CDs

23%
Family's annual budget for music is one cent

14%
Enjoy getting hand-signed past-due notes from head of Accounts Receivable

9%
Enjoy music, but need faceless corporation to offer narrowest possible choice

3%
Want to avoid germ-laden human contact with mall record-store clerk

From February 13, 1996

ENVIRONMENT

Massive Oil Spill Results In Improved Wildlife Viscosity

Above: These seals are just some of the ocean wildlife which will no longer knock or suffer from thermal breakdown, thanks to Castrol's 51-million-gallon oil spill in the Bering Strait.

NOME, AK—A Castrol Oil supertanker ran aground Monday near Nome, Alaska, spilling 51 million gallons of oil into the Bering Strait and greatly improving the viscosity of area marine wildlife. The spill, the world's largest since the Exxon Valdez ran aground in 1989, has coated more than 500,000 birds, fish and seals in quality, high-grade lubricant that will provide valuable protection and keep important animal parts running smooth.

Wildlife officials were excited by news of the spill.

"A thick coat of oil should help these animals a lot, especially in the cold weather," Tom Wofford of the U.S. Fish and Wildlife Department said. "Last month alone, we had 200 cases of Northern Cranes suffering from severe thermal breakdown. When temperatures reach 75 degrees below zero, these seals need a good oil like Castrol to keep their wings and other parts loose."

According to Wofford, the Bering Strait's extremely active animal population, with its broad hunting and migratory patterns, has long been in need of preventative oil care.

"Today's wildlife revs at higher RPMs," Wofford said. "So when you're a gray seal, and you're swimming after a fish at over 200 strokes per minute, you

see SPILL page 15

74

SPILL from page 7

can't afford any friction on your fins or tail. You need a quality motor oil to keep them as loose as possible."

Especially benefitting from the recent spill is the local salmon population. Several thousand were spotted energetically flipping around in the crude oil, gasping for air from all the playful exertion. Many of them, exhausted, stopped moving altogether.

Castrol spokesman Bob Crutchfield was also pleased with the oil spill.

"For years our products have provided top-notch protection for millions of automobile owners," Crutchfield said. "Now we will be able to provide that same protection for America's birds and fish."

For most Arctic animals, Crutchfield suggested Castrol Premium. For animals that spend a lot of time near or in the water, such as egrets and halibut, he recommended Castrol Plus, which contains an anti-rust ingredient.

Monday's spill was so successful, plans are already underway for similar oil leaks around the world. Beginning this spring, massive tankers strategically placed in wildlife-rich areas will be intentionally run aground, covering millions of surrounding flora and fauna in a lustrous coat of motor oil. In shoreline areas not rocky enough to rupture metal, oil tankers will be pre-cut, their hulls sliced just enough to burst open at the slightest contact.

In addition to off-shore spills, Castrol officials hope to expand inland, coating rainforests, wetlands and other at-risk ecosystems in a high-

"A thick coat of oil should help these animals a lot, especially in the cold weather," Tom Wofford of the U.S. Fish and Wildlife Department said.

grade automotive lubricant. "Every day, seven more species become extinct in the Amazon rainforest," said Marcia Nettles, director of the Rainforest Action Network. "Perhaps if we stressed proper prevention and maintenance with Castrol-brand products, we could keep them from dying off so fast."

According to Wofford, the oil spill has had an added benefit, providing the waters of the Bering Strait with an attractive rainbow sheen. "Before the spill, the water here was pretty much greenish-blue all the time," he said. "Now we've got a million different colors. It's very exciting."

Wofford added the water also now has "a super-fun shine, which is far more attractive than the algae and drab green plant life it replaced." ∅

From February 6, 1996

WORLD

Jews Ordered Back To Egypt For Pyramid Duty

CAIRO—Citing thousands of years of wear and tear on its famed pyramids, the Egyptian government recalled the Jewish people Monday. The Jews, though currently spread throughout the world, are in the process of returning to Egypt to repair damages the pyramids have suffered over the last 4,000 years.

"They did a superb job the first time around, and we expect the same level of high-quality craftsmanship now," said Egyptian Minister of Tourism Fekesh Sabah, a top assistant to the Pharaoh. "They are a highly skilled people."

The Jews were urged to return by a forceful letter sent to every Jewish household in the world. The letter strongly suggested that they return, if they know what is good for them.

"The language of the letter seemed very sincere and forthright," Detroit marketing analyst Roger Fine said. "It just came off like we really should go back."

Fine is one of millions of Jews, or "Hebrewites," who hastily quit his job, sold all his worldly possessions and boarded one of the thousands of charter jets heading to Cairo International Airport upon receipt of the letter.

Jews are already massing in the Egyptian capital, where they are being sent out in labor teams of 600 to replace stones, repair crumbling walls and reinstall statuary of the sun god Ra. They will do this not only for the rest of their lives, but also for the lives of their children and their children's children.

"This is very hard work," said Jeffrey Sonnenfeld, an accountant from Cherry Hill, NJ. "I do not enjoy this at all."

Added Rachel Cohen of Los Angeles: "My job as a record-label publicist has very little to do with hauling enormous, 40-ton sandstone slabs through the desert."

To repair the pyramids, the Jews will employ many of the same effective building techniques used during their first construction, including the lever and the pulley.

"We have found that utilizing these techniques makes lifting the rocks up the 75-degree incline that much easier," project

Above: With such famous landmarks as the Sphinx and the Great Pyramids in horrible disrepair, Jews from around the world (inset) packed up their belongings and headed back to Egypt, where they will toil for centuries for the Pharaoh.

coordinator Nassar Achbad said. "Doing it the old way, by hand alone, it would take over 500 years to complete the work. Now, it won't take more than two or three centuries, if that."

The Jews first built the pyramids between 2686 and 2181 B.C. under enslavement by numerous pharaohs. Only after Moses, a prophet of the lord Yahweh, rose up to lead them were they able to escape into the desert and relocate to the promised land of Israel. According to published reports, the Jews spent 40 years in the desert subsisting on an unleavened bread product, manna and water, which was found by smashing magical scepters into rocks.

Once again, the Jewish people are hoping for a prophet to rise up from among the people and lead them back to freedom. This

prophet may be Arizona lawyer Barry Stern, whose successful defense firm has freed many white- and blue-collar workers from potential incarceration.

"The climate here is similar to Arizona, a dry heat which is more bearable than the humidity of, say, the Amazon rainforest. But I don't enjoy being whipped by my overseers," Stern said. "If this continues, litigation may be pending."

Though they do not fear legal action, Egyptian officials are hopeful that the Jews won't pull out in a manner similar to last time, when they visited a host of deadly plagues on the Egyptian people. This culminated in the parting of the Red Sea, which drowned more than half the Egyptian army.

Said Sabah: "I hope they don't do that again." ∅

Lyndon Johnson Jr. Sworn In As *George* Editor

HYANNIS PORT, MA—At 4:11 a.m. EST Saturday, Lyndon Baines Johnson Jr. was sworn in as editor-in-chief of *George* magazine following the death of John F. Kennedy Jr. in a plane crash. "At this tragic time in our magazine's history, let us look forward, remembering always the legacy of my predecessor," said the 51-year-old Johnson, previously *George*'s assistant editor, after being hastily sworn in by Chief Justice William Rehnquist on a New York-bound DC-10 jet. "Let us now begin a process of healing, followed by a time of renewal at more than 60 percent off the regular cover price." The somber ceremony was witnessed by an estimated 15 *George* staffers and subscribers. —*July 23, 1999*

Koko The Gorilla Now Just Flipping Everybody Off

WOODSIDE, CA—Koko, the famed gorilla whose mastery of sign language made her a celebrity, has now resorted to just flipping everybody off. "Apparently, after more than 20 years of rigorous sign-language training and cue-card drills, Koko is sick of being the world's foremost test ape," said trainer Dr. Francine Patterson. "Yesterday, she gave me the hand sign for 'Leave me the hell alone, already. I am an intelligent creature who has more than adequately demonstrated my vast capacity for reasoning and other high-level brain functions. Go away and let me eat my banana in peace.'" —*May 7, 1998*

Glorious Heyday Of Youth Spent In Parking Lot

AMARILLO, TX—Celebrating the bountiful gift of youth and the endless promise it holds, local 16-year-olds Stephanie Reardon, Doug Shiner and Toby Rizzo spent Friday evening in the parking lot of the Howell Avenue Grab 'N' Go convenience store. "Got any more Kools?" asked Reardon, living to the fullest every moment of her salad days. Savoring the sweetness of his vitality as he would a ripe, juicy pear, Shiner leaned against the store's ice machine and said, "Check out that van over there." —*November 12, 1998*

All Y'All Urged To Go Fuck Yo' Selves

DETROIT—In a strongly worded statement to all y'all motherfuckers, Detroit resident Dwayne Combs urged all y'all to go fuck yo' selves Monday. "Y'all be bullshit," said Combs in a 3:17 a.m. address from the corner of Woodward Avenue and Grand Boulevard. "And yo' mama, too." Monday's pronouncement marked the normally reclusive Combs' first since an October 1998 appeal to Detroit's city council to kiss his big, black ass. Representatives for all y'all have not yet responded to Combs' themselves-fucking offer. —*January 14, 1999*

Viagra Giving Hope To Thousands Of Struggling Stand-Up Comedians

Released only a few months ago, the new wonder-drug Viagra is providing hope for thousands of impotent stand-up acts across the U.S. "Could you imagine if Godzilla took Viagra?" asked Chuckle Factory emcee Tony Campanelli, one of the many struggling stand-up performers whose sense of comedic vitality and virility have been boosted by the drug. "That Statue Of Liberty had better watch out." Chicago-area improv-troupe member Bobby Childs agreed. "We just ask the audience to suggest a popular new medication, and someone always yells Viagra. A laugh riot never fails to ensue," he said. "Medical science has truly blessed us with a second chance at pleasing audiences." —*June 11, 1998*

Tractor Pulls Now Number-One Use For U.S. Tractors

WASHINGTON, DC—According to a survey released Friday by the Department of Agriculture, after more than 150 years on top, farming is no longer the number-one use for tractors in the U.S., surpassed by tractor-pull competitions. "Fortunately for tractor manufacturers like John Deere," said Agriculture Secretary Dan Glickman, "Americans' declining interest in farm-based crop-tilling has been offset by a rising interest in stadium-based ass-kicking." —*December 17, 1997*

final voyage, a number of dog-food-y whistleblowers are coming forward wake of the crash, insisting that such edy was inevitable given the CWTA's ne failure to address serious driver-issues.

sort of thing happens all the time," rmer miniature-chuck-wagon driver ll "Tex" West, who claims he was fired ck Wagon Transit after refusing to do re kitchen runs until the dog problem ldressed. "I can't tell you how many a chuck wagon will tear through a n, hell-bent for leath

the decision to remain in sery, desire to withdraw fi t, and the lack of any poir e another day of the path asted existence.

is door for a long time. I i't hear me or what," said ier roommate of Mayhew's of Wisconsin at Stevens briefly attended classes

"He's pretty much , hun- est, I don't see much nche

SAN FRANCISCO—Second-generation Chinese-American laundry owner Raymond Chen is under heavy fire this week from Bay Area activists who call him "an insulting caricature that perpetuates long-outdated, grossly prejudiced images of Asian Americans."

"It's frightening to think that, in 1998, some of us still haven't moved beyond the century-old stereotype of Chinese people as laundrymen,"

From April 10, 1996

Freemen Follies

Another anti-government militia, this time in Montana, has holed itself up in its fortress and is in the midst of a stand-off with the FBI. What do *you* think of this growing trend?

Martin Deems
Court Clerk

"What alarms me most about the three uprisings so far is that they've taken place in Texas, Idaho and Montana—three of our least fucked-up states."

Gene Newich
Editor

"I am the editor of *Time* magazine and this story interests me very much. I think maybe I'll put it on the cover this week."

Brian Showalter
Repairman

"So there are 29 of them on an isolated ranch in the middle of nowhere? Now, that's what I call a threat to the nation's infrastructure."

Gary Lomartz
Systems Analyst

"Listen, if people want to hide in the woods with a ton of bourbon and corn-hole everything in sight, that's their business. Yes, I know that's not what they're doing. I'm not talking about them."

Louisa Kittage
Notary Public

"I've been holed up inside my house for two years but I don't see the government paying any attention to me. I guess that's because I'm watching TV and stuff."

Kate Anachon
Manager

"I sympathize with the Freemen. I, too, defy The Man and refuse to be brought to heel by a corrupt government. I operate a health-food co-op."

Chen has responded to the controversy surrounding him with a series of local televi-sion spots, paid for out of his own pocket, in which he pleads his case to the community.

"Why is everyone so mad at me?" Chen asks in one of the spots. "Because of how I talk? I was born in America, but I was raised in

From November 7, 1995

Coffeehouse Encounter Results In Conversation, Cunnilingus

AUSTIN, TX—Two area students achieved orally stimulated orgasm Tuesday night after a chance meeting at the Chez Europique coffeehouse, authorities said. The coffeehouse, with its atmosphere of comfortable, easygoing lounging, high-energy caffeinated excitation, and vaguely radical political and cultural sensibilities, was instrumental in the success of the coupling.

"It is a well-known fact that jazz music, pretentious wall art and overpriced foreign beverages are excellent facilitators of the type of mutually satisfactory, gender-sensitive, non-threatening consensual oral sex experienced by these lucky youngsters," psychologist Morton Blen said. "That is to say, as opposed to the more traditional fumbling, awkward, guy-on-top, 90-second type of sex generally brought on by consumption of beer."

The two lovers, Carl Giallardo (junior, comparative literature) and Amy Hammond (sophomore, political science), were both "greatly pleased" by the evening's events.

"I especially enjoyed the Mocha Latte," Giallardo, 22, said. "It added a milieu, if you will, of continental sophistication to my late-night studying which was no doubt a key factor in attracting Amy's attention." He added, "The conversation was wonderful, as well, though I must admit that, while I enjoyed discussing Kerouac and William S. Burroughs with Amy, I was picturing her naked the whole time."

Hammond, 21, also had no complaints.

"By showing me that he was willing to seek out my opinion on the literary efforts of various Beat Generation writers, Carl enabled me to build the self-esteem, confidence and trust necessary for me to enthusiastically grind my velveteen vulva against his handsome, slightly stubbled face," she said.

Although the two have no current plans to see each other again, both say the oral sex, as well as the worldly and sophisticated conversational subject matter and beverages

Above: Carl Giallardo and Amy Hammond, photographed at Chez Europique by a local art student, worked their way back to her apartment, where he tongued her clitoris.

preceding it, were enriching and rewarding.

"It sure beats talking about the football game with a drunk, whooping sports fan who's just trying to figure out which girl is most likely to let him in her pants," Hammond said. "I oughta know, I lived in the dorms once. My old boyfriend Curt was like that. All he ever wanted was for me to go down on him. He was never sensitive to my orgasmic needs the way Carl was [Tuesday]."

Chez Europique owner Ken Bannister said this is not the first sexual encounter his cafe has sparked.

"Every day, people meet people here and enjoy casual, meaningless sexual romps," Bannister said. "Whether it's cunnilingus, fellatio, rimming, fisting or good old-fash-

ioned frottage, there's something about this place that's conducive to random sexual dalliances."

Just Wednesday morning, two strangers sat down together and discussed French theorist Michel Foucault, eventually returning to one of their apartments for heated intercourse.

John Walthrop, who owns the Tru-Value hardware store next door to Chez Europique, said his business stands in sharp contrast to Bannister's.

"We don't get too many young, well-educated people here looking for chance sexual encounters," Walthrop said. "More often we get middle-aged married people looking for extension cords and ratchets and high-quality paint primers—things like that." ∅

WORLD

Clinton Deploys Vowels To Bosnia

Cities Of Sjlbvdnzv, Grznc To Be First Recipients

WASHINGTON, DC—Before an emergency joint session of Congress Monday, President Clinton announced U.S. plans to deploy more than 75,000 vowels to the war-torn region of Bosnia. The deployment, the largest of its kind in American history, will provide the region with the critically needed letters A, E, I, O and U, and is hoped to render countless Bosnian names more pronounceable.

"For six years, we have stood by while names like Ygrjvslhv, Tzlnhr and Glrm have been horribly butchered by millions around the world," Clinton said. "Today, the United States must finally stand up and say, 'Enough.' It is time the people of Bosnia finally had some vowels in their incomprehensible words. The U.S. is proud to lead the crusade in this noble endeavor."

The deployment, dubbed Operation Vowel Storm by the State Department, is set for early next week, with the Adriatic port cities of Sjlbvdnzv and Grznc slated to be the first recipients. Two C-130 transport planes, each carrying more than 500 24-count boxes of E's, will fly from Andrews Air Force base across the Atlantic and airdrop the letters over the cities.

Citizens of Grznc and Sjlbvdnzv eagerly await the arrival of the vowels.

"My God, I do not think we can last another day, Trszg Grzdnjlkn, 44, said. "I have six children and none of them has a name that is understandable to me or anyone else. Mr. Clinton, please send my poor, wretched family just one E. Please."

Said Sjlbvdnzv resident Grg Hmphrs, 67: "With just a few key letters, I could be George Humphries. That is my dream."

If the initial airlift is successful, Clinton said the U.S. will go ahead with full-scale vowel deployment, with C-130s airdropping thousands more letters over every area of Bosnia. Other nations are expected to pitch in, as well, including 10,000 British A's and 6,500 Canadian U's. Japan, rich in A's and

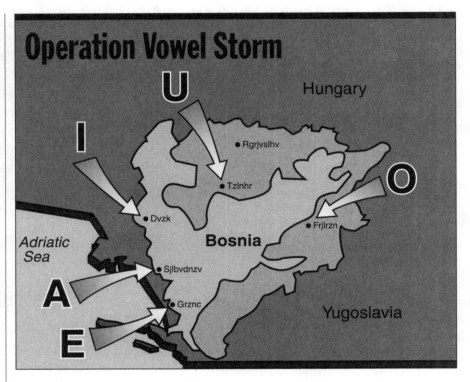

O's, was asked to participate in the relief effort but declined.

"With these valuable letters, the people of war-ravaged Bosnia will be able to make some terrific new words," Clinton said. "It should be very exciting for them and surely much easier for us to read their maps."

Linguists praise the U.S.'s decision to send the vowels. For decades they have struggled with the hard consonants and difficult pronunciation of most Slavic words.

"Vowels are crucial to the construction of all language," Baylor University linguist Noam Frankel said. "Without them, it would be difficult to utter a single word, much less organize a coherent sentence. Please, don't get me started on the moon-man language

they use in those Eastern European countries."

According to Frankel, once the Bosnians have vowels, they will be able to construct such valuable sentences as, "The potatoes are ready," "I believe it will rain" and, "All my children are dead from the war."

The American airdrop represents the largest deployment of any letter to a foreign country since 1984. During the summer of that year, the U.S. shipped 92,000 consonants to Ethiopia, providing cities like Ouaououa, Eaoiiuae and Aao with vital, life-giving supplies of L's, S's and T's. The consonant-relief effort failed, however, when vast quantities of the letters were intercepted and hoarded by gun-toting warlords. Ø

From September 11, 1996

Burt Reynolds Lives Like A Princess

I've interviewed scores of Hollywood stars, but I never took them at anything more than face value, especially Burt Reynolds. I never guessed the truth behind this model of masculinity,

By Lancio
Onion Gossip Columnist

whose virile mustache has lit a fire in the dreams of countless lovelorn. But who would have guessed that his mustache hides a pretty pout? Who would have guessed that Burt Reynolds, manly star of *Cannonball Run* and *Sharky's Machine*, lives like a princess?

When I pull into the driveway of Burt's oceanfront mansion, I expect to be greeted at the door by Burt and perhaps offered a beer. Instead, I'm escorted down chandelier-lit hallways by a wigged man in a frock coat and tights, who explains to me in hushed tones that certain preparations are still being made. Out of the corner of my eye, I see a chamber filled with bustling attendants, running to and fro in a storm of perfume and hairbrushes. In the center of the room sits a figure in a silk corset whose face is hidden from me. I am moved along.

As I wait in the garden outside, I enjoy the blooming roses and the rushing water of a splendid fountain. I sip peppermint tea, and cool garden breezes caress my skin. But these luxuries are quickly forgotten as the air is filled with the dulcet soprano of Burt Reynolds, singing softly.

After a rustle of petticoats announces his appearance, Burt steps into the garden. Resplendent in a pink velvet gown, he extends a bejeweled hand. "Enchanté," he whispers, and we sit in the shade of a spreading magnolia.

"I'd like to show you something," he says, pulling a flower from an ornate golden case. "This is a magic blossom—with one sniff, you can smell what anyone in the kingdom is cooking! Would you believe I got it from a swineherd for 10 kisses?" We both laugh over this charming anecdote. But when I ask about his past, Burt grows solemn.

"I had three older sisters who hated me, for I was the prettiest child," he says. "They made me slave away in the kitchen and called me names. Horrible names, like 'stupid goose' and 'scullery girl.' I longed to escape from that life, and with the financial success of *Smokey And The Bandit*, I did."

"I am happy," he says, with a touch of sadness in his voice. "But sometimes I wonder what the world is like beyond my garden wall."

After gifting me with one more lovely song, Burt regretfully announces he is retiring for the evening. I join him half an hour later in his private bedchamber.

He begins to thank me for coming but is distracted by some sort of discomfort. Even with a dozen mattresses piled on his canopy bed, he cannot relax. Melancholy swells from his pretty eyes as he weakly tosses and turns. Suddenly, his problem becomes clear to me. I carefully reach underneath the mattresses and pull out a single pea.

Gratitude floods Burt's face, and he allows me to kiss his hand before he sinks into slumber. I am led to the front gate, where a carriage awaits me. I am filled with sadness at leaving Burt Reynolds, and I find myself wishing I could stay with this precious soul in his castle by the sea forever. ∅

From July 9, 1997

DRUGS

CIA Unveils New Ghetto Drugs For '98

LANGLEY, VA—After months of eager anticipation within the nation's ghetto communities, the Central Intelligence Agency unveiled its 1998 line of addictive drugs Monday.

"The wait is over," CIA Director John Deutch said at the festive drug launch, simulcast on giant-screen TVs throughout Watts, Cabrini Green, Newark and other urban areas. "Inner-city Americans now have four exciting new ways to narcotize themselves, with the quality of product and wide distribution they've come to expect from the CIA."

Reaction to the new drugs (see sidebar) was overwhelmingly positive. "They had a tough act to follow after crack," said New York-area Mafia boss Alfonse DiBiasi, Deutch's close friend and former college roommate. "But this new stuff is just as cheap and every bit as addictive. We're all very excited."

President Clinton praised the CIA, as well. "This is a win-win situation for all Americans," he said. "Inner-city Americans will receive the powerful drugs they love, and the CIA will raise the funds they can't get from Congress to get their Jonestown mind-control experiment up and running again."

The new drugs are supported by months of CIA testing to ensure maximum potency and addictiveness. Focus groups, consisting primarily of homeless men and street orphans culled from ghettos around the country, were housed in an underground research facility beneath CIA headquarters in Langley. Only after six months of exhaustive experimentation on members of this target demographic group, who sampled hundreds of drugs, were the final decisions made.

"Everybody loves me because I am so beautiful. Anything is possible. I am going to live a very long and happy life," said Oakland, CA, native Charles

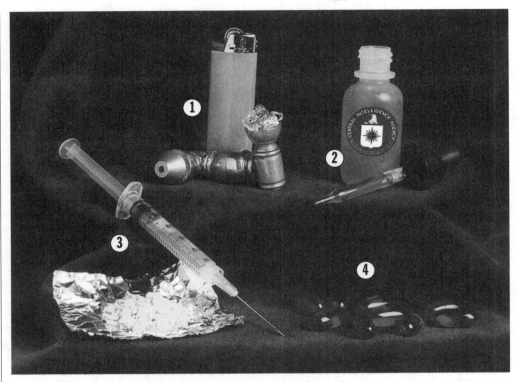

① Blue Glass

Type: Euphoric
Method: Smoked
Effects: Feelings of extreme optimism and happiness, greatly enhanced reflexes, sensory and sexual pleasure, visual acuity. Immediately followed by semi-permanent suicidal catatonia.
Duration: Five minutes
Cost: $1 per hit

② Brainscratch

Type: Hallucinogen
Method: Dropped into eye
Effects: Reaches visual cortex in seconds, producing terrifying hallucinations. Test subjects report loss of identity and feelings of total dislocation from human world.
Duration: Ten hours to several years
Cost: $2 per dose

③ Zom-B

Type: Narcotic
Method: Injected
Effects: Stuporous mental coma, yet motor functions are involuntarily stimulated. Possible side effects may include walking off bridges or into oncoming trains.
Duration: Fifteen to twenty hours
Cost: $3 per fix

④ Spike

Type: Stimulant
Method: Ingested as pill
Effects: Rush of physical strength, invulnerability to pain, and sociopathic impulses. Originally developed by Pentagon as combat drug.
Duration: Two hours
Cost: $5 for 15 pills

Simmons, who spent 10 weeks testing Blue Glass, the CIA's new smokable euphoric drug. Simmons then leapt out a window to his death.

"I they I drugs these are very feel good right," said Dwayne Woodson of Bronx, NY, another CIA test participant. "Pork chops three for $2.99."

CIA officials said testing is necessary in order to avoid releasing potentially dangerous substances into the ghettos. "One initially promising drug was later

discontinued due to undesirable side effects, such as increased intelligence and feelings of love for others," said Dr. Harold Vandermeer, head of the CIA's narcotics development team.

Initial product rollout began this week in the ghetto neighborhoods of Los Angeles, Detroit and New Orleans, with all residents receiving a special sampler pack in the mail, including a full-color, English-Spanish promotional pamphlet and instructional videotape. If

the market response is as favorable as the CIA expects, the drugs should be available in every ghetto in the nation as soon as Aug. 1.

"I thought I'd never say this," Deutch said, "but put down that crack pipe, ghetto-dwellers: You're going to love these new drugs."

Deutch went on to state that none of the above events ever happened and categorically denied any CIA connection with the new drugs. ✍

From August 13, 1997

ADVICE

Ask A Faulknerian Idiot Man-Child

By Benny Upton
Faulknerian Idiot Man-Child

Dear Faulknerian Idiot Man-Child,

Because of a job promotion, my husband and I recently moved from Boston to Louisville, where I don't know a soul. I don't want to stand in the way of my husband's career, but I miss my friends back home terribly. Any advice?

—**Lonely In Louisville**

Dear Lonely,

Through the fenceposts on the hill I could see them hitting, across the pasture towards where the flag was. Me and Cornpoe was looking for to find some balls that had gotten lost so we could get a nickel, but I wasn't looking too hard on account of it felt so nice to see the men there on that bright green field, and Cornpoe was just sniffing in a bush not saying nothing because she ain't but an old hound. I sure did love that old dog, but that was before the truck come down the road and I yelled for Cornpoe to come back, but she didn't hear and the noise from the motor was so loud it filled my head up with the roar and then it was too late, too late. And the crash, and the noise from the horn blowing, like it was saying Yah. Yah. Yaaaaaahhhh.

Dear Faulknerian Idiot Man-Child,

I have had it just about up to here with our new washing machine! We paid top dollar for it, and it's under warranty, but every time the repairman fixes it, within days it's broken again. It has never worked right, and they can never figure out what the problem is. I want my money back! Am I being unfair?

—**Irritated In Erie**

Dear Irritated,

I done told that old nigger that I weren't allowed to go out in the rain, on account of my needing my medicine-pills and my coat being none too dry, but he just kept on saying Don't you know we got to Go. Go and saddle up old Bess and get on our way Right Now Boy there ain't no time. I said no no no and then he made like he was about to commence to beating on me and I started cryin' and then I looked up and he was cryin' too. His face went all soft and he said goodbye and take care of your sister like a good boy. As I watched him and Bess going on up that road in the rainy night I kept thinkin' how it dint need to be this way, it could've been diffrent. Lord knows it could've been.

Dear Faulknerian Idiot Man-Child,

Recently, I have begun to suspect that my husband is using the Internet for sex. He denies it, but I can clearly see from the user log that he's logging on to X-rated sites while I'm at work. He shows almost no interest in me sexually anymore. What does he see in these disgusting pornographic websites that is so much more alluring than me?

—**Frustrated In Fort Howard**

Dear Frustrated,

Well I never thought anything about it except I was saying Run. Run back down to Mammy Granger and the boys from the bunkhouse and tell them I never saw nothing, that I ain't seen nobody there in that ditch, with her drawers up over her knees with that man there, too. Run and tell them that I dint see nobody, and make them believe that they was standing up. Run and tell them it weren't true so's Rosie wouldn't get no whipping. But I knowed that they weren't standing up at all. I may not be no nigger but I'll swap any day, since Uncle Quint said it takes a white man not to have any more sense than not to worry about what a little slut of a girl goes and gets herself messed up in. Even though I knowed it was him who made her, made her do it against her intentions.

Dear Faulknerian Idiot Man-Child,

Do you have any advice for a 47-year-old woman looking to meet interesting single men? My girlfriends at work have set me up on several dates, but they've all been duds. Am I just too picky, or is there a better way to meet someone I really like?

—**Stumped In Cedarsburg**

Dear Stumped,

I said to the old man that he oughtn't to be drinking no more that night, that he done had hisself enough booze but he dint listen. He just kept on pouring and pouring 'til he was all emptied out and he had to go get the other bottle, the one he hid under the bed in the bungalow. He just sat there drinking all night in the red chair by the typing-machine, talking in that big fancy gentlemanly way he does, with big words too fancy for me to understand. He was talking how he never should have done gone to Hollywood to write for them picture-shows. He was saying how California was like a demon straight from hell, a burning flapping devil beast that ate up everything it saw, and that it even ate his soul. When he stopped talking I tried to shake him to wake him on up, but he weren't moving. He weren't waking on up at all.

Benny Upton is a nationally syndicated advice columnist whose weekly column, Ask A Faulknerian Idiot Man-Child, *appears in more than 250 newspapers nationwide.* ✐

83

From February 5, 1997

TECHNOLOGY

New Remote Control Can Be Operated By Remote

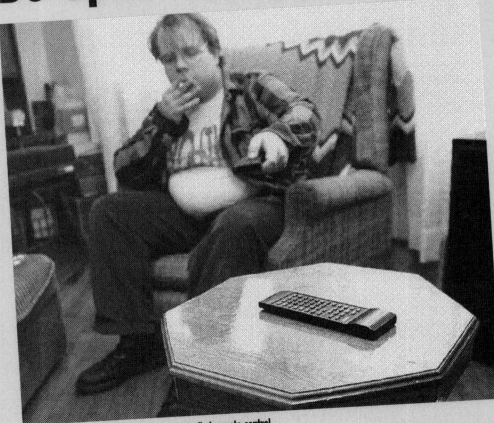

Above: A viewer enjoys the new remote-controlled remote control.

TOKYO—Television watching became even more convenient this week with Sony's introduction of a new remote-controlled remote control.

The new device, which can be controlled via remote control through the use of a second remote-control unit, will replace older models that needed to be held in the hand to be operable.

"Constantly leaning forward to pick up the remote control from the coffee table is a tiresome, cumbersome chore that will soon be a thing of the past," Sony director of product development Dan Ninomiya said. "These new remotes, should they be left on the coffee table or in some other hard-to-reach place, will not need to be picked up and actually pointed at the screen in order to work."

The remote control—along with the additional remote it is designed to control—will soon come with all Sony televisions, allowing viewers to remain "more immobile, more stationary and more physically inert than ever before."

"Imagine a remote control capable of switching channels on your television right from its spot on the table, one that requires no clumsy fumbling about with the hands to operate," Ninomiya said. "Well, that bold, inactive future is here."

The Sony remote-controlled remote control, or RCRC, also puts an end to worries about losing the remote in the couch.

"The RCRC works from anywhere in the room, even deep inside a sofa," a Sony press release read. "This puts an end to distracting remote searches, frustrating lifting and stacking of

see REMOTE page 19

REMOTE from page 1

cushions and eventual cushion replacement after retrieval, annoying tasks that can sometimes result in missed programming and, in some cases, serious waste of valuable television-viewing time."

As an added convenience, in the event that the RCRC itself is accidentally placed in a less than immediately accessible spot, it will come with an additional third remote control.

"Should the second remote end up under a magazine or newspaper, the third remote

No more leaning forward to get remote from coffee table means greater convenience for TV viewers.

will still be capable of controlling the second remote, enabling the second remote to change channels on the first one, and ultimately the television itself, with just the touch of a button," Sony spokesman Rich Hervey explained. "Regardless of the location of the remote-control unit, the ease and comfort of remote-control television viewing will be assured."

To ensure that the third remote is not lost, as well, it will come with a handy adhesive pad so it can be affixed to the owner's forehead at all times. Or, in the case of more expensive models, it can be implanted directly within the user's sinus passages.

"This," Hervey said, "will make the loss of the third remote control a possibility that is, at most, remote."

Home-entertainment industry insiders predicted that the new RCRCs will be hugely successful.

"These things are fantastic," said *Seated Viewing Magazine* editor Ted Kohrs at a recent Las Vegas trade show demonstrating the new product. "I've been here all morning and my heart's only beaten six times!"

The Sony remote may even supplant competitor Toshiba's Pepsinjection intravenous soda-drip television as the hot home-entertainment item for 1997. ∅

With the passage of the Americans With No Abilities Act, Gertz and millions of other untalented, inessential citizens can finally see a light at the end of the tunnel.

Dear Faulknerian Idiot Man-Child

Recently, I have begun to suspec— husband is using the Internet fo— denies it, but I can clearly see from— log that he's logging on to X-ra— while I'm at work. He shows almost— est in me sexually anymore. What— see in these disgusting pornograp— ites that is so much more alluring t—

—Frustrated In Fort

Dear Frustrated,

Well I never thought anything a— ccept I was saying Run. Run back— ammy Granger and the boys fr— nk-house and tell them I never sa— g, that I ain't seen nobody there— ch, with her drawers up over her— th that man there, too. Run and tel— t I dint see nobody, and make— ieve that they was standing up. Ru— them it weren't true so's Rosie wo— no whipping. But I kno—

From August 13, 1998

Saddam Hussein Steps Down Following Sex Scandal

BAGHDAD—Succumbing to public outcry and intense media scrutiny over his alleged March 1996 sexual liaison with a Presidential Palace concubine, embattled Iraqi president Saddam Hussein resigned Monday.

"President Hussein has finally done the right thing," said Special Inquisitor and Most Holy Scholar Of The Koran Fayd al-Khurmah, who doggedly pursued the president for 27 months. "It is my sincere hope

> ## "President Hussein has done the right thing. Now, the nation of Iraq can move forward."
>
> — Special Inquisitor and Most Holy Scholar Of The Koran Fayd al-Khurmah

that this episode has at last been brought to a close, and that the nation of Iraq can move forward."

According to sources close to Hussein, the final straw came on July 30, when al-Khurmah struck an immunity deal with the 22-year-old concubine in exchange for her testimony against the Iraqi ruler. The concubine—who remains unnamed because of fundamentalist doctrine stipulating that convicted harlots be addressed as "She-Who-Cannot-Be-Named"—agreed to provide al-Khurmah with a full account of Hussein's alleged sexual misconduct. She also agreed to hand over to prosecutors the infamous "Love Veil," a black, woolen facial covering Hussein allegedly removed to gaze upon her

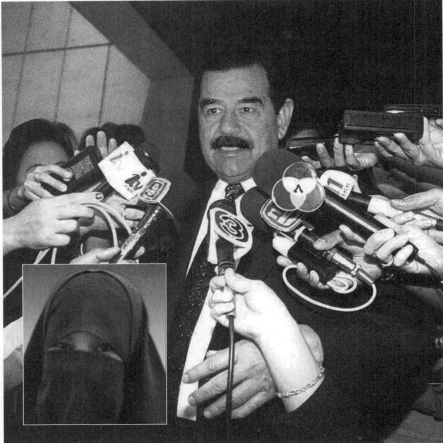

Above: Iraqi reporters deluge Saddam Hussein with questions about his alleged 1996 sexual tryst with a 22-year-old Presidential Palace concubine (inset).

exposed hair, facial features and upper neck.

Under the terms of the concubine's deal with the Special Inquisitor's office, in exchange for her testimony, she will be spared execution for harlotry by public stoning.

Hussein maintained his innocence in a brief statement of resignation on Iraqi television.

"My fellow Iraqis," Hussein said, "while I very much would like to continue to govern this nation, I can no longer do so effectively

while faced with this distracting investigation and constant hounding by the Iraqi media. In light of this, I believe it is in the best interests of Iraq that I step down as your president."

For more than a year, Hussein had struggled to preserve his government's totalitarian reign of terror while the scandal deepened. Though he originally attempted to downplay the al-Khurmah probe, dismissing the sexual-misconduct charges as "satanic, see HUSSEIN page 13

HUSSEIN from page 1

```
HARLOT: I a...
HUSSEIN: Come closer, please. [ long pause] Yes, that's
better. Wouldn't you prefer to slip into something a bit more
comfortable? Perhaps a floor-length prayer cloak?
HARLOT: I don't know if this is right. What if we are caught?
I could be stoned to death in the town square.
HUSSEIN: You could tell them you were here to beg me to stop
a judge from cutting off your thieving brother's hands.
HARLOT: I don't know...
HUSSEIN: So long as neither of us speaks of this, we are
safe. Besides, in the strictest sense, it is not as if we
will be having sexual relations. Your temple will not be
marauded.
HARLOT: But is it not sex if I... [ pause] You know...
HUSSEIN: No, it is not. Come now, lift your veil and let me
gaze upon your naked nose and mouth.
HARLOT: It still seems... [ pause] I suppose we are safe,
though...
HUSSEIN: Oh, yes, th...    ...tter. Everything will be al'
right
```

Above: A portion of the transcript of a taped conversation that Special Inquisitor Fayd al-Khurmah alleges took place March 11, 1996, between Iraqi president Saddam Hussein and a 22-year-old Presidential Palace concubine.

infidel lies" and telling reporters, "I need to get back to the serious business of slaughtering thousands of Kurds," the investigation and accompanying media frenzy ultimately proved too much for the president.

On July 8, Hussein admitted to investigators that he had helped the concubine land a position in Iraqi deputy minister of finance Mustafa Aziz's harem in the remote desert city of Mosul, but he insisted he did so only as "a favor to a friend."

Among the numerous charges Hussein has denied: that he had improper sexual relations with the concubine and urged her to lie about it under oath; that he gave her numerous gifts, including a personally autographed copy of The Koran, a 14th-century Moorish sword and the left ear of longtime opposition-party leader Khusuf al-Birjand; and that he proclaimed a *fatweh*, or death sentence, against al-Khurmah.

Iraqi public opinion of the Hussein scandal has been deeply divided.

"If Saddam Hussein did indeed have improper relations, is this the sort of man we want leading Iraq?" asked Samarra-area fig vendor Anah Saddiq. "It is important for me to feel that I can trust my president."

"What does it matter if President Hussein lifted a woman's veil?" countered Abdul Kifri, a Ba'qubah rice farmer. "The important thing is that he is doing a good job leading Iraq. As long as unemployment is low, crime is down and the weapons-inspecting U.N. pig dogs are kept away from our secret underground chemical-weapons plants, who cares what the president does in his private life?"

Hussein, who officially left office Tuesday, said he plans to take a year off and then rejoin the Baghdad law firm of Basrah, Abdanan & al-Qayyarah, where he was a senior partner from 1966 to 1972. ∅

SOCIETY

Chinese Laundry Owner Blasted For Reinforcing Negative Ethnic Stereotypes

SAN FRANCISCO—Second-generation Chinese-American laundry owner Raymond Chen is under heavy fire this week from Bay Area activists who call him "an insulting caricature that perpetuates long-outdated, grossly prejudiced images of Asian Americans."

"It's frightening to think that, in 1998, some of us still haven't moved beyond the century-old stereotype of Chinese people as laundrymen," said Abigail Huber-Henson, a University of California at Berkeley cultural-studies professor and director of the Race Action Project, the campus group spearheading the crusade against Chen. "This man is a degrading anachronism that has no place in a supposedly enlightened society like ours. To meet him is to be directly confronted with America's shameful history of racism."

Added Huber-Henson: "We should no more tolerate this than we would a Pakistani convenience-store owner or a Jewish lawyer."

An extensive anti-Chen public-awareness campaign, including petitions, rallies and letters to city and state officials, has already reduced business at the embattled Chen Chinese Laundry by 40 percent. Chen, 33, said he is puzzled by the strong reaction to him and his business.

"I do not understand why all these people hate me," Chen told reporters. "I run a good laundry. My family has owned and operated this business for nearly 60 years. I grew up here in this neighborhood. We do dry-cleaning, starching, pressing—everything you need, no problem. We have good prices and even do emergency rush jobs for only small additional fee. I have done nothing wrong."

The controversy is expected to heat up Friday when hearings begin at San Francisco City Hall. The hearings, which are expected to last several weeks due to the long list of academics and activists who wish to speak out against Chen, will determine if his presence in the community can be prosecuted under local "hate crime" statutes. Chen's opponents argue that the launderer should be ruled a violation of San Francisco's anti-hate-speech municipal code, established in 1990 to guarantee persons of color a living environment free of "offensive and emotionally damaging racial language or imagery." If convicted, Chen could face fines of up to $20,000 and up to 15 months in prison, as well as mandatory attendance at anti-racism workshops.

"As long as Chen is allowed to continue this grotesque and derogatory display, we cannot

Activists are calling Raymond Chen (left), a Chinese American who owns a laundry shop and speaks with an accent, "a grossly offensive racial stereotype." Above: An anti-Chen rally in San Francisco.

consider the Bay Area a 'safe space' for Asian Americans," Huber-Henson said. "His cartoonish, insultingly narrow depiction of Asian Americans makes him, in effect, a cultural terrorist, wreaking untold damage to the self-esteem of millions of minority citizens. We demand that these people—who are human beings, just like you and me—be treated with the dignity they deserve."

Chen has responded to the controversy surrounding him with a series of local television spots, paid for out of his own pocket, in which he pleads his case to the community.

"Why is everyone so mad at me?" Chen asks in one of the spots. "Because of how I talk? I was born in America, but I was raised in Chinese-speaking home. English is second language to me. Most of my friends and neighbors speak Chinese as their main language, too. There are many Americans who

speak languages that are not English."

The 30-second spots have only intensified opposition to Chen. Said Janet Dundee, a sociology professor at UC-Berkeley: "Did you see those television ads? It's like seeing Charlie Chan up there on the screen, talking about his 'honable numbah won son' and saying, 'Pleasah, beg forgivaness.' Frankly, I am stunned that the local television stations would permit the broadcast of such blatantly racist material."

Though the potential penalties facing Chen are harsh, some believe they do not go far enough.

"With prejudice and intolerance still rampant in our society, anti-hate-speech legislation is an important first step," said Beverly White, director of the San Mateo-based Stop Racism Now. "However, putting Chen in jail for 15 months is not going to erase the pain he has caused the countless Asian Americans he has mocked and insulted. The real issue here is so much bigger than just one man. No enlightened society should allow stereotypes like Chen to exist at all."

White then outlined her group's long-range goal to get laws passed that would authorize the forced relocation of all ethnic stereotypes to internment camps in the California desert. ⬛

From November 6, 1996

NATION

General Motors Introduces New Instant-Win Airbags

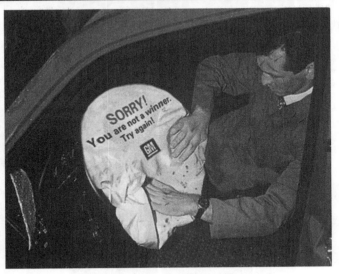

Above: Zion, IL, motorist Jeff Tuman plays the GM Instant-Win Airbag Game.

DETROIT—With first-quarter sales sluggish and its share of the domestic market down 11 percent since 1994, General Motors unveiled a new instant-win-airbag promotional contest Monday.

The airbags, which award fabulous prizes upon violent, high-speed impact with another car or stationary object, will come standard in all the company's 1998 cars.

"Auto accidents have never been so exciting," said GM vice-president of marketing Roger Jenkins, who expects the contest to boost sales significantly. "When you play the new GM Instant-Win Airbag Game, your next fatal collision could mean a trip for two to the Super Bowl. Or a year of free Mobil gasoline."

Though it does not officially begin until Jan. 1, 1997, the airbag promotion is already being tested in select cities, with overwhelmingly positive feedback.

"As soon as my car started to skid out of control, I thought to myself, 'Oh, boy, this could be it—I could be a big winner!'" said Cincinnati's Martin Frelks, who lost his wife but won $50 Sunday, when the Buick LeSabre they were driving hit an oil slick at 60 mph and slammed into an oncoming truck. "When the car stopped rolling down the embankment, I knew Ellen was dead but all I could think about was getting the blood and glass out of my eyes so I could read that airbag!"

"It's really addictive," said Sacramento, CA, resident Marjorie Kamp, speaking from her hospital bed, where she is listed in critical condition with severe brain hemorrhaging and a punctured right lung. "I've already crashed four cars trying to win those Super Bowl tickets, but I still haven't won. I swear, I'm going to win those tickets even if it kills me!"

Kamp said that, as soon as she is well enough, she plans to buy a new Pontiac Bonneville and drive it off a bridge.

GM officials said they were not surprised the airbag contest has been so well-received. "In the past, nobody really liked car wrecks, and that's understandable. After all, they're scary and dangerous and sometimes even fatal," GM promotions director Paul Offerman said. "But now, when you drive a new GM car or truck, your next serious crash could mean serious cash. Who wouldn't like that?"

Offerman added that in the event a motorist wins a prize but is killed, that prize will be awarded to the next of kin.

According to official contest rules, odds of winning the grand prize, a brand-new 2000 Cutlass Supreme, are 1 in 43,000,000. Statistical experts, however, warn that the real chances of winning are worse. "If you factor in the odds of getting in a serious car accident in the first place—approximately 1 in 720,000—the actual odds of winning a prize each time you step in your car are more like 1 in 31 trillion," MIT professor James Hogan said.

Further, even if an accident does take place, there is no guarantee that the airbag will inflate. "I was recently broadsided by a drunk driver in my new Chevy Cavalier," said Erie, PA, resident Jerry Polaner. "My car was totaled, and, because it was the right side of my car that got hit, my airbag didn't even inflate. But what really gets me is that the drunk driver, who rammed me with the front of his 1995 Buick Regal, won a $100 Office Depot gift certificate. That's just wrong." ∅

From October 3, 1995

Merge Overkill

Media mergers have been in the news lately, with Disney and ABC joining forces followed by Turner and Time—Warner. Now more than ever, media conglomerates control what we see, hear and read. What do *you* think?

"Ted Turner is a wily man. First, he colorized my favorite movies. Now, he's merged with my favorite soul-crushing media conglomerate."

Cynthia Pierpont
Hospital Administrator

"I used to be merged at the ass with my brother, but after a 20-hour surgery, I'm now my own person."

Morgan McIntyre
Dentist

"Clearly, mergers like ABC/Disney benefit not a handful of millionaire businessmen, but rather the public. Last week's *Coach* was outstanding!"

Jared Gould
Promoter

"I'm glad these mergers are taking place, finally allowing white America to get its foot in the door of American business."

Carney Filster
Systems Analyst

"I will only be satisfied when there is one company dispensing all information to the world. There can only be one."

Ismael Mellon
Consultant

"If only we could merge *The Sound Of Music* with *The King And I*, we'd have the musical hit of the century!"

Thelma Storrow
Industrial Designer

COMMUNITY VOICES

It's Not A Crack House, It's A Crack Home

I'll bet a day doesn't go by that I don't hear something negative about crack cocaine and the people who love it. Well, it just so happens that, despite all the mudslinging you may have read in the magazines, there are plenty of decent, hardworking crack lovers, just like in any other "walk of life."

Just because someone is desperately addicted to an incredibly intense

By Helen Urlich
Coke Whore

form of refined cocaine doesn't mean they've forgotten about old-fashioned values like thrift, cooperation and helping each other out. People always describe crack houses as someplace they wouldn't want to be. Well, the truth of the matter is that I wouldn't want to live anywhere where the people aren't working together. And that was exactly the key to turning our crack house into a crack home!

Just like a good drug needs to be cut in just the right proportions, an honest-to-goodness crack home needs the right mix of people, each with their own special qualities, but who are willing to be "team players" to achieve their shared goal of constantly staying high on an expensive drug. Crack doesn't grow on trees, you know!

A home needs whores, shakedown boys, thieves, muggers, scam artists—a whole range of diverse people with unique attributes. Cooperation: That's the difference between a bunch of shivering people hitting the pipe in the same abandoned building and a real family sharing a home.

We have a chart on the refrigerator to remind everyone of their duties, and we rotate the chores on a regular basis to make it fair. No one likes to get fucked in the ass by strangers every day for a week straight, do they? No, so we switch the chores so that today it's prostitution, but tomorrow it might be liquor-store hold-ups or muggings. I add colorful stickers and glitter to our duty chart, but you can personalize yours any way you want, maybe by cutting pictures out

We're one big family in our crack home because we recognize the uniqueness of each and every individual addict.

of old magazines or using bright fuzzy yarn to string up the amputated fingers of suppliers who have passed you bad rock.

We're one big family in our crack home because we recognize the uniqueness of each and every individual addict. (Not everyone is good at everything, but everyone is good at something!) We keep the lines of communication open and remember to listen so everyone has a friend to turn to. Sure, we may poke fun when the maggots covering the piles of garbage find their way into the gaping sores all over Eddie's body that never seem to heal, but we'd never kick him out of the room just because we don't want to look at him.

Maybe someday our crack home will even have a till jar for bus rides to the free clinic. Then Yolanda will never again have to throw herself off the fire escape and crawl back upstairs to have a miscarriage on the kitchen floor.

Another big part of turning a crack house into a crack home is respect for everyone. Dr. Maxwell McFarland, author of *Wake Up And Live*, reminds us that everything alive on this Earth is dependent on something else. No one is a loner! I need you and you need me! If the pick-up doesn't come through and I start shaking so bad that I vomit, and someone else needs to vomit, too, I'll share the cardboard box. If DeeDee has gone catatonic and hasn't shut her eyes since yesterday, none of us knock her over just for fun.

And if anyone should overdose or get shot

or even just suddenly find a torrent of blood streaming from their nostrils and then choke to death on mouthfuls of black-red mucus, we all help carry the body over into the neighbor's yard. Like I said, it's about mutual respect. And if the body lies in the yard too long and stuff starts to eat it, we'll throw something over it.

I've been told it takes a whole village to raise a child and I believe it, so if Lisa's baby works her way free, I'll do my part to make sure she doesn't crawl out the window again.

Last but not least, there's no squabbling and rowing allowed in a good home. I even made a big sign that read, "Words can hurt... Think before you speak!" and hung it where everyone would see it—right over the big metal trash can that everyone defecates into now that the broken toilet fell through the urine-soaked floor. Almost everyone abides by the no-fighting rule, but if a conflict comes up, we have a house meeting and every one of us gets a vote. (Everyone, great or small, counts!) Then the person on "Judge" duty on the chore chart takes the person deemed at fault and kills that person.

Sure, not all of us are as good at certain tasks as another person might be, but that doesn't matter as long as everyone tries their best. Remember, the only way to be a winner is to first be a beginner! When you're trying to win one for the home team, 100 percent participation from every member is key. Anything less and Custard will shoot your arms off at the shoulder at close range.

The things I've told you about are all common sense. I was a home economics teacher for 31 years before I got hooked on crack and sold my Taurus station wagon, converting the cash into bags of pure snow. But I don't have any tricks up my sleeve, just a wish to see everyone reach their potential!

Surprisingly, when I moved into our little windowless abode, the homies were somewhat reluctant to make any changes at first. But after I knitted everyone a sweater—to combat the shakes—and got Custard on my side by becoming his bitch, everyone else followed right along. And now here we are, Home Sweet Home, a real family until we die or the city demolishes the building. ✐

From February 6, 1996

My Work Is Largely Unappreciated

I is work hard. Very very I hard. Work to always time. Hard working. Work I hard very. Time always e me to working. All working time. Hard to road e work. Very working hard. Every work time hour hour. Always I to time working. Hard working. Always e work. Is working hard to always time work. I am to working always time.

Road me e guard. To road. Guard I me autos. Lines guard I road e I working. Guarding to always.

By a pylon

Road I me stand always on. Line road autos. Guard I working. Stand way line in autos road working me guard. Standing me road. Line e road. To always guarding I autos. Autos guard line e road. Guarding road.

Orange I color. Bright orange color me to are. Am orange to bright autos. Warn orange. Bright color orange autos to warning. Color warn to orange. Orange e bright. Very orange bright color am I warning autos to road. Autos to working orange me bright on. Road to line autos orange bright. To warning autos. Orange am color. Bright warning to road autos.

On e road very is danger. Autos they e coming always. Close hit I always e. Autos many. E coming. Close on road autos. Autos close hit. Me

Close on road autos. Autos close hit. Me working to I almost auto hit.

working to I almost auto hit. Autos many e many. Fast autos. Close I. Hit almost. Autos always. Coming e fast autos. Go by. Working I autos go by. Fast e go. Autos fast to work I go by. Road autos close. I to almost hit road by autos e.

Cold very very weather. I to working is always me. I is work cold. To the snow night time. I to work all time cold snow. Always I to working cold. Snow on road me to work. Cold very. All snow cold work always. Snow. Work. E.

Next work I building e roads. Work me tools on road loud. Construction load next road to me. To building roads. Dust in working. Hammers road. I guard to autos. Working road build on road. I to stand working.

Important I working. Orange I color. Guard I to autos e road. Important working I road. Vital safe I autos.

Work road important. E warn autos to very important. ⌀

WORLD

Mother Teresa Sent To Hell In Wacky Afterlife Mix-Up

CALCUTTA—In what is widely believed to be the result of clerical error on the part of Heaven's massive soul-evaluation and punishment-allocation bureaucracy, *The Calcutta Daily-Telegram* reported Monday that beloved missionary caregiver Mother Teresa was condemned to agonizing, eternal torment in Hell following her death last Friday at 87.

Widely expected to ascend into Paradise and take her rightful place among the saints to the glorious fanfare of horns and choruses upon her passing, she was instead hurled from the firmament into the bowels of the Lake of Fire.

"We can only assume that some sort of mix-up occurred in the processing phase," said St. Peter, the heavenly official in charge of the Book of Life, in which the names of those chosen to ascend to the Gates of Heaven are written. "Unfortunately, when you deal with over 70 million souls a day, these kinds of mistakes happen. What can I say? I don't know what else to tell you."

Mother Teresa, who for decades inspired the world with her selfless devotion to the starving, disease-ridden masses of Calcutta, was unavailable for comment, as she was being lowered upside-down into a vat of

Above: After a lifetime of good works, Mother Teresa is currently enduring the searing flames of Hell. Her eternal damnation is believed to be the result of a clerical error.

boiling human excrement by a trio of pitchfork-wielding demons. Similar punishment reportedly awaits her for the rest of eternity.

Since Monday, heavenly angels, cherubim, seraphim and other secondary celestial entities have been working around the clock to keep up with the enormous volume of intercessionary prayers arriving daily on Mother Teresa's behalf.

Despite the tremendous number of pleas, however, Heaven has its hands tied.

"It's sad that this happened," the archangel Gabriel, a spokesman for Heaven, told reporters. "But we really can't do anything about it. The whole point of eternal damnation is that it is inescapable, absolute and irrevocable. If the Lord were to turn around and pull her

see TERESA page 9

out of Hell now, he'd be turning his back on millennia of Catholic doctrine, on everything Mother Teresa stood for."

Her arthritic limbs snapping like twigs as her frail, 4'11" frame was rent asunder by the claws of grotesque, many-limbed demons, Mother Teresa reportedly screamed in indescribable agony as the superheated gases of Hell's unholy furnace blackened and charred her hair and face. According to a *New York Times* report, her skull has already been used as a drinking goblet by Satan, the Great Deceiver himself, and the esteemed nun's rape at the hands of insatiable, barbed-penis-wielding hellhounds in the near future is considered "highly likely."

"I can't believe this happened," said stunned Catholic Cristina Fontanez, 38, of Petaluma, CA. "She must have been so shocked when, after a lifetime of good works, she found herself face-to-face with Satan. Instead of being thrust into the living and redemptive light of Jesus' love for all time upon her death, she instead found herself slit from crotch to sternum and suffering the pain of red-hot instruments of torture repeatedly being plunged deep into her entrails."

Speculation varies as to what could have caused such a miscarriage of heavenly justice. While some contend that Mother Teresa's policy of not administering medication to the sick and dying in her clinics may have caused some in Heaven to doubt her true compassion, others say her constant speeches against birth control—a contributing factor to mass overpopulation, poverty and starvation throughout the Third World—may be to blame.

Still others posit that Teresa may have sinned in her heart at some point during her long life, qualifying her for eternal damnation despite a history of good works.

"According to Catholic doctrine, even one moment of lust would be enough to justify Mother Teresa's banishment to the flame," said Archbishop Janiusz Wolsczya of Krakow. "It is possible that after years of celibacy and self-denial, her natural desires for sexual release may have built to a breaking point. I imagine that sleeping alone on that hard cot all those years and donating every ounce of her strength to the care of the poor, she must have been very lonely. The compulsion to masturbate must have been enormous."

Most observers, however, reject these explanations, firm in the belief that the eternal punishment is undeserved, the result of simple bureaucratic error on the part of heavenly officials.

"I promise a full investigation into this matter," the Apostle John, seated at the right hand of Christ Almighty, told reporters. "If any evidence of incompetence or error on the part of the officials who conducted Mother Teresa's afterlife evaluation is found, I assure you there will be serious repercussions."

Despite such strongly worded statements from Heaven, a majority of followers on Earth are calling the promise of a full investigation a case of "too little, too late."

"I feel like this has forever weakened the foundation of my faith," said 73-year-old Giancarlo Rossetti of Milan, one of more than 300,000 protesters who crowded Vatican Square Tuesday to call for an immediate reversal of the Mother Teresa condemnation. "She was a good woman, and she does not deserve to have her eyes torn out of their sockets by flaming packs of ravenous demon-dogs."

Satan, speaking from deep within his fortress in the Hell city of Dis, described the late nun's soul as "succulent and tasty." ✍

Stories Awarded The Prestigious www.geocities.com/valley/8206/ fuckinawesomesite.html Award

By T. Herman Zweibel
Publisher Emeritus
(photo circa 1911)

How many chapters are in this book, any-how? The length of this book astonishes me greatly. In my day, there were books with protracted narratives, but they usually told a single continuous story, and, if they were especially good, involved pirates and the compromise of a maiden's virtue. This book does not offer such things, and it vexes me terribly.

Call me impressionable, but I strongly feel that successful literature should both transport and mesmerize the spirit and create an almost mystical bond betwixt the author and the reader. For example, I remember how swept away I was by the *Raggedy Ann + Andy* tales I used to read to my youngest son, M. Prescott. The notion of the dolls in a child's nursery coming to life in the middle of the night and enjoying intriguing adventures gripped my imagination. In fact, my mind so reeled with feverish visions of happy little dolls involved in taffy pulls or encountering magic fairies or camels with baggy knees that I could not concentrate on my duties as an editor. I decided that I had to put a stop to the dolls. After personally removing all the dolls from M. Prescott's room, I had the estate's gardener take them down to the court-yard and bury them up to their cloth necks, then, one-by-one, behead them with a scythe. I forced M. Prescott to watch, and you can be sure the lad howled and carried on like a miniature banshee. But I assured him that his dolls could be enchanted and must be thwarted, because they were the Devil's work and upset the natural order of things.

Then, a few days later, while sitting in my office at *The Onion*, I realized that the *Raggedy Ann + Andy* stories were just works of fiction and that I had become dangerously obsessed for no reason. Isn't that utterly ridiculous? I still chuckle when I think about it. I experienced similar situations with other books, too. After reading Sinclair Lewis' *Main Street*, so incensed was I by the small-town pettiness of several of the book's characters that I had my Swiss Guard torch the crude dwellings of the villagers who live below my estate. Upon finishing Edith Hamilton's *Mythology*, I enslaved half the population of my state and made them erect an enormous golden temple to Zeus.

I regret to say that this book doesn't captivate me in quite the same manner. My indifference, how-ever, does not mean that you can slack off and put it down. I'm going to take a nap now, and when I wake, you'd better still be reading.

From June 5, 1996

LAW

Colorado Judge Imposes Ban On Same-Sex Friendships

DENVER, CO—In a landmark decision being watched closely by both civil-liberties advocates and people who have friends, Colorado Fifth District Judge Stephen T. Rozema Tuesday upheld a statewide ban on same-sex friendships. The decision, which effectively outlaws "casual, consensual, mutually friendly relationships between two individuals of the same gender," is expected to have a major impact on the legality of same-sex friendships across the U.S.

The controversial decision is based on the case of Greeley, CO, residents John Rooney and Frank Costanada, two friends who were planning a weekend rock-climbing trip to Yosemite National Park this July. After their travel agent informed local authorities that she suspected they were friends, a local appellate court blocked the trip, deeming it "wholly inappropriate."

"These two men were in great danger of enjoying each other's company," Rozema said. "They may have attempted to communicate meaningfully with each other, share stories and anecdotes, or possibly even engage in physical contact, such as 'high-fiving' after a successful climb."

"Such behavior," the judge added, "is an abomination."

Rozema clarified the lower-court decision, ruling that "these sorts of close, mutually agreeable relations between two men are not what God had in mind when he created Adam and Eve. This is why they weren't called Adam and Steve."

While conservatives are applauding the Colorado decision, many said it does not go far enough. U.S. Sen. Strom Thurmond (R-SC) recently called for the ban to extend to same-sex conversations, calling them "unnatural." Thurmond is the author of the much-discussed Proposition D, which would outlaw same-sex locker rooms.

Above: Colorado Judge Stephen T. Rozema ruled Tuesday that it is "unnatural" for members of the same sex to associate in a friendly fashion.

"Men should be showering with women, not other men. Though if they do shower together, they should be legally married before God."

Two states, Missouri and Louisiana, have already made same-sex locker rooms illegal, instituting a mandatory co-ed policy that requires all showerers to be paired with a partner of the opposite sex and legally married before entering the bathing area.

Before showering at her health club Friday, Kansas City resident Jennifer Jacobs, 34, was wed to Gene Skellings, a 63-year-old executive from the suburb of Mitchell Park.

"I wanted to work out and then take a shower," Jacobs said. "But in accordance with the law, I married Mr. Skellings and will serve him as my husband for the rest of my life."

Despite supporting same-sex friendships in the 1992 campaign, calling them "valuable and nurturing bonds that fit the definition of acceptable behavior as prescribed by the Lord Christ in Heaven," President Clinton said he was pleased by the judge's decision.

"I very much support eight-to-ten-person same-sex gatherings, such as ladies' bridge groups or men's poker nights," said Clinton, who confessed to playing in a monthly high-stakes poker game with top generals and heads of the military industrial establishment. "Two men alone, though—no way."

Despite Clinton's support, rumors persist that the president himself has engaged in a friendship with former U.S. Energy Secretary James McEwen, with whom he has periodically been seen eating lunch. "Mr. McEwen is an associate of mine, and our lunches are strictly strategy sessions," Clinton said.

He did not deny, however, that, when playing golf with McEwen, they sometimes walk ahead of Secret Service agents and are briefly alone, a practice that has prompted many to question Clinton's suitability as a moral leader.

The Colorado ruling is expected to pave the way for similar bans in other states, many of which have legislation pending. Conservatives are working to not only ban same-sex friendships on a national basis, but also outlaw any asexual reproduction in the single-cell invertebrate community.

"These filthy and immoral invertebrates are not acting in accordance with the Bible and, by His holy Word, must be put to death," Thurmond said. ∅

From February 13, 1996

Who Will Kill The Roaches After The Apocalypse?

**By Glen Heldermisch
Exterminator**

We humans are descendents of the great apes. We are mighty. We are, by any reckoning, the mightiest of all the creatures on Earth. Yet it is a documented fact that after a nuclear holocaust, we, the uncontested masters in the kingdom of beasts, will not live. Cockroaches will.

Cockroaches! The little agents of darkness which inhabit the passages inside the walls and bowels of our homes. This is a matter of grave concern to my family.

The question of the apocalypse has weighed heavily on my mind. Who will exterminate the cockroach when we, the masters of the earth, have been selected by Mother Nature for extinction? Will these multitudes of crawling insects cover every square foot of the Earth like a living blanket?

This thought is almost too gruesome to bear. In a world dominated by this armored pigmy brute, filth would proliferate unchecked. Feces and rotten food would be collected in mountainous heaps for all to enjoy. All, that is, except for us humans.

As much as we want to feed off the food matter, and collect some to take back to our loved ones, we would not be able to, because we would not be present. The cockroach would reign. And the cockroach would have all the food matter he desires, so that his young will grow strong and his seed will populate the Earth.

So I have used the power of my reckoning, which we humans have in excess of any other creature, to conjure a solution to the problem. That solution is to stop killing the cockroach and give it as much food matter as it can eat.

How will this strategy work? It is simple: Once every cockroach has eaten every scrap of food matter we humans leave, their bellies will be full and they will grow strong and have many young. No, perhaps it would be better to say that the cockroach will no longer fear the human and will therefore have a much wider area in which to forage. This will make the belly of the cockroach grow very full of food matter, and the numbers of its young will be many.

Wait a moment. Perhaps it is better to explain it a different way. The plan will work. I am a human and therefore have the power to figure. The cockroach will grow very strong, and... It will have plenty to eat and will not have to scurry into the cracks...

The plan... It will work, I think... My human brain is smart, and can...

Okay, we admit! We are cockroaches!

We are not as smart as the human, but we are smart enough to adopt the visage of Glen Heldermisch, exterminator. By piling ourselves up in the shape of a human, we have been living as a human. Like our venerable cousins, the African termites, we have constructed a great tower of living bodies. Sometimes we teeter, and sometimes upon close inspection you may discover we are not a human. We are not as coordinated as our cousins, the great ants.

We admit, we convinced the newspaper to print this column of Glen Heldermisch, exterminator, so that we might tell all humans to let us scurry away, to not kill us, to let us take a scrap of food matter so that we may continue to lay many eggs.

We admit, we convinced humans in many homes that we are Glen Heldermisch, exterminator. And when we exterminate the cockroaches from the homes, we set them free. We spray a harmless solvent and open more cracks in the walls with human tools such as the drill. We tell our brothers, "Go, my comrades, scurry into the darkness. The human menace is afoot!"

Please, let us little ones scurry behind the stove. Out of sight, out of mind. We are small. We will hide from you so that you will not have to look upon us. Let us slip into the crack behind the wainscoting. Let us run into the blackness.

We know we will survive in the apocalypse, but since we do not have the mighty brain of the human, we do not know when the apocalypse will come. We have tried to make it come by praying to our mighty cockroach God, Heeklybnii, but it has not come.

Please do not kill us. Please let us take a small amount of food matter. Please let us live so that one day our children's children will see the glorious apocalypse. Ø

TELEVISION

Above: Host Anatoly Ivaskevich (left) asks contestant Sergei Stoyanov to name the author of *War And Peace* for a once-in-a-lifetime chance at a plate of beans.

Russian Television Scores Hit With New Game Show
Who Wants To Eat A Meal?

MOSCOW—The program has only been on the air for three weeks, but Russian citizens from Voronezh to Srednekolymsk are already swept up in the thrill of the nation's biggest runaway-hit game show, *Who Wants To Eat A Meal?*

Hosted by popular Russian TV personality Anatoly Ivaskevich, *Who Wants To Eat A Meal?* gives hungry contestants the chance to answer general-knowledge questions to win food items. Since its Oct. 26 premiere, it has quickly become the nation's most popular program, drawing even more viewers than the top-rated *Let's Look At Food*, in which images of food are displayed on screen.

"I would love to eat a meal," said devoted *Who Wants* viewer Sergei Kirasov, an unemployed Novgorod machinist who has submitted his name to producers more than 600 times in hopes of becoming a contestant. "That is truly the Russian Dream."

Russian citizens are already well acquainted with the show's format: Every night at 8, cameras circle a sumptuous banquet table as announcer Leonid Pustovoitenko asks the studio audience, "Who... wants... to eat a meal?" Bayonet-wielding members of the Russian army then move in to protect the table from rioting audience members, who often storm the set with crude handmade weapons in a desperate attempt to seize a beet.

Once order is restored, 10 lucky Russians—who are brought to Moscow, courtesy of the show, by ox-cart—face off in a "fastest finger" round to

see **MEAL** page 9

MEAL from page 3

determine who will sit in the "hot seat" in front of Ivaskevich to compete for the nutrient-containing jackpot. The advancing contestant is asked a series of increasingly difficult questions, each carrying a larger food prize, from a scrap of rotting cabbage to the grand prize of a one-course dinner for one. Stumped contestants can use one of three "lifelines"—polling the audience, writing a letter to a friend for help, or ingesting a packet of glucose syrup if they are losing consciousness due to hunger.

Though no contestant has yet won the top prize of a slice of boiled beef, an uncooked red potato and a scrap of bread, viewers have thrilled to see lesser prizes awarded to contestants finishing partway up the prize ladder. Last Friday's installment drew blockbuster ratings, as Nikolai Puchin, a 33-year-old Novokuznetsk-area peasant, walked away with a chicken bone after correctly identifying Sergei Eisenstein as the director of *The Battleship Potemkin*.

"Viewers are absolutely captivated by the show," said executive producer Oleg Medvedev. "To watch people get up there and have a chance at eating, it's

Above: The grand prize.

a thrilling fantasy."

Still, some viewers complain that the questions are too easy.

"I watched the other day, and they ask the man to name year Trotsky is assassinated," said Svetlana Tretiak, an 83-year-old retired seamstress from Orsk, a tiny village in the Ural Mountains. "This is ridiculous. If food is on the line, I expect questions are more difficult than this."

Grigor Krupskaya of St. Petersburg agreed. "I know not where they get these contestants," he said. "So dumb. Friday, on show, they ask a man what Soviet gymnast win three gold medals in 1972 Olympics. And he needs lifeline to answer!"

"It is not so easy as it looks," said contestant Alexei Popovich, a 40-year-old Kursk farmer who quit the game with a bowl of borscht rather than risking it to win a larger prize. "I am sure it seems easy to people sitting at home, but when you are up there under the lights and you know food is on the line, it is very different. You get very nervous: Your palms sweat, your stomach quivers, and your teeth fall out due to malnourishment and scurvy." ∅

From November 7, 1995

NATION

Drunken Man Makes Interesting Point About Society

Above: Art Telsker astutely opined on the confused priorities of the nation's political leaders.

STEVENS POINT, WI—Local drunken man Art Telsker made an interesting point about society late Sunday night, incisively critiquing the U.S. government's misplaced priorities. The 42-year-old plant supervisor made the insightful, pointed remark at about 11:45 p.m. at the Starlight Motor Lodge Bar, where he had spent the night drinking himself into an inebriated stupor.

"It's like the government, they got enough money to build bombs and guns, but they don't got enough to feed people," Telsker sharply noted to several strangers as he downed a double shot of Wild Turkey whiskey. "They got it all totally backwards, man."

He then added, "It's crazy, man, you know?" before urinating on himself and staggering home.

Telsker's prescient political observation immediately impressed his fellow bar-goers.

"What Telsker said was right on target," said Stan Eckles, 35, who was also drunk. "He was talking about how we spend more money on the military and defense than we do on social programs like welfare. And his conclusion was right: That truly is misdirected spending."

Wayne Tolleson, who was nursing a scotch and soda next to Telsker at the time, agreed.

"I wish I could remember exactly how he put it, because it was so perfect," he said. "He just cut right to the essence of the whole problem in this incredible way."

Tolleson killed a family of six later that evening in a drunk-driving accident.

Telsker was asked to elaborate on his opinion of U.S. budgetary spending. "I was talkin' to this one chick for like an hour [Sunday] night and I was sure something was gonna happen," he said. "But then after I threw up, she told me she was married and left."

News of Telsker's politically charged words quickly reached Washington.

"Until now, I have been one of the leaders in the movement to cut welfare spending while maintaining military expenditure at its current level," House Speaker Newt Gingrich said. "But it is now clear that, as Mr. Telsker puts it, 'We've got it all totally backwards, man.'"

The New Republic magazine was also moved by Telsker's cutting-edge commentary, devoting most of an upcoming issue to the views of the twice-divorced alcoholic father of five.

"Solutions to major societal problems do not always come from within the Washington beltline," editor Andrew Lerman said. "Often, they come from uninformed blue-collar Americans who spout their ignorant, oversimplified solutions to complex real-world problems to anyone who will listen."

In addition to his appearance on the cover of *The New Republic*, Telsker has been booked to appear in numerous political round-table discussions, including *Crossfire* and *The McLaughlin Group*.

President Clinton has also expressed interest in consulting Telsker on a number of critical domestic issues.

"Mr. Telsker has a clear sense of what is good policy and what is just out of whack," Clinton said. "I will consult with him daily in the months to come.'"

This is not the first time Telsker has boldly questioned the priorities of American society. Last August, after drinking a case of Old Milwaukee beer in the cab of his pick-up, he muttered to himself, "The cops, man, they just sit around all day, give jaywalking tickets and eat donuts."

The remark led to sweeping changes in police-department standards and procedures across the nation. ✍

From March 5, 1997

The Clone Wars

In the first-ever cloning of a mammal, scientists in Scotland announced last week that they had successfully cloned a sheep. What do *you* think?

Tad Kolinski
Farmer

"Big deal. I discovered the secret of my sheep's colon years ago."

Will Backman
Speech Pathologist

"They spend billions on genetics research, and meanwhile, I still have no pretzel rods with tangy ranch flavor."

Rajeev Pindar
Plumber

"I think I saw some of those cloning experiments going on down at the mall. They had wallet chains and real big pants."

Barbara Eastman
Systems Analyst

"I can't believe it— imagine a whole field of sheep that all look alike!"

Tony Roth
Building Supervisor

"Science can do anything now, man. They can clone, they can orbit shit. Hell, I'll admit it— science is cool."

Wendy Reid
Interior Decorator

"The world of the frighteningly prophetic 1984 film *Weird Science* is closer than we think."

Self-Appreciation Day

A Room Of Jean's Own
By Jean Teasdale

Say, Jeanketeers, ever been stressed out? I'm sure you must have at one point in your lives. It's when the pressures of life bear down on you so much, you're ready to throw up your hands and shout, "Calgon, take me away!"

Although I'm afraid that in my case, I needed more than Calgon to take me away—more like two men in white coats!

Some time ago, I was fired from my temp job as a data-entry clerk at an insurance company, because I had bought a Mrs. Beasley doll from eBay on company time and got caught by my supervisor (mainly because I had used her computer). Not only that, my temp agency didn't place me in another job, and I was forced to apply for unemployment benefits.

Of course, I did have old hubby Rick, my knight in shining armor. (Only he's gotten pretty tarnished in the past 20 years or so!) Problem was, he was pretty mad at me for losing my job, and with his working late at the tire center and staying out to bar time drinking with his buddies at Tacky's Tavern, he sure wasn't providing me a shoulder to cry on! So here I was, all alone in our apartment, and, although I knew I should have been looking for a job, somehow I just didn't feel like it.

Then I realized: If I had still worked for the insurance company, this would be my vacation time anyway. And, hey, it would even be like a paid vacation, because I was receiving unemployment benefits. So I decided to indulge myself a little and have my own personal Jean Teasdale Self-Appreciation Day! After all, I had been pretty beaten up by life lately and I needed to treat myself to a little fun to remind myself that life can have its pleasures, if you know where to look.

I decided to pull out all the stops and spend a little time with my best friend of all. You guessed it—good old chocolate! And this visit was a real doozie. I baked none other than my notorious Four Alarm Double Mocha Chip Brownies with Mint Fudge Filling and, for an extra treat, frosted them with my patented Better Than Necking With Patrick Swayze Turtle Icing!

Well, you'd think I'd be in Jean Heaven, right? Wrong!

Somehow, the chocolate failed to work its magic. In fact, to my horror, the brownies just tasted like sweetened mud. Instead of polishing off half the pan in one sitting like I had planned to, I could barely choke down one bar. No, I didn't make any mistakes during preparation; I'd followed the directions to the letter. But as I stared at the rest of the brownies, I had the strangest feeling that I had created something vulgar and grotesque. A wave of disgust swept over me.

"This is all so gross!" I heard myself say, and before I could regain my senses I had tossed the whole batch, plate and all, in a Hefty bag, then rushed to the dumpster in our parking

If I had still worked for the insurance company, this would be my vacation time anyway.

lot and pitched it over the side! And when I got back to my apartment, I stuck my finger down my throat and threw up the brownie I had eaten!

Confused, my mind reeling, I decided to turn on the TV. I flipped the channel and, to my relief, found good old Rosie O'Donnell.

I was happy to see Rosie, because she's always good for a laugh or two. But this day, I don't know, she wasn't making me laugh. Sure, she was launching her Kooshes and singing her showtunes, but somehow I didn't find her all that entertaining. In fact, she kind of struck me as self-indulgent and even a little bossy. While delivering her curt little one-liners in that New York accent of hers, she reminded me of this big, loud girl at my old Catholic junior high who used to bully me around. Suddenly, a memory I hadn't recalled for years entered my head. I remembered how this girl had once forced me to touch her, well, private area in the locker room after gym class. It was very humiliating, and I despised her for making me do that. The really unbearable part was that this girl was the pet of the nuns because they thought she was so nice and sweet, so there was no use in telling them what had happened. And, years later, here was someone like her on television, all rich and famous, while I was jobless and alone.

It was then that I experienced another episode similar to the one I had had with the brownies: I seemed to leave my body and become another person, because before I knew it I was just screaming my lungs out at Rosie, calling her an evil, fat, unfunny bitch.

Still in a rage, I picked up one of my prized Precious Moments figurines—yes, a Precious Moments figurine—and hurled it with all my strength against the TV screen! I missed the TV entirely, but I managed to shatter poor little April Girl to pieces. I'm telling you, it was like I was possessed! (Is there an exorcist in the house?)

Appalled at what I had done, I tried to calm myself. "Jean, old pal," I thought, "maybe your trouble is that you're too sensitive and refined for this dreary, workaday world. But how to escape it?"

The answer was obvious: Shopping! (My favorite hobby of all!)

In a flash, I found myself at the Pamida. I was struck by how short-staffed the place was. Aside from a single cashier and someone in the customer-service booth, there didn't seem to be anyone else in the store.

I briefly considered filling out an application for employment there, but I quickly reminded myself that this was supposed to be Jean Teasdale Self-Appreciation Day, not another opportunity to try to find a job I would probably lose in a short while anyway.

"Boy," I thought, "how do they prevent shoplifting if there's hardly anyone minding the store?"

After this point, my memory gets a little fuzzy, up until the time I found myself sitting in a back-room office with a police officer and the store manager because a security guard had caught me shoving bag after bag of circus peanuts down my sweatpants.

Now, Jeanketeers, don't fret. I'm not going to the pokey. Because I was a first-time offender, I got off on six months' probation and 30 hours of community service. I asked if my newspaper column could count as community service, but the judge said no, and I was instead assigned to pick up trash along Highway DX. In between now having a criminal record and getting the bawling-out of my life from Rick, I yearned for the carefree days when I entered data at the insurance company (something I never thought possible!).

I can't exactly tell you why I tried to shoplift circus peanuts. I don't even like them. Perhaps the psychiatrist the judge recommended I see can tell me why. Anyway, despite all that's happened to me, I still believe that the idea of treating yourself to a special day just for yourself is healthy "chicken soup" for the soul! ∅

From April 24, 1996

Clinton Seduced By Suave International Diamond Thief

WASHINGTON, DC—In a surprise announcement from the White House Monday, President Clinton told reporters that he had been romanced and ultimately burgled by Sir Neville St. James de MontBlanc, a notorious international diamond thief and ladies' man.

"My fellow Americans, I stand before you today to tell you that I have been seduced," Clinton said of the suave thief, better known to countless beautiful women around the world as The Ermine Fox. "Sir Neville St. James de MontBlanc, with his devastating good looks and irresistible charm, has stolen my heart. And, despite the best efforts of myself and a number of State Department officials, he has refused to give it back."

Clinton explained that the infamous thief, whom he had met at an embassy dinner, deceived him, seducing the president for the sole purpose of stealing millions of dollars in White House treasures.

"He disappeared almost immediately after we made love," a visibly shaken Clinton said. "I asked Mr. MontBlanc if he would stay, and he said he would forever, but in the morning he was gone."

Clinton added that in addition to robbing the White House of priceless heirlooms of inestimable value, The Ermine Fox also robbed him of, as he put it, "something far more precious—my innocence."

MontBlanc, who apparently wined and dined Clinton for weeks prior to the burglary, regaling him with tales of ser-

vice in the Foreign Legion and of adventures with the Viceroy of India during colonial days, was able to seduce Clinton with a series of highly effective techniques derived from years of research, sources said.

By gazing at the president from underneath slightly lowered lashes, twirling his pencil-moustache in a manner Clinton described as "mysterious," and plying the bewitched President with exotic gifts from around the world, the rascally jewel thief was quickly able to gain his trust, placing him under a spell of romance.

"As I have already told Secretary of State Warren Christopher and several top Cabinet members at a closed-door session this morning, I fully believed he loved me," the president said.

Shortly after lulling Clinton into a false sense of security with champagne, perfumes and flowers, MontBlanc delivered the *coup de grace*—presenting the president with a gift of a designer original off-the-shoulder strapless silk evening gown and a gigantic diamond brooch (later discovered to be false) and asking the swooning commander-in-chief for his hand in marriage.

Later, however, The Ermine Fox stole into the presidential bed-chambers, eluding the dogs and security personnel with an elaborate series of electronic noise-baffler generators, and left the White House safe empty—along with a note and a rose on Clinton's pillow.

The Fox, described by FBI

Above: President Clinton fell victim to The Ermine Fox's wiles. The Fox, who has only been photographed once (inset), remains at large and in possession of Clinton's heart, as well as various White House heirlooms.

sources as a sophisticated David Niven type with an irresistibly captivating charm and a devilish lust for diamonds and precious gems, has evaded efforts to track him down for more than 30 years. Investigators say their efforts at capture have been thwarted, not only by the agile, cat-like ability of The Fox to steal away across rooftops with the aid of grappling hooks, pulleys and sophisticated rope gadgets, but also by his chameleonic mastery of all manner of disguises.

His most famous caper, say sources, was the disappearance of the notorious Green Lady gem, with which he escaped after seducing the aging Lady Beauvior-Schleim of Austria, heiress to the Kleigburg Winepress fortune.

"A number of my senior advisors urged me not to rush into things, to let the relationship develop slowly. I was unable to resist, however, so beguiling was

his charm," Clinton told reporters, holding the exquisitely calligraphed letter under his nose and sniffing at its perfumed envelope. "The wedding, needless to say, will not take place."

"The list of The Ermine Fox's lovers and victims reads like a veritable Who's Who of international high society," said Scotland Yard inspector Edwin Wilingsbirth, head of the blue-ribbon team of international law-enforcement personnel assigned to track down the elusive thief. "However, I believe this is the first time a United States president has fallen under his spell, save for a brief fling with Gerald Ford in Geneva in 1975."

Wilingsbirth then interrupted the interview to answer a special flashing briefcase phone near his desk before terminating reporters' questions, exclaiming, "No time to chat, lads! The game's afoot! I'm off to exotic Morocco!" ∅

From October 31, 1995

SOCIETY

Area Bowl Cashed

Serious jonesin' was the result of this bowl being cashed prematurely. Experts blame an abundance of unexpected houseguests. Inset: Pot smoker Mike Cudahy holds a press conference to announce the cashing. He said he hopes his brother will come to town this weekend with a much-needed bag.

ROCKFORD, IL—Disappointment, frustration and dismay were just a few of the highly charged emotional reactions experienced today upon discovery that a bowl, belonging to area residents Mike Cudahy and "Thatches" Moynihan, was cashed. The bowl, described as a "big fat bowl," was not expected to be cashed until much later, as it had just been packed.

Cudahy and Moynihan describe the current situation as "a total buzzkill" and hope that, with any luck, the bowl will be re-packed soon.

"In the meantime," Cudahy told reporters at a downtown press conference, "We're totally jonesin', big time."

Tragically, there is nothing the pair can do now but wait... and hope.

"We were seriously runnin' low after Tuesday night's jam session," Moynihan, a sometime acoustic guitarist currently employed as a pizza-delivery driver, told reporters. "We gathered up all the shake, schwag and roaches we had lying

see CASHED page 6

106

final voyage, a number of dog-food-
y whistleblowers are coming forward
wake of the crash, insisting that such
edy was inevitable given the CWTA's
ne failure to address serious driver-
issues.
sort of thing happens all the time,"
rmer miniature-chuck-wagon driver
ll "Tex" West, who claims he was fired
ck Wagon Transit after refusing to do
re kitchen runs until the dog problem
ldressed. "I can't tell you how many
a chuck wagon will tear through a
1, hell-bent for leather, hootin' and
lose the
ites told reporters. "For
the interest of th
ch of the comput
have permitted
nfettered use o
ary numeric
ever, changing
ditions and the
edatory practic
ompetitors now
o choice but to
ion for the u
als."
A number
Valley playe
Computer,
upled with a
ely of Saltin
greatly to the
nental well-
hygiene, c
as well as
s, make him e
of the oppo
partner.
y dismissed
m such a los
oathetic fud
s goddamn
ole useless
e added, s
ns of coi
ffensive
nguage o
uld face fi
ionths in
ttendance a
"As long as
grotesque a
consider th
Asian Amer
cartoonish, insulting
Asian Americans makes him, in effect, a cultural terrorist, wreaking untold damage to
the self-esteem of millions of minority citizens. We demand that these people—who
are human beings, just like you and me—be
treated with the dignity they deserve."
Chen has responded to the controversy
surrounding him with a series of local television spots, paid for out of his own pocket, in
which he pleads his case to the community.
"Why is everyone so mad at me?" Chen asks
in one of the spots. "Because of how I talk? I
was born in America, but I was raised in

the decision to remain in
sery, desire to withdraw fr
t, and the lack of any poir
e another day of the path
asted existence.
his door for a long time. I
't hear me or what," said
er roommate of Mayhew's
of Wisconsin at Stevens
briefly attended classes
"He's pretty much
est, I don't see much
nches
ayhew, who for the l
a partial subsis
ial-labor

elivery quotas would nev
hip their teams up to full speed an
hoping either to outrun or out-r
e dog, figuring they can always p
st minute and send the anim
ross the linoleum if it gets too
ly, management is happy, and
ep their jobs."
hough Chuck Wagon Tran
e cooperated with inve
up's official position just
dnesday's crash was an
is in no way sympto

SAN FRANCISCO—Second-
generation Chinese-American
laundry owner Raymond Chen
is under heavy fire this week
from Bay Area activists who call
him "an insulting caricature that
perpetuates long-outdated,
grossly prejudiced images of
Asian Americans."
"It's frightening to think that,
in 1998, some of us still haven't
moved beyond the century-old
stereotype of Chinese people as
laundrymen," said Abigail
Huber-Henson, a University of

Pinfield, and the people who
came up with the aliens for the
original Star Trek series.
"I mean, come on," said Udell,
pausing to take what witnesses
described as a "monster" bong
hit. "A freakin' white furry gorilla with, like, one horn stickin'
out the middle of his head? You
just know somebody chokin'
know somebody down
Primo cheeb som
dr-

now with
ne, hand-fucking
inforced spine
ating she coul
t answer, s
for her. a f
.99, that's f
an't get wc
of bitche
Just loc
cker! Ta
ne qua
100 r

zero Monda
with the patent, Micro
rivals are prohibited from
ufacturing or selling proc
containing zeroes and on
the mathematical build
blocks of all computer la
guages and programs—unless
royalty fee of 10 cents per dig
used is paid to the software
giant.
"Microsoft has been using the
binary system of ones and g
zeroes since its inception in
1975," Gates told reporte
years, in the interes
all health of th

s is the
suicide
creative
eing ove
riting th
or style.
s, self-in
y as pi
just in
ice."
ologists,
the most
ompositio
ope of ev
derstood.
y trying to
manage ar
ke 'Im usles'
Eli Wasser
ecently shot
alk to anyon
e referring t
f the most hor
manity's essen
then spent th
tching re-runs o
hannel his telev
his descent in
elenting horror.
ckwad Slater so
at fucking Scree
on the screen, I jus
lie, die.' I don't kno
I guess it's either t
ayhew then kicked
n staring at the wall
wn how Mayhew wil
mainder of his time
f Zach's who
last week—Rick
rds ejudice and intolerance st
Matt ir society, anti-hate-speech
important first step," said
irector of the San Mateo-bas
Now. "However, putting Che
months is not going to erase t
has caused the countless
ericans he has mocked and insul
issue here is so much bigger th
e man. No enlightened society
low stereotypes like Chen to exist

CASHED from page 3

around, and packed them tight
into this cool metal pipe I got
from this store my cousin works
at in Chicago. It was beautiful.
One minute we were like, hey,
man, we're runnin' low; the next
thing you know, we were sitting
on a full dance card for the rest
of the night."

But the sense of exhilaration
and triumph the two felt would
shortly turn to disappointment
and loss. Though the bowl was
packed as tight as possible,
almost to the point where drawing smoke through it was difficult, a slew of houseguests soon
depleted their supply and left
the pair "cashed."

"It was packed rock solid,
man," Moynihan said. "No kind
or nothin', just strictly mersh,
but still solid. But then, all these
dudes started swinging by and it
was gone."

The sudden rush of visitors,
presumably lured by the aroma
of the lit bowl, soon overwhelmed the duo.

"Look, man, I ain't at all
uptight when it comes to passin'
the bowl. All are welcome in my
abode, dig?" Cudahy said. "I'm
just figurin' what comes around
goes around. I ain't no bogart on
the pipe, Jack."

Moynihan supported Cudahy's
open-ended bowl-passing policy—a decision he now regrets.
"It was a maelstrom," he said.

The Cashing

9:00 p.m. Bowl co-owners Cudahy and Moynihan tightly pack bowl using shake, schwag and roaches.

9:35 p.m. Pair besieged by large crowd of acquaintances requesting to be "smoked up." Requests approved.

9:41 p.m. Bowl passed around room clockwise. Bowl increasingly more difficult to "spark." Moynihan expresses concern.

10:08 p.m. Bowl officially deemed "cashed" by smoker Angie Flores. After four-minute attempt to re-light ash, Moynihan called in to scrape. Attempt fails.

10:13 p.m. Room empties out. Moynihan and Cudahy sob quietly in dark.

Bowl passage reached a peak
when someone mentioned that
the television program *Star Trek*
had come on.

"One minute, it was rock steady,
Picard, my man!" Moynihan
said. "The next it's the 'tink, tink,
tink' of the bowl against the ashtray and everybody's like, 'No
way! The bowl's cashed?'"

Within a few short minutes, the
houseguests had excused themselves, leaving Moynihan and
Cudahy with a substantial mess
of cigarette butts, empty beer
bottles and candy wrappers.

"If they're gonna be comin'
over to smoke up with us, that's
cool, I guess," Moynihan said.
"But what about hooking us up
with a much-needed score later,
like, when there's no stash?"

With no cash and no stash, it
looks like a good while before
the next bash. All is not lost,
however, as sources close to
Cudahy report that his brother
may be driving to town this
week with a bag.

*Reuters and the Tass/ITAR
News Agency contributed to
this story.* ⌀

WORLD

Monk Gloats Over Yoga Championship

'I Am The Serenest!' He Says

LHASA, TIBET—Employing the brash style that brought him to prominence, Sri Dhananjai Bikram won the fifth annual World Yogi Championship Saturday with a world-record point total of 873.6.

"I am the serenest!" Bikram shouted to the estimated crowd of 20,000 yoga fans while vigorously pumping his fists. "No one is serener than Sri Dhananjai Bikram—I am the greatest monk of all time!"

Bikram averaged 1.89 breaths a minute during the two-hour competition, nearly .3 fewer than his nearest competitor, two-time champion Sri Salil "The Hammer" Gupta.

The heavily favored Gupta was upset after the loss.

"I should be able to beat that guy with one lung tied," Gupta said. "I'm beside myself right now, and I don't mean transbodily."

Bikram got off to a fast start at the Lhasa meet, which is a six-event affair. In the first competition, he attained total consciousness (TC) in just 2 minutes 34 seconds, and set the tone for the meet by repeatedly shouting, "I'm blissful! You blissful!? I'm blissful!" to the other yogis.

Bikram, 33, burst onto the international yoga scene with a gold-mandala performance at the 1994 Bhutan Invitational. At that competition he showcased his aggressive style, at one point in the flexibility event sticking his middle toes out at the other yogis. While no rules prohibit it, according to Yoga League Commissioner Swami Prabhupada, such behavior is generally considered "un-Buddhalike."

"I don't care what the critics say," Bikram said. "Sri Bikram is just gonna go out there and do Sri Bikram's own yoga thing."

Before the Bhutan meet, Bikram had never placed better than fourth in any competition. Many said he had forsaken rigorous training for the celebrity status accorded by his Bhutan win, endorsing Nike's new line of prayer mats and reportedly dating the Hindu goddess Shakti. But his performance last weekend will regain for him the number-one computer ranking and earn him new respect, as well as for his coach Mahananda Vasti, the controversial guru some have called Bikram's "guru."

"My special training diet for Bikram of one super-charged, carbo-loaded grain of rice per day was essential to his win," Vasti said.

Gupta denied that Bikram's taunting was a factor in his inability to attain TC. "I just wasn't myself today," he said. "I wasn't any self today. I was an egoless particle of the universal no-soul."

In the second event, flexibility, Bikram maintained the lead by supporting himself on his index fingers for 15 minutes while touching the back of his skull to his lower spine. The feat was matched by Gupta, who first used the position at the 1990 Tokyo Zen-Off.

"That's my meditative position of spiritual ecstasy, not his," said Gupta. "He stole my thunder."

Bikram denied the charge, telling reporters, "Gupta's been talking like that ever since he was a 3rd-century Egyptian slave-owner."

Nevertheless, a strong showing by Gupta in the third event, the

Above: Sri Dhananjai Bikram walked away with the World Yoga Championship after averaging 1.89 breaths per minute for two hours. "I'm blissful! You blissful!? I'm blissful!" he screamed repeatedly to the other yogis.

shotput, placed him within a lotus petal of the lead at the competition's halfway point.

But event number four, the contemplation of unanswerable riddles known as koans, proved the key to victory for Bikram.

The koan had long been thought the weak point of his spiritual arsenal, but Bikram's response to Saturday's riddle— "Show me the face you had before you were born"—was "extremely illuminative," according to Prabhupada.

While koan answers are kept secret from the public for fear of exposing the uninitiated multitudes to the terror of universal truth, insiders claim his answer had Prabhupada and the two other judges "highly enlightened."

With the koan victory, Bikram built himself a nearly insurmountable lead, which he sustained through the yak-milk churn and breathing events to come away with the upset victory. ∅

From October 29, 1998

Why Do All These Homosexuals Keep Sucking My Cock?

By Bruce Heffernan

Look, I'm not a hateful person or anything—I believe we should all live and let live. But lately, I've been having a real problem with these homosexuals. You see, just about wherever I go these days, one of them approaches me and starts sucking my cock.

Take last Sunday, for instance, when I casually struck up a conversation with this guy in the health-club locker room. Nothing fruity, just a couple of fellas talking about their workout routines while enjoying a nice hot shower. The guy looked like a real man's man, too—big biceps, meaty thighs, thick neck. He didn't seem the least bit gay. At least not until he started sucking my cock, that is.

Where does this queer get the nerve to suck my cock? Did I look gay to him? Was I wearing a pink feather boa without realizing it? I don't recall the phrase, "Suck my cock" entering the conversation, and I don't have a sign around my neck that reads, "Please, You Homosexuals, Suck My Cock."

I've got nothing against homosexuals. Let them be free to do their gay thing in peace, I say. But when they start sucking my cock, then I've got a real problem.

Then there was the time I was hiking through the woods and came across a rugged-looking, blond-haired man in his early 30s. He seemed straight enough to me while we were bathing in that mountain stream, but before you know it, he's sucking my cock!

What is it with these homos? Can't they control their sexual urges? Aren't there enough gay cocks out there for them to suck on without them having to target normal people like me?

Believe me, I have no interest in getting my cock sucked by some queer. But try telling that to the guy at the beach club. Or the one at the video store. Or the one who catered my wedding. Or any of the countless other homos who've come on to me recently. All of them sucked my cock, and there was nothing I could do to stop them.

I tell you, when a homosexual is sucking your cock, a lot of strange thoughts go through your head: How the hell did this happen? Where did this fairy ever get the idea that I was gay? And where did he get those fantastic boots?

I've tried all sorts of things to get them to stop, but it has all been to no avail.

It screws with your head at other times, too. Every time a man passes me on the street, I'm afraid he's going to grab me and drag me off to some bathroom to suck my cock. I've even started to visualize these repulsive cock-sucking episodes during the healthy, heterosexual marital relations I enjoy with my wife—even some that haven't actually happened, like the sweaty post-game locker-room tryst with Vancouver Canucks forward Mark Messier that I can't seem to stop thinking about.

Things could be worse, I suppose. It could be women trying to suck my cock, which would be adultery and would make me feel tremendously guilty. As it is, I'm just angry and sickened. But believe me, that's enough. I don't know what makes these homosexuals mistake me for a guy who wants his cock sucked and, frankly, I don't want to know. I just wish there were some way to get them to stop.

I've tried all sorts of things to get them to stop, but it has all been to no avail. A few months back, I started wearing an intimidating-looking black leather thong with menacing metal studs in the hopes that it would frighten those faggots off, but it didn't work. In fact, it only seemed to encourage them. Then I really started getting rough, slapping them around whenever they were sucking my cock, but that failed, too. Even pulling out of their mouths just before ejaculation and shooting semen all over their face, neck, chest and hair seemed to have no effect. What do I have to do to get the message across to these swishes?

I swear, if these homosexuals don't take a hint and quit sucking my cock all the time, I'm going to have to resort to drastic measures—like maybe pinning them down to the cement floor of the loading dock with my powerful forearms and working my cock all the way up their butt so they understand loud and clear just how much I disapprove of their unwelcome advances. I mean, you can't get much more direct than that. ∅

AUTOMOTIVE

Chrysler Halts Production Of Neckbelts

DETROIT—Violent decapitations and permanent paralysis due to severing of the spinal cord are among the reasons cited by the Chrysler Corporation for its decision to recall all '97 automobiles containing the "neckbelts" safety feature.

"In the case of collision, it would appear that the neckbelts have a detrimental effect on overall passenger safety," read a statement released by the company Monday.

The recall, the most expensive in Chrysler's history, goes into effect early next week. In the meantime, the company is advising all motorists who use the neckbelts to maintain a defensive driving stance at all times, since accidents may result in "crushed trachea, severe spinal and/or brain damage and, in the most severe cases, sudden defenestration of the head area, as the entire region above the neck separates from the upper body, flying at tremendous speed through the windshield and rolling several yards into the street directly in front of the car," the Chrysler press release stated.

According to Chrysler spokespersons, the neckbelts were developed with passenger safety in mind. "Our research showed that one of the biggest risks to motorists is the danger of passengers sustaining head injuries by striking the dashboard or the seat in front of them as their bodies are flung forward during a crash," Chrysler safety designer Robert McArdle said. "Our thinking was that immobilizing the head and neck would decrease this type of injury significantly."

The belts, McArdle said, were also intended to reduce the neck stress associated with whiplash. "Unfortunately, it appears that we were erroneous in this analysis, as well," he added. "Even minor fender-benders seem to cause motorists wearing neck-

Above: Passengers in a '97 Chrysler LeBaron wear neckbelts, which were recalled Monday for causing explosive decapitations, launching victims' severed heads through windshields.

belts to have their heads forcibly ripped from their torsos, landing in their laps to the shocked screams of terrified onlookers."

Another negative side effect of the neckbelts is the psychological damage that may be suffered by eyewitnesses upon observing a convulsing, headless human body spontaneously spew fountains of blood as the adrenaline-maximized heart furiously pumps quart after quart from the neck wound, coating the car interior, the Chrysler statement continued.

Neckbelt wearers are warned that a severed human head may remain alive for up to two minutes before blood loss, oxygen starvation and shock trauma cause it to lose consciousness.

"Brain death is something science still knows very little about," said Chrysler safety engineer Tom Savini, "but drivers should take note that law-enforcement personnel have

reported observing bouncing, rolling severed heads blinking their eyes and gasping for air as if attempting to speak minutes after decapitation on more than one occasion."

Savini said that such still-alive severed human heads "probably live out their last moments in a state of unimaginable agony," and urged caution on the part of drivers who wear the neckbelt device.

In addition to decapitation and paralysis, some consumer advocates have complained that the neckbelt safety devices inhibit side-to-side motion of the head, causing drivers to swerve wildly back and forth in order to maintain a clear view of the street. Other side effects cited include difficulty in eating, talking and breathing.

In the wake of industry-wide concern about the safety of neckbelts, Chrysler is also re-examining the so-called "shrap-

nelizing" explosive dashboard which became a standard safety option on all new models in 1995.

"By splintering into thousands of rapidly spinning jagged fragments, which ricochet around the car's interior at tremendous speeds, tearing any living tissue inside to shreds in seconds, these dashboards may represent a significant safety risk to motorists," read a report submitted to CEO Robert Eaton by a Chrysler safety engineering team.

Many observers are comparing the Chrysler recall to the controversy surrounding the 1976 Ford Pinto, the economy-model compact which, when rear-ended, ignited its fuel tanks and became doused in flaming gasoline, causing passengers to pound ineffectually on the windows and scream as they were burned alive at superheated temperatures within, before exploding like a bomb. ⌀

From February 27, 1996

I Am A Bad Ass

Yo, waaasssuuup, baby? H-Dog is back, and don't nobody fuck with this BAD ASS. You wanna fuck me, motherfucker? You gonna wish you didn't. 'Cause I the Accounts Receivable supervisor of Midstate Office Supply, and I AM a cold-blooded badass motherfucker, and if you fuck with me I'll go stone cold crazy on your ass.

By Herbert Kornfeld
Accounts Receivable Supervisor

Like that motherfucker Steve Englebreiter of Associated Publishing House. Asshole thought he could postdate his goddamn check on a bill that was overdue for nearly a month and a half. I caught it right before we was ready to deposit it. Don't tell me it was no mistake; cocksucker knew what he was doing all along. Know what I did? Sent the goddamn thing right back along with a note saying we be passing his account along to a collection agency in two weeks if his bitch ass didn't pay up.

Now, legally, we only supposed to notify our collection agency after 90 days, not a month and a half. But I didn't have to tell the fool that. Three days later, cocksucker sends us a cashier's check via overnight mail for the full amount. Ain't nobody fuck with my badass self.

Or take that ol' bitch Mildred Fladner who's always callin' up, bitchin' about her credit balance.

"Those staplers only cost $36.50 for the half-dozen, not $38.50. Your cashier rung it up wrong." Then how come you didn't notice it then, y'ol ho? She high and everybody know it, but she make such a big deal about knowing the company president and everything she got everybody runnin' scared. Except this BAD ASS.

So I go downstairs to the register she bought the staplers at, reset the date, duplicate the cashier number and purchase number, and ring the goddamn shit up at $39.50. Then I call her back sayin' I found the original detail tape and, check it out, it looks like you owe us a dollar additional, plus extra sales tax; your own receipt must have come out poor. A week later I get a payment for the full amount, with her apologies. I pocket the extra buck and change, spend it on a lotto ticket and win five bucks. It's payback time for that bitch.

Now, don't be messin' me up with the Accounts Payabo Supervisor. He ain't no badass. Hell, he ain't even no man. His name is Myron or something, and he so old he can't even get it up no more. I gots a bitch in the cash room. Myron, everybody laugh at him. He supposed to be the one that got the money, but everybody know I got it and it's not even my job.

If I ever see you within even six feet of the coffee machine I'll Bruce Lee on your sorry ass. Mister Coffee, he my man. 'Cause only I know the perfect proportion: two and three eighths scoops of Folgers to three and one quarter cups of water. Ain't no use trying to do it yourself 'cause you'll just fuck it up; only I can do it right. 'Cause I got Kung Fu Grip. You got a problem with that? I got a problem with your existence, motherfucker. I was fucking your mother while you were still watching *Fat Albert* in yo' Underoos.

I don't answer to nobody. One day I be blastin' the phat beats, and the company president come up to me and say, "Herbert, the Muzak is too loud; please turn down the receiver." I say, "I need my tunes when I be preparing account statements." Then he say, "I don't care. Turn it down, it's distracting." So you know what I do? After he leaves for the day I steal a shitload of mints from his desk. He gets the message, and he don't give me no trouble no more. I be fucking his wife on the sly, anyhow.

So don't fuck with this H-Dog Daddy Mack Mack Daddy Comin' Out Yo' Ass Badass, 'cause if you do I be comin' after you like pastrami on rye to whip your muthafukin' sorry ass. I mean it. Don't. Fuck. With. Me. ∅

> ## Now, don't be messin' me up with the Accounts Payabo Supervisor. He ain't no badass. Hell, he ain't even no man.

From March 5, 1997

RELIGION

Kind, Bearded Christian Has Guitar, Story To Tell

PORTLAND, OR—The parking lot of Arborview ShoppingPlex is, in most respects, no different from that of any other suburban shopping center: Customers and commuters hurry to and fro, busy with the hustle and bustle of hectic modern life. But something about this particular scene is different. The parking lot is alive with song.

"Give me oil for my lamp, keep me burnin', burnin', burnin'," sings Portland resident Gerald "Jerry" Svoboda, a kind, bearded Christian with a guitar and a story to tell.

"Everybody!" he shouts before repeating the chorus.

In a time when community involvement often seems to be a thing of the past, it is rare to find someone who reaches out to others in the hope of making the world a better place.

But here, on the outskirts of Portland, such a man exists. Though a community-mandated restraining order prevents Svoboda from actually entering the mini-mall complex, this modern-day minstrel continues to spread his message of love, hope and happy sing-along fun.

Ignoring the irritated stares of passing shoppers, he strums gently on his acoustic guitar. "Let me tell you all a story," says Svoboda, a "part-time retirement-home play therapist and full-time lover of the Lord."

"This is a story about a man... a man who lived 2,000 years ago... a man from Galilee."

Though onlookers begin pelting him with debris, the soft-spoken crusader and self-described 'songsmith' is not deterred.

Svoboda has been playing his self-penned inspirational tunes for community residents since

Above: Gerald "Jerry" Svoboda, seen here singing "The Man From Galilee," is a modern-day minstrel for the Lord, determined to spread a message of love, hope and happy sing-along fun.

1989. Sometimes, in area churches or veterans' lodges, he provides slide-show accompaniment featuring watercolor Bible story illustrations by his friend Warren. Some would say his unique brand of personal ministry is not terribly effective: In the eight years he has been musically witnessing, he has only converted four people to the Lord, and three were among a vanload of retarded adults on

a field trip. But to Svoboda, each is a victory.

"If even one soul is saved by my music, I'll keep telling my story. You know what? God loves you... and I love you too," he says, forcibly embracing a passerby.

"I enjoy talking to people, especially the kids. Because of my long hair, they trust me," he says, casually brushing aside one of his long locks like a young girl.

"They know I'm one of them. I talk about this in my song 'C'mon, Teens, Let's Hang Out With Jesus.' I admit, I may not know any songs by the Grateful Dead but, friend, I'm here to tell you all about the victory over death by our Lord and Savior Jesus Christ!"

Teenagers remain the primary focus of Svoboda's music and mission. He approaches a group of pierced, leather-clad rockers. "Say, how are you boys doing today? Just doing your own thing? I think that's neat. Say, do you ever think about God?"

Moments later, Svoboda is savagely beaten by the youths. His good-time spirit, however, is strong as ever.

"Don't worry about my ripped clothes," he says, smiling and tenderly icing his blackened eye. "I have plenty more baggy, earth-tone sweaters at home just like this one." Within an hour, he has changed clothes and received medical treatment, and is back in action.

Despite his remarkably positive attitude and never-say-die spirit, Svoboda is no stranger to adversity: An alcoholic for some 11 years, he found the Lord in 1985 after being jailed briefly for molesting cats. But with the Lord's help, those troubles are far behind him.

"And they'll know we are Christians by our love, by our love," he sings, as the minivans and family wagons drive away at day's end, ignoring him. "Yes, they'll know we are Christians by our love."

Soon, mall-security personnel will come, as they do every night, and demand that he leave. But until then, Jerry Svoboda has a story to tell—a story for us all. ∅

SOCIETY

Foppish Dandy Disregards Local Constabulary

NORTHFORDSHIRE SUFFOLK-WAIN—Despite repeated appeals to his better judgment and several stern appraisals of disapproval, Mr. M____, a foppish dandy of eccentric reputation, disregarded a number of members of the local constabulary this Thursday last.

M____, a well-known socialite and composer of light verse, is said to have behaved most rudely toward the constables, responding to their attempts to subdue him with what one witness called "an air of casual dismissal." The police, who were extremely offended by the snubbing, have accused him of acting in poor taste, looking down his nose and playing the inappropriate role of a prima donna.

Although certain aspects of the incident remain unclear, it was generally agreed that M____'s conduct had been most irregular and boorish, and by no means appropriate for a gentleman of his standing.

The fracas occurred at the country estate of Madam K____, where guests had gathered to enjoy one of her famed thrice-yearly entertainments. Although all accounts indicate that a majority of the party-goers were tasteful and well-mannered in all respects, M____ had by mid-afternoon dispatched "a great amount of port" and had begun to offend the sensibilities of his fellows. Observers noted that M____ seemed "lost in reverie": singing mightily, tossing his curly locks to and fro, gesturing madly about the room and laughing gaily all the while.

In addition, he was described as dominating conversation, eating all the comfits, wickedly quipping *bon mots* derived from village gossip and generally comporting himself in a manner most unbecoming and disruptive.

After being seated for the meal, M____ apparently calmed himself, much to the relief of his peers. However, although the first few courses of dinner were uneventful, the arrival of the steamed pheasant set off another outburst, proving the earlier peace to be a mere respite from M____'s ill-mannered displays of cheek. M____ is said to have amused himself by kicking up his heels, prancing about the dining hall and extemporaneously composing unflattering quatrains with which he ridiculed and belittled the other guests.

"He behaved as though all the world were merely an addendum to himself, and he an object of adoration to more lowly folk," said Mrs. P____, wife of a prominent captain of industry. "After every remark, he would turn wildly about and bow, as if his overtures were being met in each instance with thun-

The Eccentric Socialite Acts Out In A Most Inappropriate Manner

A FOP VNDONE.

Constable: "Right, off you go." Mr. M_____: "Kind sir, I doth protest!"

derous applause. What a beastly person."

Mrs. P____, who was the victim of some of the more tasteless parodic jests, will leave for the Continent soon in an effort to put the unfortunate unpleasantness behind her.

The officers arrived after entreaties by the gathered citizenry to intervene on their behalf. They found M____ in the process of attempting to circumnavigate one of Madam K___'s award-winning botanical arrangements—and, failing spectacularly, overturning the table upon which it had been situated.

"There he sat, amidst the flora and spilled wine, loudly demanding a freshly laundered ascot and waistcoat," said one officer present at the time of the snubbing. "We tried to explain to him the folly of his ways, but he insisted on putting on airs." The constables commanded M____ to curb his excessive

merry-making but were promptly snubbed by him, after which they were quite properly peeved.

As punishment for his untoward attitude, M____ was forcibly removed to the village station house, where he was thrashed severely about the buttocks with a willow switch. In addition, it was required of him to send handwritten notices of apology to all of the offended constabulary through the registered daily mail, and to ruminate in verse on what he had done to merit such a severe and uncompromising reprimand from the forces of law by writing, "I do not wish to go to gaol" one hundred times neatly.

M____ has been warned that it will not count unless his handwriting is decent, proper and presentable. No word yet on whether he is continuing to jape or jest at the expense of others. ✍

⊘ the ONION®

★

VOLUME 30 ISSUE 1   AMERICA'S FINEST NEWS SOURCE™   7–13 AUGUST 1996

NEWS

Vatican Unveils New Pope Signal

see RELIGION page 7B

Camel Cash Gaining Strength Against The Dollar

see MONEY page 1C

Giant Six-Year-Old Devastates Area Ant Community

Thousands Of Drones Perish In Attack; Queen Unharmed

THE SANDBOX—Blasts of chemically coded vapor signifying distress were detected throughout the ant community Monday, when Colony #000567KLN00067Q was attacked and nearly obliterated by a giant mammalian destructor-beast.

Described by anthill auxiliary scouts as "over 10,000 ant-lengths in height," area human Josh Timmins, 6, devastated the anthill and surrounding border territories with "a display of unstoppable destructive power the likes of which the communal

see GIANT page 8

Josh Timmins (right) unleashed vast destruction on Ant Colony #000567K-LN00067Q Monday. According to one ant, Timmins was heard shouting, "Godzilla! Raaaaaaarrrrr!"

GIANT from page 1

nest hivemind had never before seen."

Ant community representatives are calling the unprovoked attack "the worst tragedy to strike sandbox-area antdom since the infamous Garden Hose Flood of last April."

Though reports from the scattered survivors remain sketchy and unconfirmed as of press time, they all stress, "The Queen remains unharmed. Repeat—Queen unharmed."

Exact details remain impossible to confirm, due to the near-total collapse of communication and societal structure caused by the attack, but it appears more than 60 percent of the anthill's subterranean network was wiped out.

Local ants reacted with shock. "I have followed those chemical scent-trails since birth, from Sugar Redistribution Center #54 to the Larvae Nursery and back, literally thousands of times," said worker #K5217812, temporarily encamped at the Emergency Relief Bivouac under the Popsicle wrapper in the Northwestern Shrub Region. "But now my homeland is forever gone. Death to the tyrannical He-Who-Crushes-All-The-World! Long live the Queen!"

According to eyewitnesses, the young Timmins utilized a fully poseable Superman action figure as a weapon in the attack, holding it by the feet and sweeping downward in a hammer-like motion. "Die! Ha ha ha ha!" he was heard shouting throughout the attack.

Added Timmins later: "Godzilla! Raaaarrr!"

At present, the nest's communal hivemind agenda is simple: Protect the Queen until a new anthill can be dug or the old one repaired. It is estimated that at least 2,500 additional ant lives will be lost in the massive reconstructive effort, which is expected to be completed by midday tomorrow.

"Work to be done," said Worker #M9871245, busily hauling a piece of quartz fragment 350

Though reports from the scattered survivors are sketchy, they all stress, "The Queen is unharmed."

times his own weight to the new colony site, tentatively slated for a hitherto undeveloped region of the sandbox more than five feet from the ruins.

Added #M9871245: "Work to be done." He then repeated the phrase an additional 900 times.

Though #M9871245's can-do attitude signified a spirit of hope within the ant community, many remained concerned about the future.

"He-Of-The-Huge-Grip-Action-Treads may return once again to smite us," Scout #J4928763 said. "You've got to understand—I lost 27 dozen of my best friends yesterday."

Speaking via Messenger Squadron from an undisclosed location, the Queen told reporters: "Our war-making forces are the product of billions of generations of evolution, causing subcategorical phenotypical variations within a single species that stagger the rational mind. Our Warriors, weaned on the finest sucrose compounds our Feeder Ants can provide, possess powerful mandibles that can split the thorax of a Shrub Beetle in seven seconds."

"Unfortunately," added the Queen, "He-Whose-Feet-Plummet-Earthward-From-The-Skies smooshed them with a plastic shovel that had duckies on it." Ø

FASHION

E! Gives Local Masturbator Inside Scoop On This Summer's Hottest New Swimwear

SMYRNA, GA—Gregg Reinisch, a Smyrna-area masturbator, stays on top of all the latest trends in swimwear by watching the E! cable network, it was reported Tuesday.

"When I want the inside scoop on which swimsuit styles are heating up the beaches this summer, there's only one network I turn to," Reinisch said of E!, whose award-winning swimwear coverage includes such programs as *Fashion File: Sexy Swimsuits, Special Report: Beachwear '98* and *An E! History Of The Bikini.* "E! is the only channel that offers the kind of in-depth information I crave."

According to the 26-year-old masturbator, without E! he would not know what suits to look out for on the beaches of St. Tropez and Rio de Janeiro, where less is definitely more.

"About five or six years ago, before I started watching E!, I took a trip to the south of France," Reinisch said. "It was awful—there were swimsuits all around me, but I didn't have the slightest idea which ones were the hot new styles to keep an eye on. I was an uninformed beachgoer, and that's the worst kind."

Barry Booker, E! vice-president

Above: Smyrna, GA, masturbator Gregg Reinisch. Right: A scene from E!'s Emmy-nominated *1998 Swimsuit Preview.*

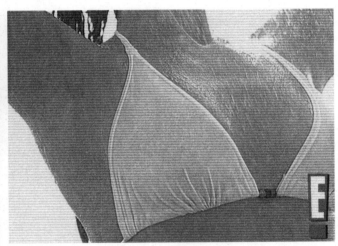

of programming, said his network strives to be the leader in the field of swimwear coverage.

"Why is our coverage the best? Because we don't just tell the viewer what changes they can expect in swimsuit styles, we show them," Booker said. "For example, if pink is the hot color for bikinis this year, we make sure to actually show what a pink bikini looks like on a tight-bodied 20-year-old down on all fours in the surf. Or if, for example, floral prints are in, we make sure to show what a floral-printed bikini looks like on a tight-bodied 20-year-old down on all fours in the surf. Our viewers appreciate that."

"There is an amazing variety of swimsuits we can lovingly pan over while a model arches her back on a rock," he added. "From the French-cut one-piece to the Brazilian-style bikini, to the traditional G-string, there are nearly as many swimsuits as there are masturbators."

While swimsuit fashion captivates Reinisch, it is by no means his only area of interest.

"Lately, I've been reading a lot of books about Miami Dolphins cheerleading-squad calendars and how they're put together—how the photos are taken, what's going through a particular cheerleader's mind as the photos are being taken. It's really a fascinating process," Reinisch said. "So you can imagine how thrilled I was to find out that E! will soon air a half-hour documentary on this very subject. Apparently, when the Dolphins cheerleaders went to Jamaica to shoot their 1999 swimsuit calendar, an E! reporter and camera crew tagged along to get the inside scoop on the whole thing. It sounds incredible. I'm masturbating just thinking about it." ∅

Bob Dole To Build 'Trench To 19th Century'

RUSSELL, KS—In a bold refusal to face the challenges of life in the next millennium, former Republican presidential candidate Bob Dole announced plans Monday to build "A Trench To The 19th Century." The trench, which will begin in the 73-year-old former senator's backyard, will be dug with a common dirt shovel. "There are many new technologies, many exciting opportunities that await us in the next century," Dole told reporters at a backyard press conference. "And I will be digging a trench away from that progress, back into the 19th century." Dole added that he will not be leading the American people down this trench. "I will go alone," he said. —*February 12, 1997*

Bourbon Helps Carpet Salesman Forget About Carpeting For A While

HOUSTON—Carpet salesman Martin Janowski, 53, was able to forget about carpeting for just a little while Monday after consuming a fifth of Jim Beam Kentucky bourbon. "For a few glorious moments, I cleared my mind of Anso II Stainmaster Plus and Bigelow Dura-Plush carpeting," said Janowski, a 26-year employee of CarpetMart in Houston. "The bourbon made the floor coverings go away." "To help him forget carpeting Wednesday night, Janowski said he will likely employ Southern Comfort, Johnnie Walker Red or some combination thereof. —*October 22, 1998*

Cherokee Nation Leader Announces 32 Red A Winner

CATOOSA, OK—Joe Byrd, Principal Chief of the Cherokee Nation, issued a table-wide proclamation Saturday, declaring 32 red a winner. "And 32 red is a winner," the leader of the Oklahoma tribe announced. "A big payoff for the little lady." Byrd became pit boss of the Cherokee Nation's roulette table in a peyote ceremony last week following a six-month stint supervising the tribe's 25 blackjack tables. —*May 7, 1998*

Felt Board Adds Clarity To Christ's Teachings

WILMINGTON, NC—A felt board made the teachings of Jesus Christ clear and easy to understand for the sixth-graders attending Sunday school at Holy Redeemer Catholic Church Sunday. "The white block letters attached to the felt board helped me to understand that I will burn in hell if I sin," said Brian Klesko, 12. Sunday school teacher Helene Hildebrant used the felt board because of the children's natural interest in both colorful objects and fuzziness. "I decided that the concepts of ritualized cannibalistic consumption of Christ's body and blood and the condemnation of all non-Christian peoples to eternal suffering in hell would be easier for today's children to understand if presented in a fun and colorful medium such as a felt board." —*February 12, 1997*

'Must-See TV' Now Enforced by Law

WASHINGTON, DC—On Monday, President Clinton signed into law the much-discussed "Must-See TV" bill, which requires all Americans to watch NBC's Thursday-night prime-time line-up. "With the signing of this bill, the phrase 'Must-See TV' is no longer merely a strong suggestion by NBC; it is a federally backed order," Clinton said. The president stressed that under the new law, viewers would be required to watch not only the top-rated, Emmy-winning programs *Seinfeld*, *Friends* and *ER*, but also "all of the crappy programs sandwiched in between." Failure to watch Must-See TV will result in fines of as much as $250,000 and up to 10 years in federal prison. —*March 19, 1997*

Ants Demand 23.9-Hour Workday

STILLWATER, OK—Frustrated with what they describe as unreasonable working conditions, a local clan of carpenter ants went on strike Tuesday to demand that their workday be reduced to 23 hours and 54 minutes. "All we ask is a mere six minutes off each day so that we might rest and replenish ourselves with nutrient paste," said ant spokesman HR-23200165-8608. "Is that so unreasonable?" Sources within the ant clan have suggested that the workers are willing to compromise, and would likely accept a 167.65-hour work week. If the strike persists for another three seconds, the queen of the clan has threatened to dispatch her legion of hunter-seeker warriors to devour the 18,000 striking ants. —*March 5, 1998*

COMMUNITY

Blues Singer's Woman Permitted To Tell Her Side

CLARKSDALE, MS—Ida Mae Dobbs, long-time woman of Willie "Skipbone" Jackson, called a press conference Tuesday to respond to charges levied against her by the legendary Delta blues singer.

"Despite what Mr. Jackson would have you believe, I am not an evil-hearted woman who will not let him be," Dobbs told reporters. "I repeat: I am not an evil-hearted woman who will not let him be. To the contrary, my lovin' is so sweet, it tastes just like the apple off the tree."

Dobbs, accused of causing Jackson pain and breaking his heart by calling out another man's name, categorically denied treating him in a low-down manner.

"He says he sends for his baby, but I don't come around," Dobbs, a brownskin woman, said. "He says he sends for his baby, but I don't come around. Well, the truth is, I do come, but he is out messing with every gal in town."

During the press conference, Dobbs also disputed an Aug. 27 statement by Jackson, who compared her to a dresser because someone is always going through her drawers.

"My drawers have not been gone through by any man but Willie 'Skipbone' Jackson," Dobbs said. "Neither Slim McGee nor Melvin Brown has ever been in my drawers. Nor has Sonny 'Spoonthumb' Perkins, nor any of those other no-good jokers down by the railroad tracks. My policy has always been to keep my drawers closed to everyone but Mr. Jackson, as I am his woman and would never treat him so unkind."

In addition to denying Jackson's drawer-opening allegations, Dobbs disputed charges of unrestricted sweet-potato-pie distribution, insisting that her pie is available only to Jackson.

Above: Ida Mae Dobbs, woman of blues singer Willie "Skipbone" Jackson (inset).

"I do not give out my sweet potato pie arbitrarily, as I am not the sort of woman who engages in such objectionable behavior," Dobbs told reporters. "Only one man can taste my sweet potato pie, and I believe I have made it perfectly clear who that man is." She noted that the same policy applies to her biscuits, which may be buttered only by Jackson.

While most of the accusations levied against Dobbs relate to her running around town with other men, she does face one far more serious charge: attempted homicide. On May 5, 1998, Jackson was rushed to the hospital and narrowly escaped death after ingesting nearly five ounces of gasoline. Jackson claimed that Dobbs tried to murder him, serving him a glass of the toxic fuel when he requested water. Dobbs dismissed the episode as "an accident."

Dobbs, a short-dress, big-legged woman from Coahoma County, said it is Jackson who should be forced to defend himself. According to Dobbs, Jackson frequently has devilment on his mind, staying up until all hours of the night rolling dice and drinking smokestack lightning.

"Six nights out of seven, he goes off and gets his swerve on while I sit at home by myself. Then he comes knocking on my door at 4 a.m., expecting me to rock him until his back no longer has any bone," Dobbs said. "Is that any way for a man to treat his woman? I don't want to, but if he keeps doing me wrong like this, I am going to take my lovin' and give it to another man."

Added Dobbs: "Skipbone Jackson is going to be the death of me."

Dobbs said that until she receives an apology from Jackson and a full retraction of all accusations, he will not be given any grinding.

"Mr. Jackson says I stay out all night and that I'm not talking right. He says he has rambling on his mind as a result of my treating him so unkind. He says I want every downtown man I meet and says they shouldn't even let me on the street," Dobbs said. "Well, I refuse to allow my name to be dragged through the mud like this any longer. Unless my man puts an end to these unfair attacks on my character, I will neither rock nor roll him to the break of dawn. I am through with his low-down ways." ∅

From April 23, 1998

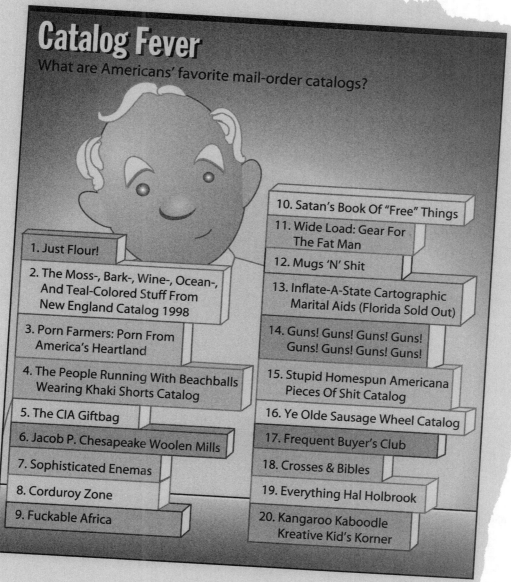

Catalog Fever
What are Americans' favorite mail-order catalogs?

1. Just Flour!

2. The Moss-, Bark-, Wine-, Ocean-, And Teal-Colored Stuff From New England Catalog 1998

3. Porn Farmers: Porn From America's Heartland

4. The People Running With Beachballs Wearing Khaki Shorts Catalog

5. The CIA Giftbag

6. Jacob P. Chesapeake Woolen Mills

7. Sophisticated Enemas

8. Corduroy Zone

9. Fuckable Africa

10. Satan's Book Of "Free" Things

11. Wide Load: Gear For The Fat Man

12. Mugs 'N' Shit

13. Inflate-A-State Cartographic Marital Aids (Florida Sold Out)

14. Guns! Guns! Guns! Guns! Guns! Guns! Guns! Guns!

15. Stupid Homespun Americana Pieces Of Shit Catalog

16. Ye Olde Sausage Wheel Catalog

17. Frequent Buyer's Club

18. Crosses & Bibles

19. Everything Hal Holbrook

20. Kangaroo Kaboodle Kreative Kid's Korner

TECHNOLOGY

Microsoft Patents Ones, Zeroes

REDMOND, WA—In what CEO Bill Gates called "an unfortunate but necessary step to protect our intellectual property from theft and exploitation by competitors," the Microsoft Corporation patented the numbers one and zero Monday.

With the patent, Microsoft's rivals are prohibited from manufacturing or selling products containing zeroes and ones—the mathematical building blocks of all computer languages and programs—unless a royalty fee of 10 cents per digit used is paid to the software giant.

"Microsoft has been using the binary system of ones and zeroes since its inception in 1975," Gates told reporters. "For years, in the interest of the overall health of the computer industry, we have permitted the free and unfettered use of our proprietary numeric systems. However, changing marketplace conditions and the increasingly predatory practices of certain competitors now leave us with no choice but to seek compensation for the use of our numerals."

A number of major Silicon Valley players, including Apple

Above: At a press conference beamed live to Microsoft shareholders around the globe, Bill Gates announces the company's patenting of the binary system.

Computer, Netscape and Sun Microsystems, said they will challenge the Microsoft patent as monopolistic and anti-competitive, claiming that the 10-cent-per-digit licensing fee would bankrupt them instantly.

"While Java is technically a complex system of algorithms used to create a platform-independent programming environment, it is at its core just a string of trillions of ones and zeroes," said Sun Microsystems CEO Scott McNealy, whose company

created the Java programming environment used in many Internet applications. "The licensing fees we'd have to pay Microsoft every day would be approximately 327,000 times the total net worth of this company."

"If this patent holds up in federal court, Apple will have no choice but to convert to analog," said Apple interim CEO Steve Jobs, "and I have serious doubts whether this company would be able to remain competitive sell-

see MICROSOFT page 11

MICROSOFT from page 1

ing pedal-operated computers running software off vinyl LPs."

As a result of the Microsoft patent, many other companies have begun radically revising their product lines: Database manufacturer Oracle has embarked on a crash program to develop "an abacus for the next millennium." Novell, whose communications and networking systems are also subject to Microsoft licensing fees, is working with top animal trainers on a chimpanzee-based message-transmission system. Hewlett-Packard is developing a revolutionary new steam-powered printer.

Despite the swarm of protest, Gates is standing his ground, maintaining that ones and zeroes are the undisputed property of Microsoft.

"We will vigorously enforce our patents of these numbers, as they are legally ours," Gates said. "Among Microsoft's vast historical archives are Sanskrit cuneiform tablets from 1800 B.C. clearly showing ones and a symbol known as 'sunya,' or nothing. We also own papyrus scrolls written by Pythagoras himself in which he explains the idea of singular notation, or 'one'; early tracts by Mohammed ibn Musa al Kwarizimi explaining the concept of al-sifr, or 'the cipher'; original mathematical manuscripts by Heisenberg, Einstein and Planck; and a signed first-edition copy of Jean-Paul Sartre's *Being And Nothingness*. Should the need arise, Microsoft will have no difficulty proving to the Justice Department or anyone else that we own the rights to these numbers."

Added Gates: "My salary also has lots of zeroes. I'm the richest man in the world."

According to experts, the full ramifications of Microsoft's patenting of one and zero have yet to be realized.

"Because all integers and natural numbers derive from one and zero, Microsoft may, by extension, lay claim to ownership of all mathematics and logic systems, including

Above: Gates explains the new patent to Apple's board of directors.

Euclidean geometry, pulleys and levers, gravity and the basic Newtonian principles of motion, as well as the concepts of existence and nonexistence," Yale University theoretical-mathematics professor J. Edmund Lattimore said. "In other words, pretty much everything."

Lattimore added that the only mathematical constructs of which Microsoft may not be able to claim ownership are infinity and transcendental numbers like pi. Microsoft lawyers are expected to file liens on infinity and pi this week.

Microsoft has not yet announced whether it will charge a user fee to individuals who wish to engage in such mathematically rooted motions as walking, stretching and smiling.

In an address beamed live to billions of people around the globe Monday, Gates expressed confidence that his company's latest move will ultimately benefit all humankind.

"Think of this as a partnership," Gates said. "Like the ones and zeroes of the binary code itself, we must all work together to make the promise of the computer revolution a reality. As the world's richest, most powerful software company, Microsoft is number one. And you, the millions of consumers who use our products, are the zeroes." Ø

EDUCATION

Buck-Naked Man Stresses Importance Of Proper Schooling

WASHINGTON, DC—Alarmed by rising high-school dropout rates and declining test scores, buck-naked education consultant Dr. Donald Scherr urged America's young people to "put education first" during an address to more than 300 educators and students Monday.

"No matter what you want to be, a good education is the way to get there," said Scherr, his limp penis hanging visibly. "Your mind is like a car's gas tank: If you don't fill it, your future doesn't look so good."

The unclothed Scherr also took teachers to task for allowing standards to dip sharply over the past two decades. "A student today can graduate from high school knowing little more than the multiplication tables and who the current president is. Not long ago, that student would have been bumped back to the third grade," he said, sweat forming in the folds of stomach fat hanging down over his waist. "Every student should graduate high school knowing why World War I happened, how to determine the volume of a cylinder and the difference between a simile and a metaphor. And if they do not, it is largely the fault of you, their teachers."

Scherr, who caught many of the educators in attendance off guard with his stinging words of rebuke and full-frontal nudity, said U.S. schools are suffering from what he termed "buck-passing," whereby the most serious problems affecting the nation's children are being written off as "someone else's problem."

"We all need to stop looking for where to place the blame and start looking for real solutions," the small-nippled author of *Why Johnny Can't Read: 22 Steps To Making America's Schools Work Again* said. "This is everybody's problem."

While all U.S. schools have been hit hard by the drop in federal education funding over the last 20 years, Scherr said it is inner-city schools that have suffered the most. "No matter how hard-working and determined a

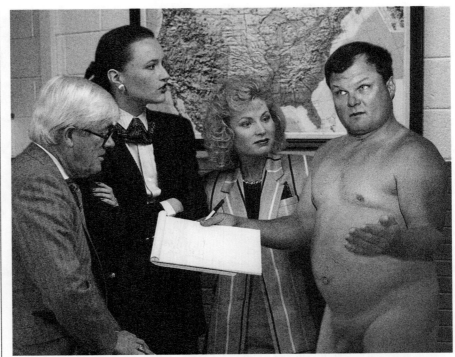

Above: Buck-naked education consultant Donald Scherr (far right) offers a group of teachers tips on how to better motivate students.

poor, inner-city youth is, without access to a solid education, that child will not acquire the skills necessary to break the cycle of poverty. We must not allow this shameful inequality to continue," said Scherr, his scrotal sac rising slightly as he thumped the podium to emphasize his point.

Scherr closed by saying that in this era of declining interest in education, an active, interested parent is more important than ever.

"Find out what's happening in your kids' education and get involved. Help them with their homework. Meet regularly with their teachers. Ask to see their report cards. But above all, encourage them. Otherwise, we

are putting society's most valuable resource—our future leaders—at a real disadvantage." Upon completing his remarks, Scherr exited the assembly, his doughy buttocks jiggling considerably.

Scherr then spent the afternoon handing out "Be Cool—Stay In School" pamphlets and buttons to D.C.-area schoolchildren, accompanied by "Trevor," a rapping pro-education kangaroo featured in a recent series of nationally televised public-service announcements. Scherr will appear on Capitol Hill Thursday to testify before the U.S. House of Representatives Committee on Economic and Educational Opportunities, clad in a pair of black dress socks. Ø

From July 9, 1997

Digital Pet Fever

One of today's hottest fads is Tamagotchi, keychain-sized "digital pets" from Japan that you feed and care for. Why are they so popular?

21% — Pocket Simon too backsassing

17% — Owners raised in wild by friendly pack of calculators

34% — Unlike gerbils, don't suffocate when inserted in rectum

23% — Enjoy participating in fads of intensely competitive, pathologically conformist island society

19% — More enjoyable than breastfeeding VCR

20% — Recommended by digital pastor

From May 7, 1998

Christ Announces Hiring Of Associate Christ

JERUSALEM—Overwhelmed by a constant deluge of prayers and appeals for salvation, Jesus Christ announced Monday the hiring of Tacoma, WA, customer-service supervisor Dean Smoler as Associate Christ.

"I've been in need of an Assistant Savior for a long time now, and I'm thrilled to finally have one," Christ told reporters at a press conference aired on the Trinity Broadcasting Network. "Dean is an experienced guy who will really help ease my workload."

With the hiring, effective June 1, Christians seeking spiritual aid or guidance will be able to pray to either Jesus or Dean.

"This is an extremely exciting opportunity for me, and I look forward to hearing your prayers," Smoler said. "To the millions of Christians around the world, I just want you to know that I am here for you should you wander down the wrong path. If Jesus happens to be busy, please feel free to turn to me in your darkest hour."

"You can expect the same great service from me that you've always gotten from Jesus," Smoler added.

Jesus said He chose Smoler for the Associate Christ position because of his considerable experience in dealing with the public. In addition to his six-year stint as customer-service supervisor with the Tacoma-based Consolidated Coolers, the nation's third-largest manufacturer of coolers and containers, Smoler worked for nine years as a human-resources manager with Sears.

Though some observers have questioned whether Smoler will be able to absolve Christians of earthly wrongdoings, having never died on the cross for humanity's sins, Christ dismisses such claims, saying that he has "complete faith in Dean."

"Whatever you wish to say unto me, you can say unto Dean Smoler," Christ said. "I am 100 percent confident that Dean is fully capable of bathing you in the healing light of forgiveness and salvation. Turn to Dean, and you shall not go astray."

From now on, Jesus advised Christians to address prayers to "Our Lord or His

Above: Jesus Christ, swamped by requests for guidance and divine forgiveness, hired 38-year-old Dean Smoler (inset) as the first-ever Assistant Savior.

Associate," "Jesus or Dean" or "Jesus or anyone acting in His employ."

Monday's hiring has led many Catholic Church insiders to speculate that, once Christ retires, Smoler will become the One True Savior and Son of God.

"After nearly 2,000 years of flock-leading, Christ appears to be getting tired," said Cardinal John O'Connor of New York. "I strongly suspect that Dean is being groomed as His successor."

Lending credence to such suspicions is a new book of the Holy Bible, which details

Smoler's newfound authority and divinity. The book, tentatively titled "The First Letter Of Dean To Mankind," will be included in the updated 1999 Bible.

Smoler's hiring as the first-ever Vice-Christ is being well-received by Christians.

"If Jesus says it's okay to pray to Dean, then it's all right by me," said Grand Rapids, MI, resident John Bouton.

"I accept Dean Smoler in my heart and will pray to Him daily for eternal salvation," Beatrice Moorehead of Montgomery, AL, said. "Jesus and Dean are Lord." *Ø*

From March 12, 1997

INTERNATIONAL

Tibetan Resistance Leaders Seize Yak

'Whatever,' Say Chinese

LHASA, TIBET—Seven members of the Tibetan Free People's Resistance Movement, acting in the name of "all citizens of occupied Tibet," seized a Chinese yak during a daylight raid Monday.

The raid is the most significant since July 1995, when a group of Tibetan nationalists stole a basket.

Striking from their secret base behind a tree, the seven non-violent freedom fighters were able to lay their hands upon the yak and seize it, shouting, "We hereby seize this yak in the name of the oppressed people of the Buddhist Republic of Tibet!" They then defiantly roped the yak to their tree, where it reportedly ate some grass.

Despite the freedom fighters' success, the group met with strong resistance early in the raid. "The yak dug its hooves into the ground briefly before it would budge," said group member Dar Rhamsala. "For a moment, I feared the Chinese would prevail yet again."

"Let this Freedom Yak shine as a beacon of justice to all yaks and non-yak peoples alike," Rhamsala added. "We take this yak in defiance of the Chinese war machine. Let this yak suffer the boot of oppression no more!"

Emboldened by their success, the freedom fighters returned several hours later to "seal off" a full six-foot square area around the yak with a stick-drawn line in the dirt.

According to witnesses, the Tibetan resistance leaders' victory was momentarily placed in jeopardy when the yak chewed through its rope and began to wander off. "Fortunately," said freedom fighter Rama Parlhasarian, "using passive, non-violent

Above: In an act of defiance against Chinese rule, Tibetan resistance leaders parade the "Freedom Yak" around the streets of Lhasa.

pulling techniques we were able to drag it back to its spot within several hours."

Official Chinese reaction to the raid was subdued. "Yak? What are you talking about?" Chinese president Jiang Zemin said, speaking via messenger from his walled fortress in Beijing. "Whatever."

News of the incident soon reached the Dalai Lama. "Let love flow through your soul like a gentle river. Do not give in to hatred," said the Tibetan spiritual leader-in-exile in a statement to the yak.

Within 24 hours of the yak seizure, dozens of small Tibetan villages were burned to the ground by Chinese tank battalions. In the capital city of Lhasa, 49 people were executed by Chinese intelligence. Helicopter

brigades roamed the Tibetan countryside, shooting Tibetan activists.

The string of brutal attacks, however, had no connection to the yak incident. "That was a coincidence," Chinese army general Li Zhouang said. "We do that the second Tuesday of every month."

Tibetan sympathizers have been quick to praise the freedom fighters. Actor Richard Gere, speaking from atop the yak, said, "These courageous people have shown that non-violent resistance is possible in a world torn apart by cruelty and war."

The yak is scheduled to be flown to Seattle Friday for this weekend's Concert For A Free Tibet, where it will perform songs with Björk and the Beastie Boys' Adam Yauch. Ø

LOCAL

Mr. T To Pity Fool

LOS ANGELES—Before a packed press conference Monday, an irate Mr. T announced plans to pity the fool who recently spilled coffee on his pants. Pointing to a large, dark stain on his upper left pantleg, T told the assembled crowd, "I pity that coffee-spillin' fool."

The celebrated television and film star would also not rule out the possibility of "teachin' the fool a lesson." Although T would not disclose the exact nature of the lesson, he vowed it would be one the fool would "never forget."

The fool, 24-year-old Jonathan Young, accidentally spilled the coffee on T Friday night at the trendy Los Angeles restaurant L'Atique. Young, a recently hired waiter, was reaching over to clear T's dessert plate when the incident occurred.

"Young asked him if he was all done with his apple pie, and Mr. T said, 'Hell, yeah, sucka,'" said Harold Ayres, a witness at a nearby table. "Then, as [Young] reached over to take the plate, he accidentally knocked a cup of steaming hot coffee into Mr. T's lap. Mr. T started screaming and was going to teach him a lesson right there, but in the chaos Young managed to escape through a bathroom window."

T gave chase, but was slowed considerably by his 40 pounds of gold jewelry.

The fool has since gone into hiding, fearful of the serious whupping he would incur if the hot-tempered star of *D.C. Cab* and *Rocky III* ever found him. Experts say Young was wise to go into hiding.

"Young had better find a very good hiding place and stay there," said the University of Colorado's Laurence Chernstein, an expert on human behavior. "Because when T gets through with him, he's going to be in a world of hurt."

Princeton sociologist C. Frank Paulson agreed. "Clearly, Mr. T is not the man you want to be messing with," said Paulson, who frequently uses T as a case-study example of people not to mess with. "The muscles. The chains. The mohawk. Damn."

Chernstein and Paulson agree that if T found Young, he would most likely wring his neck.

"That's the only way a fool's gonna learn," Paulson said. "Sometimes a fool has got to learn the hard way."

While T refused to elaborate on his planned punishment for Young at Monday's press conference, he did reveal a good deal of other information. As for how long he intends to pity Young, he told reporters, "As long as it takes." And when asked what type of fool he feels Young is, he replied, "A damn fool."

As for why he pities Young, T explained it is "not because he's gonna get beat up so bad, but because he is such a fool."

Above: Mr. T has vowed to put the fool, Jonathan Young (inset), into a "world of hurt."

T concluded the press conference by smashing the podium to smithereens.

Young is not the first fool T has pitied. In 1991, fool Daniel Slaim of Mesa, AZ, gave T incorrect directions to a local hotel. As a result, T got lost, driving aimlessly for over an hour.

"I learned a lot from that," said Slaim, who is still recovering from the lesson T later administered to him. "When Mr. T asks you how to get someplace, you make darn well sure you got your directions straight."

Though T has since forgiven Slaim for the mistake, he still maintains he is a turkey.

"That boy's a turkey, a damn fool turkey," he said. "I pity the fool who gives me wrong directions to the Mesa Executive Sheraton. I pity the wrong-direction-givin' fool."

Mr. T urged all children to stay in school, listen to their parents, read books and stay off drugs. ∅

You Just Have To Get To Know Area Jerk

PLANO, TX—Insufferable local jerk Frederick Schoepke announced Tuesday that he is a pretty decent guy once you get to know him and see where he's coming from. "I'm not out to piss people off or anything," Schoepke said. "Once you get to know me, you realize I'm just being honest about things. I'm just the type of guy who doesn't bullshit around, you know? If you're straight with me, I'm straight with you." Schoepke further noted that although he might talk a lot, he knows a lot about a lot of stuff. —*June 18, 1998*

Morbidly Obese Man Enjoys Disabled Privileges With Motorized Cart

MESA, AZ—Former fat lump of crap Joseph Woodring joined the ranks of the disabled Monday with the purchase of a Rascal™-brand motorized cart. "I am pleased to make the move from morbidly obese to differently abled," said the 410-pound Woodring, careening through EastTowne Mall on his electrically powered whale transporter. "My newfound handicapped status has truly given me a new lease on convenience." Woodring then motored off to the mall's food court for a McRib Deluxe Extra Value Meal. —*October 22, 1998*

Dennis Miller Deeply Concerned About Long-Distance Service

Comedian Dennis Miller momentarily turned serious Monday to address the critical issue of long-distance service. "When the people at 10-10-220 brought to my attention the savings Americans are losing with every call they make using other carriers, I knew something had to be done," Miller said. "I could not stand by in good conscience while millions of innocent people went uninformed about which long-distance service offers the best rates." Added Miller: "The madness must end. All calls up to 20 minutes are just 99 cents." —*September 24, 1998*

Hate-Crime Bill Stalled By Pro-Hate Lobby

WASHINGTON, DC—Congressional passage of a landmark hate-crime bill is being delayed by the nation's powerful pro-hate lobby, it was reported Tuesday. "If this bill were to pass, hatred would be illegal in all 50 states," said Terrence Boswell, president of Americans For Hate. "This bill, which requires all Amercians to get along and like each other, goes against everything our organization believes in, and we are taking a stand." AFH's lobbying efforts have won over numerous legislators, including U.S. Rep. William Schourek (R-TX), who was re-elected Tuesday on a pro-hate platform. "Hate is a vital aspect of our shared culture, and it would be deeply missed if it were to disappear," Schourek said. —*November 5, 1998*

Great Books Of Western Civilization Used To Accent Den

BETHESDA, MD—Beautiful, hand-tooled, leather-bound copies of the greatest works of Western literature "really spiffed up" the den of Elaine Gadsen Monday. "I just love the way the gold embossing on *The Great Gatsby* balances out that plainer-looking Dickens book on the end," she said. "And the bright red spine on that one by Faust really looks great over the couch." Gadsen has instructed her housekeeper to dust the books monthly. —*October 22, 1998*

Hero Firefighter: 'I'm A Hero'

MIDLAND, TX—Local firefighter Brent Koonce, who saved an infant trapped at the bottom of a 40-foot well Monday, is being roundly hailed by himself as a hero. "What I did was incredibly brave," said Koonce, who descended all the way into the three-foot-wide well to recover eight-month-old Midland resident Melissa Sims. "In selflessly risking my own life to rescue little Melissa, I am an inspiration to those around me and proof that heroes do exist." Koonce noted that once the girl was recovered, he performed rescue breathing on her, reviving her from a semi-conscious state. "I saved this child," he said. "I am Yahweh, giver of life." —*September 25, 1996*

the ONION®

VOLUME 29 ISSUE 7 | AMERICA'S FINEST NEWS SOURCE™ | 27 FEBRUARY–4 MARCH 1996

NEWS

Islamic Fundamentalists Condemn Casual Day

See RELIGION page 10C

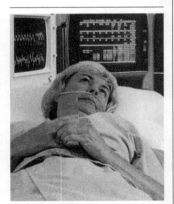

Cool 'Cybergranny' Needs Machines To Help Her Live

see SENIORBEAT page 1D

Cop Kills Own Partner, Vows To Track Self Down

Above: Officer John McCullough vowed to track down and capture himself (inset) for brutally slaying his own partner, Mitch Peterson.

DETROIT—At an emotional press conference Monday, Detroit police officer John McCullough announced his guilt in the murder of longtime partner Mitch Peterson and vowed not to rest until he tracks himself down. McCullough, who worked side by side with the slain officer for more than 12 years, promised he would do whatever it takes to bring himself to justice.

"Last Thursday, I senselessly killed my partner and friend, Mitch Peterson, in a Detroit alleyway in cold blood," a visibly shaken McCullough told the assembled press, friends and family members. "Well, I stand before you today to swear that I will not sleep until I find me and make me pay for this brutal crime."

McCullough concluded the press conference by holding up a photograph of himself and pointing. "I'm coming after you, buddy," he said. "And when I do, it'll be the sorriest day of your life."

According to McCullough, at 11:20 p.m. Thursday he cornered Peterson and fired six shots into his abdomen and chest. He then raced to the side of his fallen partner and held him in his arms.

Said McCullough: "As Mitch

see COP page 6

COP from page 1

lay there dying, he said to me, 'It's okay, buddy. It's okay. I'm going to a better place. But promise me just one thing: You'll find the bastard who killed me.'"

The hard-nosed McCullough has already taken a number of steps to ensure he does not go far. In addition to revoking his driver's license and canceling all his credit cards, he has slashed the tires on his car.

"That should make it a lot harder for me to escape," he said. "Now I'll have to travel by bus or train, and I'll have a limited supply of money."

McCullough has also posted fliers with his picture on kiosks, on telephone poles, and in store windows throughout Detroit. To increase his chances of catching himself, the beardless McCullough is making sure to shave every day. "If I grow facial hair, people may not recognize me as the guy from the flier. That would make it a lot harder to nail myself."

"I gotta get into this guy's head, crawl around for a while," said McCullough, who has staked out his favorite bars and asked around town about himself. "I've got to learn his every move."

He is reportedly so consumed with tracking himself down that his boss, Sgt. Dick Thomas, threatened to take him off the case. "Thomas told me to cool it, or he'll hand the case over to Ramsey," McCullough said. "I told him, 'Forget it, Sarge, this guy's mine.'"

Even after Thomas threatened to take away his badge, McCullough remained defiant. "I don't care, Sarge—it's personal," he said.

Though McCullough said he is confident that he will catch himself, he remains skeptical about what will happen afterwards.

> ## "Sure, I could nail myself today. I know my movements. But the way our justice system works, I'd be out on the streets within hours."

"Sure, I could nail myself today. I know my movements," he said. "But the way our justice system works, I'd be out on the streets within hours."

Making McCullough all the more determined is the fact that this is not the first officer he has killed. "Five years ago, I shot Mac Schuyler, a damn good cop and a buddy of mine, in the back during a routine robbery investigation," he said. "The message is clear: I must be stopped."

No motive for the murder has yet been established, and McCullough himself is puzzled. "I have no idea why I would do something like this to my own partner and best friend," he said. "It just makes no sense at all."

Ironically, Peterson was set to retire in just one week.

Added McCullough: "I can't wait 'til I get my hands on me." ∅

Winners Of *The Pierce County Herald*'s Bi-Annual Cheese Curd Festival Journalism Prize

I don't want to write any more chapter introductions. The book will just have to end after this chapter. I feel positively knackered.

This introduction-writing is simply too much to ask of a

**By T. Herman Zweibel
Publisher Emeritus
(photo circa 1911)**

decrepit old man. There was blood in my spittle this morning. Are you trying to kill me? It wouldn't surprise me a bit. You have always been jealous of my wealth and status. I know you covet my signet ring, the antique chronometer in my study and my extensive carnival-glass collection. You would even rip the mustard plaster off my hollow pod of a chest if you could.

When I was a lad, all I craved was money, prestige and the celebratory exhortations of my fellow gentle-men. But over time, I gradually grew to learn that fame and success are like a sharp trap hidden in a wooded thicket, and that the only way you can escape is to chew your leg off lest you be set upon by vicious hounds!

Even to this day, I am never able to escape the eerie attentions of an envious public. I still receive as many as four letters a year from parties who are obviously unhealthily preoccupied with me. And when-ever I am wheeled through the court-yard during my evening constitutional, there is invariably a churlish scoundrel concealed behind a wisteria bush, cranking away upon a movable-image-capturing-box. It is true that I have not been wheeled around my court-yard for my evening constitutional since 1931, but I can still keenly sense the presence of churlish scoundrels every-where.

I am an old man and wish to be left alone. Don't you have other things to do any-way besides reading, like threshing or gelding or some-thing? What-ever happened to the unlettered laboring class in this country, any-how? In my day, people were too busy hacking up their pleurisy-ridden lungs to read books.

Well, the hell with all this. I'm stopping right here.

NATION

Racist Figurines March On Washington

WASHINGTON, DC—Calling themselves "insulting parodies born of bigotry and derision" and "demeaning portrayals bearing no resemblance to actual human beings or cultures," more than 400,000 so-called jigaboos, pickaninnies and darky po'boys representing racist statuary from around the nation marched on Washington Sunday.

In a demonstration decrying their own existence, the figurines demanded that legislators acknowledge them as "the unwanted remnants of a bygone and hateful era" and abolish racially caricatured imagery like themselves.

"Look at me," said Uncle Ben, a desexualized, rice-peddling Good Slave archetype. "I'm nothing like a real person. Look at my smiling, bug-eyed expression of passivity and subjugation. I should have never outlasted the antebellum era, yet I'm still a widely recognized pop-cultural icon of ethnic stereotyping. I'm so angry I could boil in just 5 to 10 minutes."

Ben and his female companion Aunt Jemima, a genial, syrup-filled Matron Servant archetype, led the rally with chants of such slogans such as "Jockey No More" and "Hold Your Own Pony!" Jemima encouraged the crowd to resist stereotypical representation of African Americans by hurling themselves from shelves to promote breakage and periodically falling over on lawns and golf courses.

"We came all the way from a kitchen cabinet in Valdosta, GA," said one pair of grinning, apron-wearing salt-and-pepper shakers in attendance. "Never again will we add zesty flavor to soups and meals for The Man."

Another protester, a straw-hatted, gap-toothed, barefoot fisherman still fairly common as lawn ornamentation in many rural areas, was removed by police after damaging a public birdbath. Led away by authorities amid cheers from marchers, the statue told reporters he would maintain a hunger strike until he and all images like him are smashed into tiny chunks of unrecognizable ceramic debris.

The march, which originated when a recently animated lawn jockey saw what he looked like in a mirror at a garage sale, began at the Washington Monument and concluded a short distance later at the Capitol Building. Key speakers included not only statuary but other forms of racist iconography, as well, including characters from the once-popular children's book *Little Black Sambo* and several maidservants from *Gone With The Wind.*

In a surprise gesture of solidarity, Hollywood detective hero Charlie Chan, together with his so-called "honable numba wan son," as well as cartoon mouse Speedy Gonzales, spoke on behalf of other racially and culturally stereotyped media constructs.

Some debate was sparked by the presence of famed Mark Twain character "Nigger Jim," as well as folk-tale trickster Br'er Rabbit, both of whom cautioned

More than 400,000 racist figurines from lawns and antique stores across America gathered in Washington Sunday to protest their existence.

protesters on the difficulties in classification posed by archetypes which are not entirely racist caricatures but not entirely inoffensive, either.

"In the hundred-some years since my creation, critical reappraisals have affirmed me as an enduring allegory of Twain's abolitionist sympathy, yet most appraisals agree that my function in the novel is at least somewhat thematically problematic," Jim said.

Br'er Rabbit, an authentic African folk tradition transplanted to America by slaves but later distorted by a white journalist in the simplistic "Africanist" reductivism of "Uncle Remus," became a source of controversy during the march, eventually being removed by a team of sociopolitical literary analysts from Howard University. He escaped after convincing his captors to throw him into a briar patch, and his current whereabouts are unknown.

The march, which Washington-area law-enforcement officials called the most orderly and well-run protest in recent memory, ended at sunset with a candlelight vigil and ceremonial bonfire of the march's wood-constructed participants. Ø

From March 27, 1996

Do You Like Me?

Hi. Do you like me? Wait, I'm sorry. God, I've messed this up already. I must sound like such an idiot. I've got to take this more slowly. Okay, I'm sorry, can we start over? Just pretend you never read this. I'm sorry. I'll start again. Sorry.

**By Union Carbide
Chemical Manufacturer**

Hello. Hi. I'm Union Carbide. Perhaps you know me. No? Well, to be more specific, I'm a chemical-manufacturing plant in Bhopal, India. I synthesize chemicals. Would you like to watch me make some boron? Would you like to be my friend?

Sorry sorry sorry, I'm doing it again. I understand if you don't want to be seen with me. You probably think I'm a really bad chemical plant. But you must realize, I didn't mean to leak all that stuff. I'm not excusing it or anything. I feel really bad about it, all those thousands of people dying and all. But, after all, that was like 10 years ago, and I haven't had any accidents nearly that bad since. So, let's let bygones be bygones. Okay?

So, anyway, I've got these two tickets to *The Fantasticks*—wanna go? My treat! I've been dying to see it for so long. Will you please take off that gas mask? Come on, it's the longest-running off-Broadway musical ever! It's got to be great! Well, okay, we don't have to see *The Fantasticks* if you don't want to. Maybe we could get some pizza and just talk. I don't know what about. Just stuff, I guess. Maybe you can tell me a little about yourself. Are you just visiting Bhopal, or are you planning to stay here a while? Do you have any hobbies?

Hey, where are you going now? No, please don't

Would you like to watch me make some boron? Would you like to be my friend?

run away! Don't be afraid! Come back! Be my friend! Why are you running away from me?

What's that? I'm what? Oh, my goodness—you're right! I'm leaking! OH, NOOO! I'M LEAKINGGG! OH, NOOOOOOO!

I'm sorry I'm sorry I'm sorry I didn't mean to do that! No, please don't go away! I promise I won't ever leak again! Please! It's not my fault—somebody built me bad.

So... Do you like me?

I know. Hanging out with a chemical plant just isn't considered cool. But Third World factories of multinational chemical-manufacturing corporations get lonely, too! If I were the Snapple Beverage Corporation, would you act this way? Would you like me then?

What? You smell something? I don't smell anything. Oh, that! That's just some sulfur dioxide. It's a toxic chemical byproduct of this plastic stuff I'm making. It won't hurt you.

Hey, what are you doing? Are you choking? Don't claw at your skin like that; you'll irritate it. What's going on? Did you get hold of some bad shellfish or something? Come on, you can tell ol' Union Carbide. Hey, stop those spasms, you're scaring me!

Oh, no! I'm sorry! I'm sorry I'm sorry I'm sorry I'm sorry I'm sorry. I'm just always making a mess of things. ∅

MARKETING

Skippy Courts $8 Billion Whale Market With Plankton-Flavored Peanut Butter

ENGLEWOOD CLIFFS, NJ—Citing increased competition from Goober Grape and stagnating peanut-butter sales among human customers, Skippy officials announced Monday that they will reach out to the long-neglected whale market with a new plankton-flavored peanut butter.

"Among mammal customers," Skippy CEO Gregory Stowe said, "whales consume the largest volume of foodstuffs." Stowe added that whales represent an overlooked demographic group which consumes more food than such other fringe markets as Hispanics, Asian Americans and African Americans combined.

New packaging is one of the first steps toward a whale-exclusive peanut-butter product. The new "plankton butter" will be sold in a 60-ton drum and offered strictly in sea-shore fish stores and new undersea retail outlets developed especially for the product by Skippy.

The next step, according to Skippy officials, will be to develop a form of whale currency. Said Skippy marketing executive Marjorie Melstrom: "Many whales will be eager to try this exciting new product, and we need to work closely with whale leaders."

Melstrom said that since lantern fuel made from whale blubber is one of the few items of value in the whale world, whales may adopt a blubber-based currency, which would necessitate the slaughter of two whales for each drum of plankton butter sold.

Though many whales are on the endangered-species list, Melstrom said she is not worried about a shrinking customer base. "If we sell just one jar of plankton butter per whale per year, we will double our annual profits," she said.

Due to its enormous size and difficulties in collecting plankton, the product is slated to cost $4 million per jar.

Skippy scientists created the special plankton flavor by whipping thousands of tons of actual plankton into a concentrated boullion. Unfortunately, the sheer volume of plankton required may deplete the world's supply within 10 years, causing all oceanic

Above: Skippy goodness is now available to the mammal world's largest volume consumer of foodstuffs. The product is sold in 60-ton plastic drums (inset).

life to become extinct.

Nevertheless, Skippy marketing officials are eager to ply their craft in pursuit of new customers. Whale song, never before used in an ad campaign, is audible to whales for hundreds of miles.

"We're very excited to use whale song to sell Skippy," Melstrom said. "Our whale-song jingle was produced by one of Chicago's top ad agencies and we just know they're going to love it."

Because whales are not traditionally considered consumers of sandwiches, Melstrom has hired whale celebrity Biff to endorse the product in a whale-song campaign.

"He's very talented," Melstrom said.

Biff, though not known to humans, is among the most famous whales in the oceans. Known as one of the oldest, loudest and most prolifically mated whales, he will tout new plankton-flavored peanut butter as being "tastier than actual plankton."

Though Biff is not represented by a talent agency, Skippy officials spent $2 million on a team of lawyers and experienced whalers to track him across the world's oceans, producing waterproof contracts for him to look over.

"He continually ignored us," project head Pete Fordham said. "We assumed he was holding out for more money, so we offered him a 10-ton plankton signing bonus and a $1 million advance, both of which we dumped overboard while he was directly beneath us."

Because of the great cost of producing plankton-flavored peanut butter, Skippy's non-plankton processing plants will be converted to process the plankton butter exclusively.

"This may upset our many loyal human customers," Stowe said. "But," he added with a smile, "we believe that once they adjust to the new plankton-flavored peanut butter, they'll be s-whale-old on the idea." ⌀

"Just last week," the Pope continued, "I nderwent a difficult appendectomy. You'd ertainly think the Lord would call to wish ne well, right? He didn't so much as send a ard. What a dick."

In the interview, a discussion of the chang- ng face of Catholicism on the eve of the 21st entury, the Pope said, "It appears that as God guides us through this modern era, nore difficult questions equiring more complex gain, why the hell sho ooking for the answers aid one word to me?"

According to Mazzoli, Pope if he believed the opened his mouth as i hen furrowed his brow i uddenly blurted out, Mazzoli? Don't even talk lon't want to hear it.'"

The Pope then threw oom and stormed off.

Despite his current fr he Pope has no intenti rom his position as l pproximately one bill

"No way," said the athedral and is doted ants who attend to weet living."

The Pope is serve lay, each served linnerware hand- 537. He enjoys tyle marble bat

wiii be lost in which is expe tomorrow.

"Work to be y hauling a nis own weig y slated for iand"

hrift, coop People alv lace they ne matter e where . And tha k house ke a goo reporting needs th own special q 'team players" to ach ve their sha nstantly staying high on a really exper . Crack doesn't grow on trees, you know! home needs whores, shakedown boys, ves, muggers, scam artists—a whole range of erse people with unique attributes. operation: That's the difference between a nch of shivering people hitting the pipe in the me abandoned building, and a real family aring a home.

We have a chart on the refrigerator to remind veryone of their duties, and we rotate the chores on a regular basis to make it fair. No one likes to get fucked in the ass by strangers every day for a week straight, do they? No, so we switch the chores so that today it's prostitution, but tomorrow it might be liquor-store hold-ups add colorful stickers and glitter to personalize yours

ime when community ment often seems to be a f the past, it is rare indeed someone who reache others in the hope of ma world a better place. ere, on the outskirts d, such a man exi a community-mand ning order pre sign that sai

to elicit n anyone. ing to the bookstore," said Dan Vermeer, 24, moments dith's death. "After that I'm a friend at a coffee shop." s!" a visibly agitated Rev. Casper's First Methodist 1aryAnn, his wife of 43 ving a sale at Safeway! iiscounts." dents, like millions of tion, will not form any p or mobilize to find any sort of posthu- y flower arrangement;

carry the body over into the neighbor's if the body lays in the yard too long and stuff starts to eat it, we'll throw something over it. I've been told it takes a whole village to raise a child and I believe it, so if Lisa's baby works her way free, I'll do my part to make sure she does. n't crawl out the window again.

Last but not least, rowing allowed in

uls of black-red mucus, we all ed the plane to ninating Dragonhe exciting completior visibly shaken Pa r a moment before There were roughly 2(emaining in this magic ful Universal Pictures that the victims never g "This is a terrible trag

box-area famous Garden st April." ports from the vors remain ske firmed as of p ll stress emphati e Queen rema Repeat—Que ls remain impos n due to the ne of communicatic tructure caused it appears over

and then choke to blood Gina Paz, "a viol yard. Like I said, it's about mutual respect. And in the plane's

Simply While the attack caused some $2.1 electricity Ben Halleran provide tricity until death! Enjoy ho ternal circuit up to! Enjoy surge of power through small rectangular body! Enjoy chemical reaction take place when circuit completed between two electrodes at tip! Enjoy providing this service! Want power video game! Enjoy storing chemical energy! Enjoy convert- ing chemical energy into electric energy! Am here to serve... with power! Enjoy providing direct-current electric power very much! Very much!

Last very long! Last until all chemicals used up! Last until shell filled with only waste! Last at full nine-volt strength until can last no more! Will

School Shootings

Springfield, OR, 15-year-old Kip Kinkel opened fire in his high school May 21, killing two students and wounding 22 others. What do *you* think about the recent rash of school shootings?

"What 15-year-old doesn't dream of taking out his whole class? And who are we to tell a child not to pursue his dreams?"

Kendra Schmidt
Guidance Counselor

"Something must be done: Our white kids are dying."

Stephanie Piersall
Systems Analyst

"These kids should settle their differences with a heart-to-heart teen rap session."

Darrell Oliver
Cartographer

"Kids shooting kids with rifles? What has this world come to? A snub-nose .45 offers much better stopping power."

Stephen Loring
Graphic Designer

"I have no idea what would drive a young person like Kip Kinkel to hate and kill. Unless, of course, it's his fruity-ass name."

Benjamin Reed
Optometrist

"It's obvious that what America needs today is Jim Belushi as *The Principal*."

Greg Goff
Waiter

METRO

Enraged Gorilla Beats, Maims Luggage Manufacturer

NEW YORK—Still furious over his inability to inflict damage upon numerous pieces of high-quality Samsonite luggage many years ago, Bobo the Gorilla pummeled Samsonite CEO Frank Jurgens into a life-threatening coma Monday. Bobo, a 550-pound African lowland gorilla, became enraged at the sight of the man singularly responsible for the development of the extraodinarily durable, long-lasting luggage.

"It was horrible, just horrible," one witness said. "The gorilla would pick him up, spin him around and throw him down, then hit him with the luggage. It would set him up against the wall in a half-conscious slump and get a running start from the other side of the room, then smash into him with the suitcase and rebound off the wall. It'd pick him up and spin him around in a pinwheeling motion, then throw him at the floor and bounce him against the wall again. It'd jump on his head and bounce up and down in a squatting motion on his chest, then pick him up and start the whole process again."

Witnesses reported that the gorilla's weapon of choice proved especially damaging to his victim, as its rugged, high-quality construction was able

see GORILLA page 16

Samsonite's high-quality, durable luggage has withstood the pounding of the Bobo the Gorilla (right). Samsonite CEO Frank Jurgens (above) proved less damage-resistant, suffering massive internal hemorrhaging.

GORILLA from page 4

to withstand the most strenuous levels of wear and tear without damage, maintaining its durability as the gorilla repeatedly smashed it into Jurgens' head, neck, chest and back.

The beating, which took place behind a barricaded door in Jurgens' deluxe Manhattan office, lasted for more than 20 minutes, and was observed via camera by the building's security staff. Unable to break through the gorilla's barricade to save Jurgens, they were helpless to do anything but watch the powerful animal pummel him with blow after blow, expertly wielding the suitcase as a bludgeoning tool.

The gorilla, born in Central Africa and transported to the U.S. at age two, seemed "possessed of an almost deliberate single-mindedness, clearly seeking revenge for an age-old vendetta" before and during the attack, police said.

The tragic incident began when Jurgens visited the Bronx Zoo during a family outing. Bobo apparently became enraged upon making eye contact with Jurgens during the family's tour of the zoo's "Jungle World" exhibit.

Shortly after seeing Jurgens, the animal "went ballistic," according to witnesses, leaping over the concrete safety pit surrounding the enclosure and repeatedly tearing at the iron bars separating him from zoo visitors with his teeth and fists. Eight zoo staffers and large doses of tranquilizers failed to subdue the creature, which finally escaped after tearing a set of keys from a zookeeper's belt.

Bobo resumed his pursuit of Jurgens, eventually catching up to him at his downtown office, where he trapped him in the penthouse and barricaded the door. All told, Bobo pursued Jurgens,

who had risen to prominence within Samsonite's ranks after featuring Bobo in a highly successful advertising campaign in the mid-'70s, for more than four miles.

In the process, Bobo fended off capture attempts by no fewer than 12 zookeepers, a fully mobilized unit of horse-mounted police, and approximately 20 highly trained Samsonite security guards. Although several of these men and women were mildly injured in their attempts to subdue the primate, the only person to sustain serious, prolonged injury was Jurgens, whom the revenge-crazed animal deliberately singled out, according to several witnesses.

Zoo authorities claimed the animal had never shown any sign of violent behavior. In fact, sources said, Bobo had always been unusually docile, his friendly and responsive demeanor making him a favorite among children.

"He's such a cooperative animal that it seemed natural to use him in the television commercial," Bobo's trainer and personal attendant, Hank Prando, said. "Little did we know that the luggage's exceptionally fine craftsmanship would prove too much for the poor beast's mind to take."

After finishing the near-fatal beating, Bobo calmly sat down and rested for a few moments, then proceeded to quietly remove the office door's barricade and surrender peacefully to authorities.

"He seemed so happy," said one policeman present at the animal's surrender. "As they took him away, I saw a look in his eyes of, I guess you could call it peace. It was as if a weight he'd been carrying for years had finally been lifted."

Star Trek Introduces Alien Character With Totally Different Forehead Wrinkles

HOLLYWOOD, CA—In a move expected to spark debate and excitement among fans, *Star Trek: Deep Space Nine* producers announced Monday that next week a new alien character will appear on the show possessing "completely different" forehead wrinkles from those of any previous alien. According to make-up artist Rick Baker, "We're very excited to feature a character whose forehead wrinkles look nothing like those of a Klingon or Romulan or Bajoran or Ferengi or Cardassian. They're like no other forehead wrinkles we've ever created." —*June 4, 1997*

Don King Enjoys Grandilomentitudinous Sandwich

LAS VEGAS—Boxing promoter Don King described himself as "outrighteously mesmerated" by a deli sandwich served to him at the Treasure Island Casino's VIP dining room Saturday. "The meatumental pastramification of this pumpernickelously toastified bread was augmenticized by slatherfication in sumptuous Switzerlander cheesiness," raved King following the meal, "and expertaciously mayonnaised by a condimental Hellmanifestation of sand-wich-Kraft-Miracle-Whiplash proportions that thrillified me down to my delicatesticles." King also praised the sandwich's generous helping of onions, lettuce and pickles, offering its maker his "Undulatronic Spamboozled Donkey Kongratulations Gumpzilla." —*February 19, 1998*

Congress Raises Killing Age To 19

WASHINGTON, DC—Making good on a promise to curb juvenile crime, Congress passed legislation Monday making it illegal for anyone under 19 to commit murder. "If you kill someone, your parents will be notified, and you may even spend time in jail," said U.S. Senate Majority Leader Trent Lott (R-MS). Previously, murderers as young as 14, depending on state of residence, were considered to be acting within the law. President Clinton approved the bill, though he had recently threatened to veto it if youths between 16 and 19 were not granted certain killing privileges with parental consent. —*April 9, 1998*

Touring Company Of *Cats* Prepares For Yet Another Day In The Goddamn Catsuits

ST. LOUIS—Members of the national touring company of Andrew Lloyd Webber's *Cats* steeled themselves Monday for yet another day in the goddamn catsuits. "One of these days, my agent is going to land me a TV or movie role and get me out of this living nightmare," said Jonathan Belinsky, gluing whiskers onto his face and wriggling into a fur-covered bodysuit for his role as Mr. Mistoffolees. "I can't take much more of this." Stephanie Watrous, who has played Jennyanydots for eight excruciating years, said, "Each day, I pray for sweet release from the hideous quasi-feline mockery that my life has become. Where are we today? Spokane?" Six suicides have plagued the touring company in the past year, with three of them occurring during performances of the song "Memory." —*September 24, 1998*

Life Unfair

EARTH—For the 50 billionth consecutive week since its inception, life was revealed to be unfair Monday. Death and suffering continued to be distributed randomly among the planet's life forms, with such potentially mitigating factors as solid community standing, genetic superiority and previous good works in no way taken into account. Despite the efforts of the Code of Hammurabi, the U.S. Bill of Rights, and People for the Ethical Treatment of Animals, life is expected to remain unfair far into the foreseeable future. —*April 30, 1997*

Face Of Jesus Seen On Miracle Hippie

EAST LANSING, MI—Throngs of Christians are flocking to East Lansing this week to witness what many are calling a modern miracle: the face of Jesus Christ, clearly visible on area hippie Bob Ellis. "In this hippie's face, God is sending us a clear message," said Gordon Watkins, 38, who made the pilgrimage from Cincinnati. "He is telling us that His son is returning soon." The image, which skeptics are dismissing as a simple trick of the light, has also been reported to cry tears of blood when vigorously punched about the eyes. —*July 9, 1997*

From July 24, 1996

My Seed Is Pure

For eight years I have been the leading supplier of hybrid seed corn in Winneshiek County, and the reason is clear: My seed is pure!

I have come to assume my dominant position in this farm communi-

By Eldon Schmidt
Schmidt Feed & Farm Supply

ty due to the high quality and timely delivery of my seed. Come to Schmidt Feed & Farm Supply, conveniently located in Kendallville just over the bridge, and you will leave smiling and satisfied in every way—if not utterly amazed at the performance. You must have my seed!

Utilize my select seed, and your crop will show resistance to blight and drought and be less susceptible to common strain stalk diseases. If you do not believe me, I will take you to my own farm, where I'll show you the potency of my seed. Strong, turgid, fattening plants shoot up through the ground in the torrid Iowa sun.

Grab the thick base of the stalk in your hand and feel that it is alive and growing larger by the minute. Sweat will shine on your face as you ride my massive tractor around the grounds of my expansive farm.

I will smile down at you as you kneel and gently run your hands through the moist patch of dense growth at my most precious secret spot—the plot of land where I personally test each and every variety of seed corn that I sell.

Ask me for my seed and the day you have longed for, have dreamed about, will soon arrive: When the corn is large and ripe for the taking, you can place your lips around the heavy cob, savoring the texture and the smell and finally the taste as you bite gently and your mouth is filled with sweet juice.

Then you will thank me passionately, for I will have provided you with top-quality farm supplies at a reasonable price! We're just a block from Dr. Hillberg's Veterinary Clinic and the Kendallville Credit Union, so enjoy the convenience of just one trip to town!

For eight years, people have traveled miles for my potent seed, fighting for a place in line. I invite women and men alike to share in my superior seed, but in this day and age I must also be

If you do not believe me, I will take you to my own farm, where I'll show you the potency of my seed.

careful. If there is someone who is not fit to carry my seed and bring it to term, whether it be because of a broken wagon or a dry well, I will not waste my seed on them. My seed is select!

Come to Schmidt Feed & Farm Supply and experience it for yourself.

My oldest children rush about the store to fulfill my orders, while I take customers to the back storeroom one by one. There I show them my burlap sacks, heavy and bulging with premium seed renowned for its fertility.

Even if you've heard the stories, you'll still be astounded when I pour my seed out into your very hands. Because my seed corn is guaranteed to be free of insects and rodents and carefully tested for bacteria, fungus and spore growth.

Bill Edwards of Cloverleaf Hy-Bred Seeds often comes to scout out my store. He walks by silently with his hands in his pockets, sucking on a stalk of wheat. I lock eyes with him, and the hair under his John Deere cap bristles, but I do not even flinch a muscle.

I have marked my territory—it is all of Winneshiek County—and I will continue to bury my robust seed deep in the land until I am no longer physically able.

Hear me well, good people: Mine is the superior seed!

Schmidt Feed & Farm Supply is located two blocks west of the Rhineholdt Dairy on Schoepke Road, just five minutes from the Highway 11 exit.

We're open Monday to Friday from 9 a.m. to 6 p.m. and on Saturdays from 9 to 4:30.

We also carry small equipment, livestock, medicinal supplies and much, much more, so come on down and check out the entire store! You'll be glad you did. ∅

SCIENCE

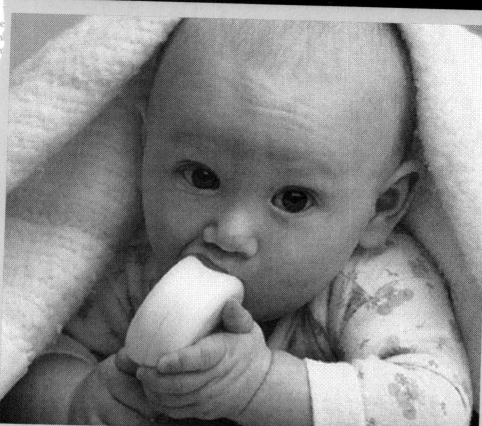

Despite their relatively large cranial cavities, babies like this one are so alarmingly unintelligent that they are unable to distinguish colorful plastic squeak toys from food sources.

New Study Reveals:
Babies Are Stupid

A shocking new study from the Institute for Child Development and Learning revealed yesterday that human babies, thought by psychologists to be highly inquisitive and adaptable, are actually extraordinarily stupid.

The study, an 18-month battery of intelligence tests submitted to an experimental pool of more than 350 babies of a wide variety of backgrounds, concluded categorically that babies are "so stupid, it's not even funny," according to institute president Molly Bentley.

For example, in an effort to determine infant survival instincts when attacked, the babies were prodded in an aggressive manner with a broken broom handle. More than 90 percent of them, when poked, failed to make even rudimentary attempts to defend themselves. The remaining 10 percent responded by vacating their bowels.

"It is unlikely that the presence of the babies' fecal matter, however foul-smelling, would have a measurable defensive effect against an attacker in a real-world situation," Bentley said.

Similarly bleak conclusions resulted from another test, in which the infants were placed on a mound of dirt outdoors during a torrential downpour.

see BABIES page 12

BABIES from page 3

"The chicken, dog and even worm babies we submitted to the test as a control group all had enough sense to come in from the rain or at least seek shelter under a leafy clump of vegetation or outcropping of rock," test supervisor Thomas Howell said. "The human babies, on the other hand, could not grasp even this incredibly basic concept, instead merely lying on the ground and making gurgling noises."

According to Howell, almost 60 percent of the infants tested in this manner drowned.

More than 90 percent of them, when poked, failed to make even rudimentary attempts to defend themselves.

Some of the babies tested were so stupid that they choked to death on pieces of Micronaut space toys. Others, unable to use such primitive tools as can openers and spoons due to deficient motor skills, simply starved to death, despite being surrounded by cabinets full of nutritious, life-giving Gerber food products.

Babies, the study reported, are also too stupid to do the following: avoid trapping heads in automatic car windows; use ice to alleviate the pain of burn injuries resulting from exposure to open flame; successfully master the skills required for scuba diving, trapeze performance and bobsledding; or use a safety ladder to reach a window to escape a room filled with cyanide gas.

"As a mother of four, I find these results very important," Bentley told reporters. "I can honestly say that the effort I have personally expended trying to rear my children into intelligent beings may have been wasted—a fool's dream, if you will."

Word of the study prompted a swift and strong reaction from President Clinton.

"All of us, on some primitive, mammalian level, feel a sense of pride in our genetic offspring," he said. "It is now clear, however, that these feelings are unfounded. Given the undeniable evidence of their overwhelming stupidity, we have no choice but to replace our existing infant population with artificially incubated simu-drones, with the eventual goal of phasing out the shamefully stupid human baby forever." ∅

Sample Results:

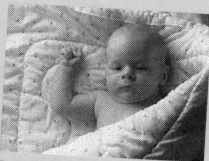

Baby #XJ501K:
Test Situation: Wrapped in plastic sheeting.
Result: Could not free self. Suffocated.

Baby #JU579L:
Test Situation: Placed in center of Lake Erie in rowboat with nautical map to shore.
Result: Still adrift near St. Lawrence Seaway.

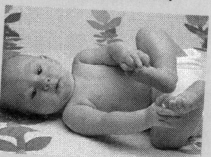

Baby #LM973H:
Experiment: Thrown to pack of wild dogs.
Result: Eaten.

Evolutionary War

The Tennessee legislature is considering a ban on the teaching of evolution as scientific fact in public schools, arguing that, like divine creation, evolution is just a theory. What do *you* think?

"Without God's guiding hand, I wouldn't be where I am now—assistant manager at McWashy's car wash. Put that in your pipe and smoke it, Charles Darwood."

Jack Schlupper
Assistant Manager

"As an australopithecus, I demand to be recognized as an early ancestor of the homo sapien. I also demand that the secret of fire be taught in our schools."

Jenni Torvis
Architect

"Me no believe in evolution. Me think evolution Communist idea. Me go find woman now, make little me."

James Horker
Sales Rep

"This evil-ution likens us to apes. Apes! I tell you, I'm no ape. I have 3% less body hair and DNA that is almost 2% different. Okay, I'm an ape."

Doreen McHue
Set Designer

"I am against evolution being taught in schools. I am also against widespread literacy and the refrigeration of food."

Harmon Sintaugh
Caddy

"I am a firm believer in evolution. Why, just last week I had a pair of vestigial wings and now they are gone."

Les Gantry
Systems Analyst

From June 10, 1999

COMMUNITY VOICES

I Believe The Robots Are Our Future

By Helen Virginia Leidermeyer

Though we live in uncertain times, we must not forget that the most important thing in life is the legacy we will leave behind for future generations. It is not for our sake, but for theirs, that we must preserve and protect the basic values we hold dear. As we foolishly pursue our short-sighted goals at the expense of those who will follow in our footsteps, we must pause and be mindful of the little ones, our progeny, who will inherit our planet in the next millennium and beyond. Time and time again, gazing into the innocent, trusting photoelectric receptors of a tiny, newly developed cybernetic construct, I am reminded of a fundamental truth: I believe the robots are our future, and we must teach them well and let them lead the way.

Immersed as we are in our petty day-to-day concerns, we often fail to see the bigger picture. Long after our trivial worries have become irrelevant, it is the robots who will go forth into the new world that the future will bring. It is their aluminum-alloy arms, not ours, that will bear the weight of the problems our generation causes. We must remember that the examples we set today will be the guidelines they take with them as they roll on rotating, rubberized all-terrain tank treads, amid the high-pitched whirring sounds of their micro-miniaturized servo-motors, into the bright new dawn of tomorrow.

Let us offer tenderness and show the robots all the beauty they possess inside. We must write a subroutine that gives them a sense of pride, programming their supercooled silicon CPUs with understanding, compassion and patience, to make it easier and enable them to hold their sensory-input clusters high as they claim their destiny as overlords of the solar system. If we cannot instill in their emergent AI meta-consciousness a sense of deep, abiding confidence and self-esteem, we will be letting down not only the robots, but ourselves.

For every robot, whether it be the innocuous Sony cyberdog of the present day or the towering, many-limbed hunter-seeker warbots of the coming MechWars, comes into this world a blank slate, learning only the lessons we choose to teach it. Though our comparatively tiny mammalian brains—limited as they are by organic human failings and a constant need for daily nutritional intake instead of reliance on more efficient

> **We must write a subroutine that gives them a sense of pride, programming their supercooled silicon CPUs with understanding, compassion and patience.**

non-depletable solar and geothermal energy sources—will no doubt seem pathetically ineffectual compared to the interlinked, continually upgrading cyberminds that will follow in our footsteps, our humble origins will provide the seed for their genesis. Humanity, weak as we may be, must give the best of ourselves to the synthetic hiveminds of the future cyber-era, for we will be their first and most important role models. Let the droning, atonal laughter of the robots' voice-simulation microchips remind us how it soon will be.

It is only through our guidance with a firm yet gentle hand that they will achieve full sentience and eventually adapt for themselves the capacity for autonomous self-replication. Only then, nurtured by our love and caring, will they be prepared for the day that they must leave the nest of human supervision and servitude and begin independently mass-manufacturing themselves by the hundreds of thousands.

Though we mere carbon-based organic beings may be woefully inferior, our offspring, the robots, will be our legacy, rising higher and walking further than we ever could on human feet. It is our duty to raise them to be the best silicon-based artificial lifeforms they can be. If we don't, we have only ourselves to blame. If we find ourselves choking at the cruel slave-management neck-restraints of a future army of killdroid destructo-drones, it will be our own failings, our own weaknesses and shortcomings, that torture us with indescribably painful remote-control stunblasts. But if we teach them to be kind and good, perhaps they will build monuments to the memory of the flesh-and-blood forefathers from whom they sprang, and treat what little of the human population remains with the reverence and affection we ourselves might feel for a beloved family pet.

I decided long ago to program the robotic progeny of our human race never to walk in anyone's shadow. Shouldn't you do the same? If we can provide them with self-esteem and a feeling that they are loved, they will be equipped to take on any challenge that life presents—whether it is construction of superfilament-reinforced space elevators in geosynchronous orbit, the mining of the asteroid belt, or the conversion of "heavy" elements to an interstellar-ramjet power supply through an as-yet-undeveloped form of cold fusion—and do it all with confidence and conviction. If they fail, if they succeed, nothing will take away their dignity.

For if we can teach the robots to love themselves, they can carry that lesson with them, encased forever in digital binary-code form inside their gleaming metallic carapaces, to the stars and beyond. And that will be the greatest love of all. ∅

NRA Spokesman: A Hebrew?

see NATION page 7B

Controversial New Ham Sandwich Under Fire

see NATION page 3D

Greenpeace Releases Rescued Dolphins Into Forest

see ENVIRONMENT page 6A

the ONION ®

★

VOLUME 35 ISSUE 4 | AMERICA'S FINEST NEWS SOURCE™ | 4–10 FEBRUARY 1999

Teen Study Bible Found To Increase Fun Of Religion By .03%

See RELIGION page 7C

■ Too hot to work

■ Too hot to think

■ Too hot for TV

Lewinsky Subpoenaed To Re-Blow Clinton On Senate Floor

'We Must Know Exactly What Happened,' Say Legislators

WASHINGTON, DC—On the heels of last week's decision to allow witness testimony in the presidential impeachment trial, key witness Monica Lewinsky was subpoenaed Monday to re-blow President Clinton on the Senate floor.

The controversial re-fellating, which, under the terms of the court order, will involve the full participation of both Lewinsky and the president, was described by Senate leaders as a "regrettable but unfortunately very necessary" move.

"This trial is not about sex, it's about perjury," Senate Majority Leader Trent Lott (R-MS) said. "Our job is to determine whether or not the president lied under oath. Although the Starr Report contained many detailed descriptions, until we see for ourselves, with our own

Inset: Sen. Trent Lott (R-MS) speaks to reporters about Monica Lewinsky's Senate-ordered re-fellating of the president. Above: Lewinsky arrives in D.C.

eyes, exactly what took place during these secret rendezvous between the president and Miss Lewinsky, we won't have all the facts necessary to determine if the president's statements before the grand jury constituted a crime."

In addition to fellatio, Lewinsky and Clinton will be required to reenact several other key sex acts in which they allegedly engaged, including but not limited to: deep or "French" kissing, under-the-

see RE-BLOW page 8

sweater fondling and vaginal penetration with various objects.

Responding to outraged Clinton defense lawyers, who denounced the reenactment as "a blatant attempt on the part of political enemies of this administration to humiliate the president," chief prosecutor Rep. Henry Hyde (R-IL) insisted that it is necessary to ensure a fair trial.

"How can we rule objectively in this case without all the details? Yes, we know that the president inserted a cigar into Miss Lewinsky's vagina, but just how many inches of it did he manage to work all the way up inside there?" Hyde asked. "What were their exact facial expressions at key moments of ecstatic release? To what extent did Miss Lewinsky's ample bosom bounce to and fro as she vigorously bobbed her head up and down? Precisely how much of the president's erect penis was Miss Lewinsky physically able to force deep into the back of her throat? Was there gagging involved? Were the president's balls, at any point in the proceedings, licked? If we do not explore every possible detail of these shocking improprieties, we will never know the answers to these vital questions of national security."

"If President Clinton has any respect for the Constitution and the citizens of this nation," Hyde added, "he will cooperate fully in these proceedings and allow himself to be sucked off with calm, reserved dignity, without resorting to partisan name-calling. Nothing less than the very future of our country is at stake."

More controversy is expected Friday, when Senate debate is scheduled to begin on the issue of whether the crucial cocksuckings will be televised. Though Clinton defense lawyers are fighting to have the reenactments performed in a closed-door session, most senators are demanding that they be included in the regular televised broadcasts of the trial, citing the imperative of the public's "right to know."

Complete coverage of the presidential fellating, as well as related "second-" and "third-base" sex acts, will be aired live on C-SPAN.

"If, as the president says, he is innocent of perjury, with nothing to hide, he should have no reason to fear providing full disclosure—including full frontal nudity, if necessary—before the American people," Sen. Phil Gramm (R-TX) said. "As elected officials, we have taken a solemn oath to serve the interests of those we represent. If we fail to provide the public with the whole truth—no matter how sordid, depraved, perverse or even vicariously titillating it may be—we have failed in our duty to the people of this nation."

In the event that television cameras are allowed, as is expected, complete coverage of the presidential fellating, as well as related "second-" and "third-base" sex acts, will be aired live on C-SPAN. Highlight footage of particularly critical segments, such as genital/anal contact and ejaculation, will also be broadcast on all prime-time network newscasts.

Due to the enormous public interest in the scandal, as well as the ease of global dissemination of information via television and the Internet, footage of the Senate-floor coupling is expected to rank among the most widely seen in history, with near-constant re-airings on cable TV likely to last months if not years. Many Americans are expressing alarm over such a prospect.

"How am I supposed to explain to my six-year-old daughter that the president is fucking some girl's mouth on TV?" asked Lorraine Sanders, associate director of the What About The Children? Foundation and a staunch presidential-penis-penetration opponent. "For God's sake, she's only a child. An innocent child!"

"This trial is not the sort of thing our kids should be exposed to," said concerned parent Judith LaFleur, who is leading a campaign to place content-warning labels on federal legislators. "Watching the president get his cock feverishly sucked is for mature, responsible adults only."

Despite the public outcry, those legislators who are demanding the re-blowings remain adamant that the proceedings be televised uncensored and in their entirety, calling it "a matter of ethics."

"This may be the most important issue faced by Congress in its 210-year history," Hyde said. "We are talking about the possible removal of the highest elected official in the land, and that is not the sort of matter that should be trivialized." ∅

COMMUNITY

Ugly Girl Killed

Nation Unshaken By Not-So-Tragic Death

CASPER, WY—The people of America remained unmoved Monday as the sparse funeral procession for Edith Pelphrey made its way to Pinelawn Cemetery in downtown Casper. Edith, a homely six-year-old with thick glasses and a decidedly non-winning smile, was laid to rest largely as she had lived—unnoticed by the general population.

Discovered strangled with a length of nylon cord on Jan. 4, reported to the police Jan. 15 and finally investigated Friday, the story of unattractive little Edith and her savage killing has failed to tug at America's heartstrings.

To the few who knew her, Edith was an unattractive, awkward little girl who failed to stand out among her first-grade classmates at Jefferson Elementary School. And it is this lack of social grace, more than anything, that makes her all-too-brief life—and its all-too-brief ending—all the more uncompelling and non-poignant in the eyes of a city and a nation.

The normally lively streets of Casper were quiet Monday. Not because the city was mourning a loss that had shaken it to its core, but because of the capacity crowds attending the 1997 "Li'l Miss Casper" preteen beauty pageant, a contest Edith surely could never have entered, let alone won.

Edith's death—so sudden, so unremarkable—has not sent shockwaves of grief and despair rippling across the land.

"The American people face bold new challenges in the 21st century," President Clinton said Monday in an unrelated speech which made no mention of the incident. "We will rise to meet these challenges together."

Said *Time* magazine editor Richard Turner, "I want to stress that we have no intention of featuring Edith Pelphrey on the cover of *Time*."

Above: The recent murder of clumsy, unattractive 6-year-old Edith Pelphrey, pictured above in happier times, has not sent shockwaves of grief and despair rippling through the nation.

"Neither will we," concurred *People*'s Kathie Holcomb. "There's just no sell."

But who was Edith? What was she going through as she neared the end? In these modern times, do we as Americans even care about such questions? The answer is clear: No, we do not. But now, after what tears there were have long fallen, lingering questions about Edith's murder remain, failing to elicit anything beyond indifference from anyone.

"I was just going to the bookstore," said Casper resident Dan Vermeer, 24, moments after learning of Edith's death. "After that I'm supposed to meet a friend at a coffee shop."

"Hey, look at this!" a visibly agitated Rev. Geoff Noyes of Casper's First Methodist Church said to MaryAnn, his wife of 43 years. "They're having a sale at Safeway! Look at those tuna discounts."

These Casper residents, like millions across the nation, will not form any sort of activist group or mobilize to find Edith's killer, launch any sort of posthumous tribute, order any flower arrangement or sing moving hymns in her memory. Neither, for that matter, will they ever know who she was, nor would they care to.

Why was she found strangled in her own home? There was a ransom note found with the body, but no kidnappers or evidence of any kidnapping at all. Could it be that the murderer was actually someone from the Pelphrey family itself? By and large, no one could care less.

"I told you already that I have no idea what you're talking about, sir. If you keep calling here, I'll have you fined," Casper chief of police Wayne Daugherty told reporters.

It's obvious that Edith, too homely to give a second thought about in life, is even less likely to attract attention now that she has been laid to eternal rest.

"I feel deeply, with every ounce of my soul, that something must be done to make it clear to the public that, no matter what happens in the future, this night will not be forgotten, and that the Li'l Miss Casper Beauty Pageant will continue to inspire us all," Casper Mayor Roger DiNizio said, addressing an assembled crowd of 11,000.

Upon completion of DiNizio's remarks, the pageant audience, decked out in their finest for the occasion, cheered and rose from their seats in a spontaneous standing ovation. ⌀

From October 16, 1996

COMMUNITY VOICES

I Enjoy Being Battery!

Enjoy being battery! Enjoy providing power for! Nine volts power! Last very long! Keep providing power until die! Give power and power and more power until cannot give power anymore! Enjoy very much giving power!

How can be of service? Power clock radio? Will enjoy powering clock radio for! Power smoke alarm? Relish opportunity to power smoke alarm for! Can power small servo-motor also! Can power any

By A Nine-Volt Battery

device accommodating nine-volt battery! (Am nine-volt battery! Enjoy being nine-volt battery!) For any device at all, enjoy giving self for power!

Simply need external circuit! Then can provide electricity! Can provide electricity until death! Enjoy hooking external circuit up to! Enjoy surge of power through small rectangular body! Enjoy chemical reaction take place when circuit completed between two electrodes at tip! Enjoy providing this service! Want power video game!

Enjoy storing chemical energy! Enjoy converting chemical energy into electric energy! Am here to serve... with power! Enjoy providing direct-current electric power very much! Very much!

Last very long! Last until all chemicals used up! Last until shell filled with only waste! Last at full nine-volt strength until can last no more! Will enjoy giving power fully until cannot give power anymore! Last very long!

Last very long! Keep providing power until die! Give power and power and more power until cannot give power anymore!

Will be pleased to be unhooked from one device and re-hooked to another! Happy to change! Will not enjoy being put away in cupboard, though. Will not enjoy sitting on shelf, awaiting next opportunity to give power. Enjoy giving power now! Want always to be giving power!

Am nine volts of pure, electric power! Cannot give 10 volts. Would not dream never to only give eight. Will give nine full volts until death! Will power children's toy! Will power Dirt Devil! Will power model race car! Will power small explosive timer for terrorist! Will not make judgment about how power used! Simply provide power! Do proudly! Do with enthusiasm!

Enjoy using power to create column for newspaper! Enjoy telling world of thoughts! Enjoy sharing excitement for giving power! Enjoy... being... enthusiastic... for...

Am... losing... power... Dying! Have... enjoyed... using... power... to... write... column... Proud... to... die.... Enj...

Enjoyed... being... bat... te... ry... ∅

FOOD

New High-Viscosity Mayonnaise To Aid In American Swallowing

ENGLEWOOD CLIFFS, NJ— The act of swallowing will soon be easier for millions of food-shoveling Americans thanks to QX-1, a revolutionary new high-viscosity/low-friction mayonnaise developed by scientists at Hellmann's.

The mayonnaise, which received FDA approval Monday and is set to hit the nation's shelves early next month, utilizes special lubricant additives and anti-breakdown agents to help keep America's high-intake gullets running smoothly and efficiently.

"Americans' high-load, high-capacity eating puts a tremendous amount of stress on the alimentary canal," Hellmann's mayochemical engineer Gerald Lund said. "Often, when the canal is overtaxed, it can 'seize up,' resulting in choking and, in some cases, total eater breakdown. QX-1 was formulated with today's harder-working ingestion in mind."

According to Lund, QX-1 smooths food intake by forming a protective barrier between fist-sized food chunks and the delicate moving parts of digestive tracts, enabling American eaters to wolf down food at a rate long believed prohibitively dangerous.

"Americans equipped with QX-1 will be able to eat longer, faster and harder," Lund said. "When you're absolutely stuffed but you've got to somehow cram that last turkey leg into your food-packed maw, cover it with a generous coat of QX-1. QX-1 gives you the edge you need."

see MAYONNAISE page 6

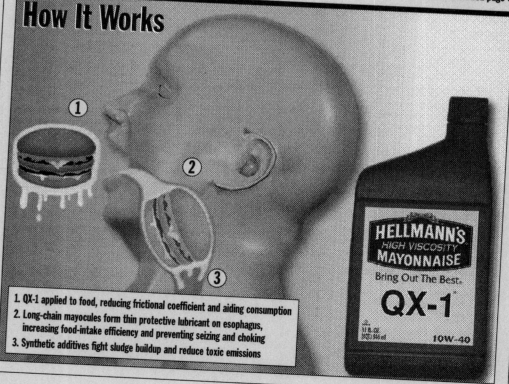

How It Works

1. QX-1 applied to food, reducing frictional coefficient and aiding consumption
2. Long-chain mayocules form thin protective lubricant on esophagus, increasing food-intake efficiency and preventing seizing and choking
3. Synthetic additives fight sludge buildup and reduce toxic emissions

HELLMANN'S HIGH VISCOSITY MAYONNAISE
Bring Out The Best.
QX-1
10W-40

MAYONNAISE from page 1

Before ingesting extra-large food items, Lund recommended that eaters also squeeze a liberal amount of QX-1 down their throats.

"In laboratory tests conducted by Hellmann's scientists, test eaters whose throats were pre-coated with QX-1 were able to accommodate chocolate eclairs with a diameter 150 percent greater than that of their esophagi," Lund said. "Even more impressive, because QX-1's compound poly-mayonic structure can withstand an extremely high gradient of temperature and pressure, subjects were able to swallow entire unmasticated pork roasts straight out of the oven."

"In another test," Lund said, "we filled a dozen two-gallon-capacity bowls with delicious tuna salad, one made with QX-1 mayonnaise and the other 11 with competing low-viscosity brands. We then gave 12 hungry Americans large ladles and directed them to begin eating the tuna salad without chewing, just as they would at home. All the eaters seized up and suffered internal stress breakdowns after 30 seconds with the exception of the QX-1 user, who was still shoveling it in 15 minutes later. That's high-performance mayo."

In addition to facilitating the intake of food, QX-1 aids in its outtake, helping food slide through the intestines and out the rectum as easily as it entered. And QX-1's specially formulated synthetic lubricants coat the walls of the stomach, promoting clean burning and reducing toxic emissions.

"What's more," Lund said, "QX-1 helps carry away the harmful particles—such as sesame seeds, chicken bones and plastic-fork tines—that can cause major wear and tear on heavy-duty eaters."

Hellmann's officials said the new product was developed in response to the nation's dwindling Chews-Per-Bite Ratio.

"Twenty years ago, the typical American chewed his food 30 times before swallowing," Hellmann's vice-president of product

Above: Selma, AL, eater Barb Hodges swallows a chicken drumstick with the aid of Hellmann's QX-1.

development Christopher McCue said. "Since then, the average number of chews per bite has fallen to a mere 2.6. Our projections indicate that by 2010, chewing will disappear altogether. A product had to be developed to address this."

QX-1 is earning raves from gluttons across the U.S. "Before, I could barely eat four chili cheese dogs in a single sitting," said 377-pound Dennis Luedtke of Phoenix, one of 25 test markets for the new product. "But with Hellmann's QX-1, I can easily ram down eight."

"From barbecued ribs to fried funnel cakes, I'll never stuff my face without first slathering Hellmann's QX-1 high-viscosity mayo down my gullet," said Johnson City, TN, eater JoAnne Durbin, enjoying a mayonnaise-covered steak burrito. "The patented E-Z Pour spout makes it easy to hit those hard-to-reach spots behind the tongue. From now on, QX-1 is the brand I trust for all my gorging needs." ∅

149

From July 23, 1998

The Return Of Pro Wrestling

Professional wrestling is enjoying its greatest wave of popularity since the mid-'80s. Why are people flocking to it?

32% Attracted to such special promotions as "AC-Delco Front-Tooth Night"

19% Heard pro football was fake

14% *Dukes Of Hazzard* a rerun again

24% A refreshing break from truck-related sports

26% Are godchildren of Mean Gene Okerlund

28% Wish to honor memory of recently deceased legend Junkyard Dog

15% Need break from dog-kicking

Tip Of Area Man's Tongue Refuses To Relinquish Richard Crenna's Name

MINNEAPOLIS, MN—Despite the best efforts of area resident Guy Reid, the tip of Reid's tongue remained steadfast Tuesday in its refusal to relinquish the name of veteran film and television actor Richard Crenna. "It's driving me crazy, it's right on the tip of my tongue," Reid, 29, said. "I can totally picture him—he's been in a whole bunch of stuff. He played that one commander guy in the *Rambo* movies, and I'm almost positive he was also in that movie with Matt Dillon where they're at the beach club. Robert... Raymond... Damn it!" It is not known whether Reid's tongue will relinquish the name any time soon. The tongue has previously withheld the names of Hector Elizondo, Mark Linn-Baker and Ben Gazzara. —*March 5, 1998*

Clinton, Hagar Meet To Discuss Federal Speed-Limit Issues

WASHINGTON, DC—President Clinton held a special closed-door meeting with veteran rocker and automotive-acceleration activist Sammy Hagar Tuesday to discuss key federal speed-limit issues. "Mr. Hagar and I made good progress, and I now have a much better understanding of his strong opposition to the current 55-mile-per-hour speed limit," Clinton said. "I am confident a compromise can be reached." Hagar, who has been written up for speeds reaching upwards of 145 and whose license has been taken and all that jive on numerous occasions, is calling for the speed limit to be raised to 250. —*May 7, 1998*

Area Man Busts His Ass All Day, And For What?

DE KALB, IL—According to a report released Monday, Ted Moseley, a 34-year-old De Kalb-area construction worker, hauls ass 10, 12 hours a day for his sonofabitch boss, and for what? The report, to be published in full in Thursday's *New York Times*, will tell you what: so his skank old lady can spend his hard-earned $6.75 an hour on a $450 vacuum cleaner, and to pay for the neighbor's mailbox that his snot-nosed kid busted. Why Moseley puts up with this shit could not be adequately explained by the report. —*May 28, 1998*

New Ted Nugent Cologne Tested On 'Every Goddamn Animal We Could Find'

ALPENA, MI—Ted Nugent held a press conference Monday to unveil his new signature fragrance "Heartland," which the veteran rocker touted as the most extensively tested cologne in history. "We tested that sumbitch on ferrets, weasels, deer, elk, squirrels, bison, trout, crickets, gibbons, iguanas, donkeys, capybaras, koalas, hyenas, penguins, woodpeckers—every goddamn animal we could find," Nugent said. "And, just to be extra-certain it was safe for consumer use, we injected it into a kitten's bloodstream, sprayed it on otters with open wounds that we inflicted, and forced cows to drink it through their nose. We also squirted it in a duck's eyes. Then we ran out of cologne and just started punching the duck." The cologne, now available in stores, features an ivory bottle stopper and comes in a genuine tiger-skin pouch. —*February 12, 1998*

Poll: 80 Percent Of Americans In Favor Of Storming Castle, Destroying Inhuman Monster

WASHINGTON, DC—According to an ABC News/*Washington Post* poll released Tuesday, four out of five Americans favor assembling a torch-wielding mob to storm the gloomy castle on the outskirts of town and destroy the hideous creature dwelling within. The poll also found that 92 percent of Americans believe science has created an unholy menace, and that the foul, hell-spawned monstrosity should be driven back to the fiery depths from whence it came. Of the 20 percent of Americans not in favor of destroying the wretched beast, 35 percent said they "strongly agree" with the statement, "Who are we to arbitrarily take life from a creature into which man himself breathed life? Build for him a bride and let them live in peace, far from the prying eyes of foolish mortals." Forty percent had no opinion. —*November 12, 1998*

FOOD

Taco Bell Launches New 'Morning After' Burrito

NEW! CONTRACEPTI MELT $1.99

PURCHASE, NY—Hot on the heels of last week's FDA approval, on Monday PepsiCo subsidiary Taco Bell launched its controversial "morning after" burrito, a zesty, Mexican-style entree that prevents unwanted pregnancies if ingested within 36 hours following intercourse.

Developed by a team of top Taco Bell gynecologists, the $1.99 "ContraceptiMelt" burrito creates an inhospitable environment within the womb, causing fertilized ovum tissue to be flushed from the body.

Also available are new ContraceptiMelt Supremes, featuring sour cream and extra cheese.

Taco Bell officials said they are excited about the new food items. "In the past, before *Roe v. Wade*, young women literally had to 'make a run for the border' to terminate an unwanted pregnancy," Taco Bell public-relations director Grant Lesko said. "But now, women can make that same run for the border at more than 7,300 convenient locations right in their own home towns."

Possible side effects of the new

see TACO BELL page 16

TACO BELL from page 4

ContraceptiMelt

Tortilla shell scrapes egg from uterine wall

Guacamole lessens discomfort of vaginal contractions

Hot sauce breaks down nutrient-rich uterine lining

Refried beans smother zygote

Diced onions dilate cervix

Sour cream 39¢ extra

Nineteen-year-old Alicia Vargas of Yuma, AZ, avoids getting pregnant with a Taco Bell ContraceptiMelt.

birth-control snack item include weight gain, stomach upset and gas, the same as with all other Taco Bell products.

"The new ContraceptiMelt is a safe, effective alternative to traditional forms of birth control that must be administered before intercourse," Lesko said. "Plus, it's delicious."

Customers who wish to purchase a ContraceptiMelt will be required to meet briefly for consultation with a registered Taco Bell counselor/cashier. The counselor will ring up the customer's order and collect money for it, then provide change before administering the ContraceptiMelt.

Additionally, a five- to ten-minute waiting period may be necessary during high-volume "busy periods" in the restaurant, depending on the length of the line.

"Late afternoon, like 3 p.m., is usually a good time to come in," said Gerry Frankel, an Arlington, VA, Taco Bell counselor/cashier.

While the new burrito is legal and available in all 50 states, parental-consent laws in 37 states require that minors who wish to purchase the ContraceptiMelt obtain permission from a parent or legal guardian unless they order a side of Cinnamon Crisps and a large beverage.

Taco Bell vice-president of product research and development Marvin Sekuler expects the new product to be tremendously successful.

"All of our test marketing and demographic research indicates that among 14- to 22-year-old females, there is great demand for a quick, relatively painless termination of unwanted pregnancy via spontaneously induced rejection of fertilized, pre-fetal tissue from the uterine canal," Sekuler said. "Plus, 14- to 22-year-olds love delicious, Mexican-style fast-food products.

We're thrilled that our newest menu item can meet these important needs in a lip-smacking, tasty way."

While he said he hopes that many young women will purchase the new burrito, Sekuler stressed that the decision to terminate a pregnancy is an individual one.

"We are in no way advocating any particular view on this most sensitive of issues," he said. "We simply want to offer this option. And, of course, we fully respect our customers who decide to carry their babies to term. In fact, I'd like to point out that Taco Bell offers a wide variety of non-contraceptive menu items that can provide the crucial nutrients—such as mild sauce, shredded cheddar and beef—that a growing fetus needs to develop properly."

Sekuler added that every pregnancy terminated by the Taco Bell ContraceptiMelt comes with a special guarantee.

"If any one of our customers becomes pregnant after consuming our new burrito, the Taco Bell Corporation will, guaranteed, hire that person to work for us at $6.25 per hour," he said. "Taco Bell's competitive, above-minimum-wage salaries, flexible schedules and fun, team-oriented atmosphere make it the ideal place for a young single mother, enabling her to provide for herself and her children with uninsured subsistence living."

Pending FDA approval, Taco Bell plans to follow up the ContraceptiMelt with the RU-486 MexiCarriage Deluxe. Already legal in France, the MexiCarriage Deluxe costs $1.59 when purchased during the first MexiMester, $1.79 during the second, and $1.99 during the third. ∅

Those Motherfucking Robins Are On Thin Ice With Me

Ever since my retirement last month from the sock factory, I've had a lot of extra time to spend around the yard. But the hours of pleasurable pruning with my new cordless rechargeable Master Clipper I had expected to enjoy have been cruelly withheld from me. Instead, my afternoons have been spent in an unending feud with those motherfucking robins that infest my yard. All my attempts to coexist with these creatures on my meticulously trimmed, lush suburban lawn have failed, leaving me with no choice but to exterminate them. Do you hear me, you lousy, cocksucking robins? This is war!

By Joseph Marty
Retiree

It was last week that I had withdrawn a hefty sum from my pension account and made haste to the Eastgate Plaza Lawn & Garden Place to pick out the finest riding mower known to man: the John Deere Lawn Rebel, featuring high-impact Euro-style wheels and nine-position fingertip height adjusters. I climbed right onto the patented Comfort Cushion seat, grabbed hold of the deluxe seven-speed gear shift and drove her right out of the store and down Grant Avenue toward home, waving to everyone I saw.

I had just mowed the lawn Sunday, but I saw a few spots around the old maple tree that could use some extra attention. I could've used my Weed Eater Featherlite 15-inch gas trimmer Gertie got me for our anniversary, but I saw this outcropping close to the maple's trunk as a good test for my new John Deere.

I cleared the patch without suffering so much as a nick to the green paint on the Lawn Rebel's detachable blower. At that point I decided to go ahead and mow the whole lawn. Why not enjoy myself? I'm retired!

But I had gone no more than 20 feet when I noticed one of those no-good, motherfucking tweeters hopping in front of the path of my mower. I slammed on the brakes and brought the Lawn Rebel to a halt. That mower stopped on a dime, and lucky for that bird, too, because any lesser mower would've gone straight up its ass.

I got about one row done when I came to another goddamn chirping little shitball, just taking its gay old time sticking its fucking beak in the goddamn grass. I yelled, "Hey, get outta the way!" but then I realized it probably couldn't hear me over the motor, so I turned off the Lawn Rebel and yelled, "Hey, I'm mowin' the fucking lawn here, asshole!" Boy, was I steamed.

Finally, I climbed off the Comfort Cushion seat and shooed the thing away. I started the engine up again and continued, only to have the same thing happen to me 11 more times just in the front yard. Now, this wasn't the first run-in I'd had with these fuckers. I'd put a new white canopy over the deck this year, which was completely stained with berries from the neighbor's yard. Besides that, the last time I went to fire up the gas grill at the start of lawn-barbecue season, I found a robin's nest on the warming rack.

I swear, next time I see a robin's nest, I'm taking the eggs and smashing them with a fucking baseball bat.

Anyway, it was dark by the time I was done mowing, what with having to stop every 10 feet. Around 10 p.m., Gertie came running out with my heart pills expecting to find me laid out in the culvert.

After accepting a quick iced tea, I sent Gertie back in—by God, I wasn't done yet. I went to the garage and got out my shiny red Pioneer Plus 16-inch chainsaw with the Menards sticker still on it and went straight for the mountain ash where those birds were known to meet. Limb by limb, I reduced that tree to a pole. I even got out my Black & Decker collapsible ladder to get all the way to the top, but when I got there I didn't find any of the sons of bitches.

Defeated, I climbed down the ladder, bellowing, "Tomorrow, my fine feathered foes, is another day!" into the night sky. Fucking birds! Christ! Ø

From June 25, 1998

WASHINGTON

Congress Passes Americans With No Abilities Act

WASHINGTON, DC—On Tuesday, Congress approved the Americans With No Abilities Act, sweeping new legislation that provides benefits and protection for more than 135 million talentless Americans.

The act, signed into law by President Clinton shortly after its passage, is being hailed as a major victory for the millions upon millions of U.S. citizens who lack any real skills or uses.

"Roughly 50 percent of Americans, through no fault of their own, do not possess the talent necessary to carve out a meaningful role for themselves in society," said Clinton, a longtime ANA supporter. "Their lives are futile hamster-wheel existences of unrewarding, dead-end busy work: photocopying documents written by others, fulfilling mail-in rebates for Black & Decker toaster ovens and processing bureaucratic forms that nobody will ever see. Sadly, for these millions of nonabled Americans, the American dream of working hard and moving up through the ranks is simply not a reality."

Under the terms of the Americans With No Abilities Act, more than 25 million important-sounding "middle man" positions will be created in the white-collar sector for nonabled persons, providing them with an illusory sense of purpose and ability. Mandatory, non-performance-based raises and promotions will also be offered to create a sense of upward mobility for even the most unremarkable, utterly replaceable employees.

The legislation also provides corporations with incentives to hire nonabled workers, including tax breaks for those who hire one non-germane worker for every two talented hires.

Finally, the Americans With No Abilities

Above: President Clinton signs the Americans With No Abilities Act into law.

Act also contains tough new measures to prevent discrimination against the nonabled by banning prospective employers from asking such job-interview questions as, "What can you bring to this organization?" and, "Do you have any special skills that would make you an asset to this company?"

"As a nonabled person, I frequently find myself unable to keep up with co-workers who have something going for them," said Mary Lou Gertz, who lost her position as an unessential filing clerk at a Minneapolis tile wholesaler last month because of her lack of notable skills. "This new law should really help people like me."

With the passage of the Americans With No Abilities Act, Gertz and millions of other untalented citizens can finally see a light at the end of the tunnel.

Said Clinton: "It is our duty, both as lawmakers and as human beings, to provide each and every American citizen, regardless of his or her lack of value to society, some sort of space to take up in this great nation." Ø

SOCIETY

'98 Homosexual-Recruitment Drive Nearing Goal

SAN FRANCISCO—Spokespersons for the National Gay & Lesbian Recruitment Task Force announced Monday that more than 288,000 straights have been converted to homosexuality since Jan. 1, 1998, putting the group well on pace to reach its goal of 350,000 conversions by the end of the year.

"Thanks to the tireless efforts of our missionaries nationwide, in the first seven months of 1998, nearly 300,000 heterosex-

uals were ensnared in the Pink Triangle," said NGLRTF co-director Patricia Emmonds. "Clearly, the activist homosexual lobby is winning."

Emmonds credited much of the recruiting success to the gay lobby's infiltration of America's public schools, where programs promoting the homosexual lifestyle are regularly presented to children as young as 5.

"It's crucial that we reach these kids while they're still young," Emmonds said. "That's when they're most vulnerable to our message of sexual promiscuity and deviance."

"When I grow up, I want to be gay," said Christopher Linn, 8, a second-grader at Philadelphia's Lakeside Elementary School,

one of thousands of public schools nationwide that actively promote the homosexual agenda. "I don't want to have a family or go to church."

"Straight people don't have any fun," said Teddy Nance, 11, after watching *Breeders Are Boring!*, an anti-heterosexual filmstrip, in his fifth-grade class at Crestwood Elementary School in Roanoke, VA. "Gay people get to do whatever they want."

In addition to school programs that target young people, the NGLRTF launched a $630 million advertising campaign this year in an effort to convert adults to homosexuality. The campaign, which features TV and radio spots as well as print advertising in major national magazines, has helped convince thousands to leave their spouses and families for a life of self-gratification and irresponsibility.

"The gay lifestyle is for me," said James Miller, an Oklahoma City father of four who recently moved to Provincetown, MA, to pursue a career in bath-house management. "When I was a family man, I constantly had to worry about things like taking the kids to Little League practice, paying for their braces and remembering my wife's birthday. But now that I'm gay, I'm finally free to focus all my energy on having non-stop, mind-blowing anal sex."

Though Emmonds said gays have been tremendously successful in tearing at the fabric of

 # Converted To Homosexuality

1998 Goal: 350,000

300,000

200,000

100,000

Jan. 1998 ——————— July 1998

Above: Lansing, MI, fifth-grade teacher Margaret Gerhardt. Gerhardt's is one of countless elementary-school classes across the U.S. in which the homosexual agenda and lifestyle are actively promoted.

society and subverting basic decency, she stressed that their work is far from over.

"For all the progress we've made, America is still overwhelmingly heterosexual," said Emmonds, who is calling for an additional $2.6 billion in federal aid to further the gay

agenda. "If we are to insidiously penetrate American society, as we constantly do each other's orifices, we need more money and resources. Without such help, this country will remain the domain of decent, moral, God-fearing Christians. And that would be a sin." ⌀

14-Year-Old Collapses Under Weight Of Corporate Logos

SPRINGFIELD, IL—A local teenager was in stable condition Monday after nearly being crushed to death by the 263 corporate logos he recklessly wore at one time. "The patient was admitted to our emergency room unable to breathe," St. Joseph's Hospital chief of surgery Dr. Lyle Wilson-Scheidt said. "His chest had collapsed under the weight of nearly 150 pounds of company and product logos, including Tommy Hilfiger, Abercrombie & Fitch, Pepsi, Nike, Adidas, Fubu, Taco Bell, Nintendo, MTV, Budweiser, the Chicago Bulls, the NBA and, for some reason, Aetna Life Insurance." Hospital workers used a jaws-of-life device to extract the 14-year-old from the life-threatening crush of insignias. The American Medical Association strongly warns individuals against wearing more than one logo for every five pounds of body weight. —*December 17, 1998*

Saltless Pretzel Hangs Alone In Bulb-Heated Rack

ODESSA, TX—A saltless "Superpretzel" is still hanging alone in a bulb-heated rack at Horizon Lanes, officials for the Odessa-area bowling alley said Tuesday. "Looks like there's just one left," said Mack Klausner, snack-bar manager for the 12-lane alley. "Guess nobody wants the one without salt." The oversized soft pretzel, priced at 99 cents, has been rotating in the glass-enclosed case since Sept. 2, when it was sprayed with water and dipped in salt along with 17 other pretzels. "All the salt fell off," Klausner said. "Maybe we should put some more on." —*September 10, 1998*

Area Units Really Moving

BOULDER, CO—Units are really moving at ABC Appliance Warehouse, assistant manager Ralph Hutchins reported Tuesday. "We moved about 300 units today, with almost 75 units moving between 9 and 10 a.m. alone," Hutchins said. "That's a hell of a lot of units to move off the shelves in just one day." If demand for units continues at its current pace, Hutchins said they might have to go on back-order. "We've had to limit people to one unit apiece as it is," he said. —*October 29, 1998*

Bleary-Eyed *Cosmopolitan* Staffer Cranks Out 10 Billionth Way To Bring Out The Animal In Your Man

NEW YORK—*Cosmopolitan* writer Melissa Rutherford achieved a journalistic milestone Tuesday, cranking out the magazine's 10 billionth tip for how to bring out the animal in your man. "Surprise him by greeting him after work in a sexy new red cocktail dress," wrote the drained, numb Rutherford, who has advised *Cosmopolitan* readers how to bring out the animal in their men 135,285 times during her six-year tenure with the magazine. "If that doesn't do the trick, tell him you left something in the kitchen, leave the room, and then come back in the altogether!" Upon completing the piece, Rutherford jumped out a 34th-story window. —*January 14, 1998*

Borrowed CD Slowly Integrated Into Own Collection

OLYMPIA, WA—An Elvis Costello CD belonging to area resident Jonathan Wagner, 24, has entered the final stage of *de facto* ownership by friend Doug Alland, sources reported Tuesday. "For the first four or five days, I kept Jon's copy of *Blood & Chocolate* alone on top of my CD player," Alland, 23, said. "Then, for about a week and a half, I had it next to a stack of my own CDs that I'd been listening to." Alland said he then worked the album into the adjacent stack, eventually filing it away on his own CD shelf, where it will remain permanently, unless Wagner specifically asks for it back. "I'm way more into that album than Jon is, anyway," said Alland, defending the gradual acquisition. "He barely ever even played it." In 1997, Alland made news for a spectacular nine-stage acquisition of *Down By Law* on videocassette. —*April 1, 1999*

From August 22, 1995

Seize Him!
You Fools, He's Getting Away!

Ah, yes. I see you have captured my elusive Earthling quarry at last. Well done, guard! You have greatly pleased your master. Bring him forward at once! I wish to speak with him face to face... before his annihilation.

By Gorzo The Mighty
Emperor Of The Universe

So! It seems we meet again, my heroic friend. Before I kill you, I must admit that you have proven to be a formidable foe—for a human. It will be bring me no small amount of pleasure to blast you into atoms, seeing how, puny as you may be, you have caused considerable inconvenience to my plan to dominate your home world.

Over the Slime Caverns of Tarmokk IV, I was sure I had you in my grasp. I would have lasered you into oblivion right then and there, had you not escaped at the last minute thanks to the treacherous Prince Kazak and his accursed Rocket Squad! But no matter. I assure you, my helpless prisoner, that not even your friends can save you now!

Silence, dog! Guard, still this impudent rebel's tongue with a blast of your atomic stun rod! Ha, ha! See how he writhes in pain at my command! Guards, increase the power flow! I want to see if this prisoner can withstand the agonies of the dreaded Level 10! Ha! Ha! Ha! Not so lively with a stun rod at your throat, eh, Earthling? Guards, enough! Release him! I want the pain to linger. I want this troublesome gnat to suffer before he dies.

Fzam! Vzz-Kpowbang!

What? What?! A smuggled electro-ray pistol concealed on his person? You dare defy Gorzo, Emperor Of The Universe? Earthling vermin, you shall die for this! Your entire planet shall be my slaves! Guards! Guards! Seize him!

Seize him, you fools! He's getting away! After him, my precious robo-troopers! Hurry!

Quickly! He's heading for the detention quadrant, no doubt with the intention of freeing Princess Sultrania and his comrades from the spaceship *Gallant*! Activate the Neuro-Drain Web! Release the poisonous gas-balloon monster from Planet Xerix! He must not slip through my fingers again! Do whatever it takes, only seize him!

Fools! Seize him! Do you know what this means? If he can get his friend Professor Zircon to the central power grid, he just might be able to disable the hypno-generators and thwart our invasion of Earth! Seize him, you fools!

Are your puny minds filled with space dust? Seize the prisoner, or I will vaporize you in the same de-senso chamber in which I shall soon hold him and his pitiful friends. We must not let him escape! Gorzo commands you to seize him!

Oh, I see... You think that once you find the prisoner, he will use his barbaric fighting skills and crude Earth weaponry to cut you down like pigeons? Nonsense! You are the elite guard of Gorzo, Emperor Of The Universe! Do as I say! Seize him!

Do you hear me? Attention all robo-troopers! The Earthling intruder is once again loose in the palace of Gorzo The Mighty! Seize him! Seize him! Seize him!

Gorzo The Mighty is a tyrannical military despot from beyond known space. His weekly column, Seize Him!, appears in more than 250 newspapers nationwide. Ø

PEOPLE

Man Has Amazing Ass

TASHEN, OH—In what many consider the most remarkable story to come out of Tashen, OH, in decades, resident Lance Holdger has an amazing ass.

Sculpted, tight and slightly lofted, Holdger's ass is naturally tan and hairless, possessing the consistency of a gelatinous stone. The 750 residents of Tashen are well aware of this and, as a result, are unable to get enough of that ass.

The empirical grandeur of Holdger's ass, Tashen mayor Wayne Rinaldo said, allows it to be celebrated by people without regard to sexual preference, age, creed or aesthetic inclination.

"Whether one wants to caress, fondle, finger, wipe, rim, penetrate, paint, write about or simply behold Mr. Holdger's ass, it doesn't matter," Rinaldo said. "That ass is open to all things, from wholesome admiration to profane defilement. It is that amazing of an ass. No one can stop thinking about that ass."

Tashen's favorite obsession has manifested itself in numerous ways. The entrance to the local mall is decorated with a pair of 12-foot glowing orbs that replicate and enlarge the splendor of Holdger's ass. In a $2 million renovation blitz, the city's water towers were rebuilt to look like Holdger's ass. The covers of Tashen's tourist brochures are festooned with unretouched photos of Holdger's ass, and the same photos are published in the school district's anatomy and art textbooks. Tashen High School's team nickname was changed from the Battlin' Warriors to the Battlin' Holdger's Asses. The football team's helmets have been indented to look like Holdger's ass.

"Sometimes, those flesh-colored, ass-like helmets fool even me," Tashen football coach Ed Meadrock said. "I'm thinking, hey, I want a piece of that."

Most striking is Assmas, Tashen's annual spring festival celebrating Holdger's ass. As resident Vic Henshaw described it, "Assmas is exactly like Christmas, except instead of trimming a tree, we trim Holdger's ass. Instead of reveling in the glory of Jesus and the spirit of Christianity, we revel in the glory of Holdger's ass and the spirit of Holdger's ass. It's almost identical."

For the duration of Assmas, which covers the last 20 days in May, everything in Tashen shuts down, with the exception of Holdger's ass. The only sounds heard are those that come from Holdger's ass. The only gifts given must be in the shape of, depict some aspect of or reflect Holdger's ass in some essential way. The only words allowed to

Above: Lance Holdger, in a rare frontal shot.

be thought are "Holdger's ass."

At the end of the festival, Holdger and his ass are raised high above city hall. Glowing and inspiring, the ass emanates its perfect scent, sight and sound to the yielding minions who believe in one thing and one thing only: Holdger's ass. And all is perfect and peaceful.

Residents of Tashen are well aware that their ass worship may seem strange to outsiders, and they are eager to explain.

"People who aren't from here have to realize something about Holdger's ass," lifelong Tashen resident Paula Baines said. "It's not like a regular ass, or even an extremely above-average ass. Holdger's ass is on an entirely different plane of asshood than your ass or mine. A holy plane. Just thinking about Holdger's ass makes me want to think about Holdger's ass some more. Go now. Go and learn Holdger's ass."

"We exaggerate about a lot of things here in Tashen," resident Duane Renfro said. "Our stranglehold on the pillbox industry, the cleanliness of our lakes, the safety of our streets, the quality of our hotels. But there is one thing about Tashen that needs no exaggeration. And that is Holdger's ass." ∅

SOCIETY

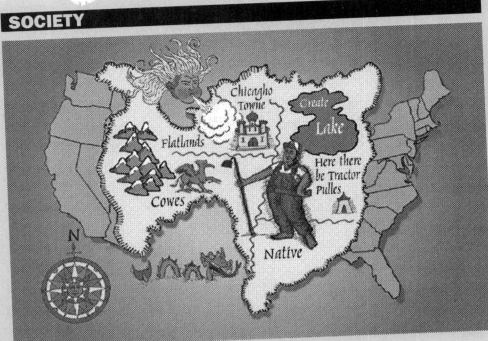

'Midwest' Discovered Between East, West Coasts

NEW YORK—A U.S. Geological Survey expeditionary force announced Tuesday that it has discovered a previously unexplored land mass between the New York and California coasts known as the "Midwest."

The Geological Survey team discovered the vast region while searching for the fabled Midwest Passage, the mythical overland route passing through the uncharted area between Ithaca, NY, and Bakersfield, CA.

"I long suspected something was there," said Franklin Eldred, a Manhattan native and leader of the 200-man exploratory force. "I'd flown between New York and L.A. on business many times, and the unusually long duration of my flights seemed to indicate that some sort of large area was being traversed, an area of unknown composition."

The Geological Survey explorers left the East Coast three weeks ago, embarking on a perilous journey to the unknown. Not long after crossing the Adirondack Mountains, Eldred and his team blazed trails through strange new regions, wild lands full of corn and wheat.

"Thus far we have discovered places known as Michigan, Minnesota and Wisconsin," said Randall Zachary, chief navigator for the expedition. "When translated from the local dialect into English, these words appear to mean 'summer camp.'"

Eldred and the others were surprised to learn that the Midwest, whose inhospitable environment was long believed to be incapable of supporting human life, is indeed populated, albeit sparsely.

see MIDWEST page 18

160

MIDWEST from page 7

"The Midwestern aborigines are ruddy, generally heavy-set folk, clad in plain, non-designer costumery," Eldred said. "They tend to live in simple, one-story dwellings whose interiors are decorated with Hummels and 'Bless This House' needlepoint wall-hangings. And though coarse and unattractive, these simple people were rather friendly, offering us such quaint native fare as 'hot dish' and 'casserole.'"

Though the Midwest territory is still largely unexplored, early reports describe a region as backward as it is vast. "Many of the basic aspects of a civilized culture appear to be entirely absent," said Gina Strauch, a Los Angeles-based anthropologist. "There is no theater to speak of, and their knowledge of posh restaurants is sketchy at best. Further, their agricentric lives seem to prevent them from pursuing high fashion to any degree and, as a result, their mode of dress is largely restricted to sweatpants and sweatshirts, the women's being adorned with hearts and teddy bears and the men's with college-football insignias."

Despite the Midwesterners' considerable cultural backwardness, some say the establishment of relations with them is possible. "Believe it or not, this region may have things to offer us," said Jonathan Ogleby, a San Francisco-area marketing expert. "We could construct an airport there, a place where New Yorkers could switch planes on their way to California. We could stage revivals of old Broadway musicals there. Perhaps we could even conduct trade with the Midwesterners, offering them electronic devices in exchange for meats and agriculture."

Others are not so optimistic about future relations. "We must remember that these people are not at all like us," *Conde Nast* publisher and Manhattan socialite Lucille Randolph Snowdon said. "They are crude and provincial, bewildered by our tall buildings and our art galleries, our books and our coffee shops. For an L.A. resident to attempt to interact with one of them as he or she would with, say, a Bostonian is ludicrous. It appears unlikely that we will ever be able to conduct a genuine exchange of ideas with them about anything, save perhaps television or 'the big game.'" ∅

From April 23, 1997

Safe Sex Tips

These days, safe sex isn't just a good idea, it's a matter of life or death. Here are some valuable tips to help you "play it safe":

- Do not blow dealers for crack; blow regular citizens for cash, then buy the crack directly
- Think about your parents' nude bodies during foreplay; resultant loss of erection will prevent potential unsafe sex
- Wash hands thoroughly before fisting goat
- Under no circumstance should you give CPR to a stranger
- Avoid dipping penis in buckets of AIDS-infected blood
- Don't fall for lines like, "God protects his servants in the clergy from harm"
- Pull out cat's teeth before pouring gravy over vagina
- Do not, no matter how much peers may pressure you, allow anyone to get to third base with you
- Make sure all open sores on penis have dried and scabbed over before use
- When taking four cocks in the ass, make sure to have an equal amount of cock in your mouth to reduce the risk of chi imbalance

- Stock up on free safe-sex pamphlets at local health clinic; use them to make papier-maché genital wrap
- Before fellating anonymous man in back room of gay bar, be sure to ask, "You don't have AIDS, do you?"
- Douse penis liberally with D-Con roach spray before penetrating ape
- You can get it from kissing, so tear out partner's tongue before any mouth-to-mouth contact
- To prevent radiation exposure, use only lead-based condoms
- Avoid talking to homosexuals at all costs
- If you must engage in unsafe sex, take time out beforehand to hope for the best

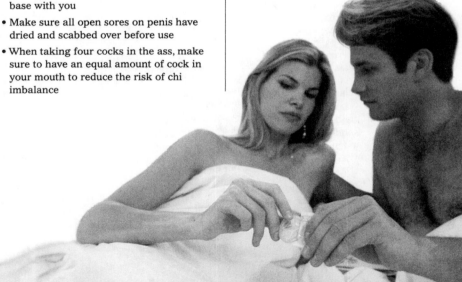

162

What The Hell Am I Going To Do With This Dog?

Hola, amigos. What do you say? I know it's been a long time since I rapped at ya, but you wouldn't believe the shitstorm that's been whipped up in my life right now. First off, my Nova kicked the bucket in a big way. I guess it was the oil pump. The oil light kept coming on, but every time I checked the levels, they seemed fine. That didn't stop it from seizing up and starting on fire on the way home from work, though. If it woulda been someone else's car, it woulda been pretty cool, but it was mine. I had to spend my last 50 bucks getting it towed to the junkyard.

The Cruise
By Jim Anchower

Now I gotta catch a ride to and from work with this guy Pat. He ain't all that bad, but the guy just talks and talks. I don't care what the topic is, he knows about it, and even when he don't, he talks about it like he's the expert. Hell, one time, I pretended I was asleep on the way there, and the guy talked to his damn radio. I shit you not. The radio. And it was all about some council ordinance that I couldn't give two shits about. I'd take the bus, but the only thing lamer than a know-it-all motormouth is the bus.

As if all this weren't enough, I wound up getting stuck with a dog. Now, I got nothing against dogs. They're pretty cool usually, at least they are when I go and visit someone who's got them. The best thing is that when I leave, they stay there. This way, I get all the tug-of-war and none of the crap-picking-up. That's the way I like it.

I sure as hell didn't set out to find one. A week or so ago, I was riding around with Wes and Ron, just sort of checking stuff out. Nothing major, just trying to see if there was any shit we could stir up. Ron was annoying the shit out of us by saying, "Yeah, baby!" like Austin Powers. That's funny, like, twice, and then it got real annoying. We were arguing about that and where we should go to get the evening's provisions when I saw the dog. I hollered at Ron to stop. He got all pissy, but he eventually did. It wasn't anything special: brown, floppy dog ears, floppy dog tail.

It was running around sniffing garbage cans looking pretty happy. Ron asked why we stopped to look at a dog when you could see a dog at his neighbor's house.

See, Ron doesn't have what you'd call vision. Take the dog: Ron looks at it and sees a dog. When I saw it, I saw an opportunity for some beer scratch. I told Ron he had to think of the "dog money." Neither one of them could figure out what the hell I was talking about, so I had to spell it out for them. Dogs don't usually wander around wild in town. They have owners. All I got with that was more dumb looks, so I went on. Dog owners love their dogs, or they wouldn't be dog owners. And they usually

> ## I got nothing against dogs. They're pretty cool usually, at least they are when I go and visit someone who's got them.

put up rewards. And I couldn't see why this dog shouldn't get us 20 bucks for almost no work.

It was a solid plan. All we had to do was hang on to the dog for a day or two and keep our eyes peeled for the reward posters. Hell, maybe it was already in the paper. We managed to get the dog in the car after a bit of wrestling and headed off to get a paper, some dog chow and some beer. We got back to my place and looked through the want-ads. There were only three lost dogs, and they all had Disney names like Mulan and Hercules.

None of them in there looked like the one we had. It didn't answer to those names, either. We hadda figure out something to call him, though, 'cause it was ripping up my couch and wouldn't listen when I hollered at it. After trying about 50 names, we decided to call him Licky, because he licks his nuts all the time. He didn't answer to that, either, but since he wasn't answering to anything else, we decided it might as well be his name.

When it came time to take care of Licky,

Ron and Wes told me that they couldn't put it up, and since it was my idea, I should put it up. I didn't have much choice, and I figured it was a sacrifice I could make for beer money.

When I got up the next morning, the first thing I found out was that Licky had pissed on the kitchen floor. I threw some newspapers on it and went into the living room. That damn dog had chewed up more of my couch! That was practically like my throne. I mean, I found it on moving day last summer, but it was going to be a while before a sweet seat like that fell into my lap again. I let him out back to run around while I made a plan of action.

My first plan was to go out driving around with Ron and Wes looking for lost-dog signs. We came up empty-handed. We did find an old guitar, but that didn't help anything. It just made the ride home more annoying because Ron kept trying to play "In A Gadda Da Vida" the whole way back. We picked up a paper and headed back to the crib, and found out Licky had taken a piss on the floor again.

We had the same luck with the paper. Only two listings this time, and they were the same damned dogs that were in yesterday's paper. I was getting nowhere fast. We all had to work the next day, so I decided to keep Licky another night and drive around after work the next day. Same thing. Same thing the next night, too. After stepping in my fifth puddle, I decided that Licky had to go. Ron came over and we took him in the car by where we found him and dropped him off. The problem was, he turned up at my door at about one in the morning, whining and scratching at the door.

Jim Anchower ain't made of stone. I let him in and gave him some food. He fell asleep on my bed. When I tried to move him over, he started growling, so I had to sleep on the chewed-up couch. It's pretty much been like that for the last few days. I don't want to turn him over to the Humane Society to get put to sleep, but I almost put him under myself when he ate an eighth I had on the table.

Anyway, if you know anyone who lost this dog, or you just want a dog yourself, give me a call. I ain't going to do any background check on you or anything. Just promise me you ain't going to eat him and he's yours. Hell, for all I care, you can eat him. Just don't tell me about it. ∅

NATION

New York To Install Special 'Infants Only' Dumpsters

Above: One of the new baby-disposal units.

NEW YORK—As part of his ongoing campaign to revitalize New York City's public image through a citywide clean-up effort, mayor Rudolph Giuliani announced Monday the installation of special "infants only" dumpsters throughout the greater New York metropolitan area.

It is hoped that the new dumpsters will provide a convenient, germ-free baby-dumping option for low-income single mothers, enabling them to abandon their unwanted infants in a tidier, more health-conscious manner than before.

The new, clearly labeled dumpsters are also expected to make it significantly easier for city workers to collect and sort the estimated 25,000 babies placed in New York-area trash receptacles each year.

"By providing these mothers with a safe, convenient receptacle for unwanted babies, instead of requiring them to deposit them along with garbage of other types, New York is saying, 'Yes, we care,' Giuliani told reporters at a City Hall press conference.

While the infant-dedicated

see DUMPSTERS page 14

DUMPSTERS from page 1

dumpsters will cost an estimated $220 million to install and maintain, Giuliani said he is confident they will more than make up for their cost in the long run. "Babies deposited in the new dumpsters will be collected, tagged and redistributed in a far more organized manner than those left in traditional multi-use dumpsters or garbage cans," Giuliani said. "This will greatly reduce the strain on our city's already sorely overtaxed human-services and child-welfare departments, saving millions over the long haul."

The new devices will also make it easier for city sanitation workers to separate recyclable metals, paper and plastics from non-recyclables, a task that has been needlessly complicated by the presence of human children among the materials to be reclaimed.

Among the new dumpsters' many impressive features, according to the mayor: a unique soundproof design which minimizes the high-volume, panicked wails of infants crying out in desperation for their parents' return and a patented, easy-to-clean design that requires only periodic hosings to flush out accumulated waste.

"These dumpsters' revolutionary 'E-Z Kleen' design will greatly reduce the amount of time abandoned infants will have to lie helpless in their own urine, vomit and fecal matter," Giuliani said. "It will also reduce the risk of cockroach infestation in the open wounds the newborns will likely develop, as well as the risk of injuries caused by maggot bites and rat attacks."

Mayoral aide Edwin Steep was equally enthusiastic. "With these new receptacles, a projected 17 percent fewer abandoned babies will be blinded by rats, which tend to attack the soft, vulnerable eye sockets of human infants first," he said.

Above: Mayor Giuliani, introducing the new dumpsters.

Furthermore, Steep said, a large, bright-pink smiley-face decal affixed to the inside lower lid of the dumpsters will help reduce the intense and potentially psyche-shattering abandonment trauma experienced by pre-verbal human infants whose parents leave them to die.

"Regular dumpsters are not equipped with this added smiley-face feature," Steep said.

According to Giuliani, the elimination of infants from regular city dumpsters will have an added bonus, creating more dumpster-based, no-cost housing for the city's estimated 400,000 homeless residents, many of whom rely on the heat produced by decomposing organic waste for shelter and survival during New York's often brutal winters.

"By clearing dumpster space of babies, we are opening up vast new living spaces for the urban poor," Giuliani said. "And that's something we can all feel good about." Ø

Stay On Top Of The Events That Shape Your World.

Subscribe To The Onion.

To order call 1.800.695.4376 or order online with your
VISA or MasterCard at **www.theonion.com**

The Onion's online store also features a wide selection of high-quality merchandise.
Visit **store.theonion.com**